Practical Web Analytics for User Experience

Practical Web Analytics for User Experience

How Analytics Can Help You Understand Your Users

Michael Beasley

UX Designer, ITHAKA
Ypsilanti, Michigan, USA

ELSEVIER

Amsterdam • Boston • Heidelberg • London • New York • Oxford
Paris • San Diego • San Francisco • Singapore • Sydney • Tokyo
Morgan Kaufmann is an imprint of Elsevier

Acquiring Editor: Meg Dunkerley
Editorial Project Manager: Heather Scherer
Project Manager: Priya Kumaraguruparan
Designer: Greg Harris

Morgan Kaufmann is an imprint of Elsevier
225 Wyman Street, Waltham, MA, 02451, USA

Library of Congress Cataloging-in-Publication Data
Beasley, Michael, 1980–
    Practical web analytics for user experience: how analytics can help you understand your users / Michael Beasley.
       pages cm
    Includes bibliographical references and index.
    1. Web usage mining. 2. Internet users—Attitudes. 3. Web sites—Development. I. Title.
    ZA4235.B43 2013
    006.3—dc23

                                                                                         2013010542

British Library Cataloguing-in-Publication Data
A catalogue record for this book is available from the British Library.

ISBN: 978-0-12-404619-1

Printed in China

13 14 15 16 17   10 9 8 7 6 5 4 3 2 1

For information on all Morgan Kaufmann publications visit our website at www.mkp.com

Contents

Part 2   Learning about Users through Web Analytics

Acknowledgments

This book exists because of the help of several people. I'd like to thank the people who have read this book and offered feedback along the way: Daniel O'Neil, Christina York, and Mark Newman whose technical review made this book considerably better; Andrew Grohowski and Barbra Wells, who was also the person who got me thinking I could write this; the people at Pure Visibility—Dunrie Greiling, Linda Girard, Jeremy Lopatin, Bill Smith, and more—who pushed me and helped me learn and gave me the space to make mistakes; awesome clients like Lisa Ocasio and Harmony Faust who asked the questions that made me dig deeper and find new ways to use data; Veronica Machak for listening to me complain and taking my first professional photo; Emily Merchant for being my writing buddy and also listening to me complain; and Melissa Bowen, who supported me and helped me clear the time I needed to work and, of course, listened to me complain. And thanks to Mom and Dad for the love and support over the years.

About the Author

Michael Beasley is a user experience (UX) designer at ITHAKA and has eight years of experience in usability testing, user interface design, and web analytics. Previously, he was the measurement team lead at Pure Visibility, where he fused web analytics with traditional UX activities to better answer clients' questions about their customers. Mike earned his MSI degree in human–computer interaction at the University of Michigan School of Information, and was active for several years on the board of the Michigan chapter of the User Experience Professionals' Association. Mike has written articles for *User Experience* magazine and has given talks and workshops on web analytics geared toward UX professionals.

CHAPTER 1

Introduction

Imagine you have just wrapped up a round of usability testing on your organization's website. Half of your 10 test participants clicked on a misleading link and then immediately clicked the Back button and tried a different link. Clearly, there's a problem here, but key stakeholders are unconvinced. They tell you that your sample size is too small to produce any statistically significant findings. Luckily, you have web analytics data available to you, and you can show that this is a common path for 63% of the website's users over the last year. In addition, users spend, on average, among the lowest amount of time on that page that they accidentally go to compared to the rest of the website. Not only do you now have more evidence to show to stakeholders, you also have a better sense of the scale of the problem.

It turns out that your organization's web analytics expert had often wondered why the average time on that page was so low, yet had so many pageviews. He knew something was wrong with those two pages because of the way users moved back and forth, but it was data from the usability test that showed exactly how the labeling misled some users.

User experience (UX) professionals have a strong track record of building bridges to other fields and finding ways to utilize whatever data they can gather. Web analytics is one such valuable source of data. Web analytics experts can be a great ally, helping UX professionals understand data and find ways to measure aspects of user behavior that they need. In turn, UX professionals provide web analytics experts with a perspective on users that they can't readily access.

However, UX professionals, like yourself, who work with websites and mobile applications (apps) can get a great deal of value from learning to work directly with web analytics. Using these tools not only allows you more immediate access to data, it also allows for the kind of open exploration and deep, iterative analysis that can be challenging when you work through an intermediary. A major drawback of relying on web analytics experts is that they won't necessarily focus on the kinds of questions that are important to you—they may focus on measuring the effectiveness of online market-ing efforts or simply filling requests for data. Adding web analytics tools as a regular part of your practice lets you build expertise in answering questions about users' behavior and measuring the effectiveness of design changes. Web analytics can also help you communicate with stakeholders about how usability problems affect users and help you argue for important design and research activities.

This book is geared toward UX practitioners, from those just starting out to management, who want to add another source of data about users to their toolkit. It is for people familiar with or experienced in other user research methods, such as usability testing and contextual inquiry, or engaged in design. Readers do not need to be familiar with web analytics, but this book will be the most valuable for people who enjoy solving puzzles and are excited by the thought of working with numbers.

WHAT IS WEB ANALYTICS?

Web analytics is a way of learning how users interact with websites and mobile apps by automatically recording aspects of users' behavior and then combining and transforming the behavior into data that can be analyzed. The scale of the data collection—that is, the large number of visits that can be recorded—and the approaches to analysis described in this book differentiate web analytics from other user research methods.

The most fundamental and useful information web analytics tools record is the pages a user views, when he or she views it, and in what order. From this sliver of insight into user behavior, web analytics tools stitch together the story of how each user moves through a website. They also capture how a user got to a website, such as by doing a search in a search engine or following a link from another website, and technical details like the user's browser and screen resolution. With the right tool or with the addition of the right code, almost anything a user can do on a website can be recorded, combined with other data, and analyzed.

These tools have matured considerably since the mid-2000s and their use has grown as a result. Much of the use of web analytics tools has been in the realm of online marketing, a field concerned with introducing a company's brand to people and enticing them to become customers. Web analytics has fueled growth in online marketing because it allows marketers to measure the effectiveness of their work, through such metrics as the number of people who reach their website and go on to buy something—data that can be com-pared to the amount of money spent to acquire those visitors.

USER EXPERIENCE AND WEB ANALYTICS QUESTIONS

The term *user experience* has different meanings depending on whom you talk to and is the subject of some disagreement. This book is not intended as an entry into any debate over the term. For the purpose of this book, *user experience* is meant to describe the practice of utilizing user research and design techniques—including usability testing, user personas, and user-centered design—to make items usable, useful, and delightful.

As UX professionals, we want to understand what users do and why they do it. Our traditional research methods have typically involved observing the behavior of small samples of representative users. The kinds of UX questions one might ask are: "What problems do users encounter when performing this task?" "How do users understand the way information is organized?" "Why do people click on this button rather than that other button on the same page?"

Web analytics data tell you what large numbers of users have done on your website. These tools capture data on nearly every user who comes to your website and allow you to answer "what" questions rather than "why" questions. That is, you can learn what the most and least viewed pages on your website are and what the people who ended up buying something on your website typed in your search box. What web analytics can't tell you is why users did or didn't view those pages, and what those users meant when they entered a particular search query.

One may ask "what" questions, such as "How many users visited the website on a mobile device last week?" For some, the answer may be useful by itself, but many people, from various fields, want to know not just this simple fact but also how the behavior of mobile users differ from that of desktop users. UX professionals are uniquely positioned to provide information that can contextualize web analytics data.

WEB ANALYTICS AND USER EXPERIENCE: A PERFECT FIT

Web analytics does not replace any UX methods. It simply adds to and complements them. For the most part, user experience is geared toward providing insight into how users behave and why, drawing on methods such as usability testing, field observations, and interviews. Web analytics reveals how large groups of users have moved through a website, expanding the quantifiable aspects of UX methods from small sample sizes to the entire universe of a website's visitors.

In practical terms, web analytics allows you to better quantify the portion of your website's users that exhibit a behavior you have observed during another kind of user research. You can find out how well the number of pageviews of different pages on your website matches the stated interests of the users you've talked to. You can find out not just how many of your users formulated their search engine query in some specific way, but also how many people typed similar searches that led them to your website.

ABOUT THIS BOOK

This book will help you utilize web analytics to answer questions about your users and how they interact with your website. Throughout this book, we will draw upon Google Analytics for examples and will occasionally refer to examples from the author's work at Pure Visibility, an Internet marketing firm that, among other services, helps clients understand why users visit their websites and how users interact with them. Examples will usually relate to marketing-oriented websites, but the principles discussed in this book will also serve you well if you work on websites devoted to other purposes.

Part 1: Introduction to Web Analytics

The first part of the book is an introduction to key, foundational concepts in web analytics. Chapter 2 focuses on the analysis process itself—an introduction to the mindset of using web analytics. It discusses the importance of viewing data in context, and balancing the desire for perfection against the reality of time constraints.

In Chapter 3 we start to focus on web analytics itself, with an introduction to how these tools work and some of the basic concepts involved. We pay particular attention to ways analytics tools organize and segment data.

In Chapter 4 we look at analytics goals and conversion rates, a way of choosing specific actions users can take on your website to serve as indicators that the website is achieving its aims. Choosing web analytics goals is a process of understanding the purpose of an organization and the role of the website in carrying out this purpose, and is key to organizing and structuring your use of web analytics.

Part 2: Learning About Users through Web Analytics

The next several chapters provide an overview of various analyses you can perform with the data from web analytics. Chapter 5 discusses analyzing the data you gather about users themselves to understand them better. Analysis of these data can provide information about where users are geographically located, what kind of technology they use to access your website, and how often they visit the website.

Chapter 6 is about studying the way users actually get to your website, with most of the chapter focusing on analyzing the words users type into search engines to arrive at your website. Keyword analysis reveals how users articulate their information needs and allows you to categorize users according to their reason for visiting.

In Chapter 7 we focus on exploring how users interact with the pages on your website, through analysis of metrics that record things like how many times users view a page and how long they spend on the page.

Chapter 8 delves into click-path analysis, a specific way of studying how users behave by following their journey from page to page on your website. Click-path analysis is challenging because of the diversity of behavior that you will almost certainly see on your website, but examining the relationships between pairs of pages can point to potential problem areas.

Chapter 9 introduces segmentation, a powerful way of filtering data that can produce answers to more complex questions. Up to this point, we will have worked with data about the entire population of users or about every user with a single shared attribute. Segmentation lets you isolate data about users according to multiple attributes so you can analyze the behavior of users who fit specific profiles, such as users who look like your website's primary persona. It is key to answering complex questions about users.

In Chapter 10 we look at ways you can integrate web analytics with traditional UX methods like usability testing and personas. The process is fully reciprocal: studying web analytics can raise questions about users that you can then try to answer through other research methods, and you can also take findings about your users from small sample studies and learn from web analytics data how well those observations reflect the larger population of your users.

Chapter 11 is about using web analytics to test the effectiveness of design changes on your website. The basic mechanism for doing so is isolating aspects of user behavior you wish to change, and comparing data from before and after the design change to assess the effect on user behavior.

Part 3: Advanced Topics

Part 3 is a sequence of chapters dealing with topics beyond the core functionality of web analytics tools. Chapter 12 looks at ways to measure user behavior within pages rather than movement from page to page, which often requires adding more tracking code to a website.

In Chapter 13 we turn to the topic of A/B testing, pitting two or more designs of a page against each other simultaneously to evaluate which one performs better. A/B testing is distinct from measuring the performance before and after a change, both because it requires specialized A/B testing tools and because it allows you to answer very narrowly focused questions.

Chapter 14 discusses ways to organize the data in web analytics tools to better support UX work. This chapter talks about how some web analytics tools display data in one or more profiles that you can filter to take out unwanted information or even display the structure of your website in new ways.

In Chapter 15 we deal with incorporating web analytics into a regular rhythm of communication with business stakeholders. Doing so entails determining metrics that you will monitor over time and report to stakeholders the context of your team's efforts.

Finally, Chapter 16 concludes this book with a look and some of the possible directions analytics will take in the future.

GOOGLE ANALYTICS

This book draws on Google Analytics for its examples and in many cases provides instructions on manipulating reports in Google Analytics (or at least, as the interface works at the time of writing). This tool is in widespread use in organizations of all sizes. At the time of writing, it is the only mainstream tool that's free—this means that if you don't have access to web analytics in your professional life, you can install Google Analytics on a personal website and begin using it.

However, the principles and approaches discussed in this book will also work with other tools, such as Omniture and Webtrends. Although the interfaces are different and there may be nuances in how different tools record and manipulate data, the ways they measure website usage are fundamentally the same.

Whether your organization uses Google Analytics or another tool, it is advantageous to gain access to the tool or tools themselves rather than asking an intermediary to produce reports for you. The most interesting analyses tend to be exploratory or have exploratory elements, meaning you need the freedom to go back and get more data when you find interesting threads to tug on. Depending on the culture of your organization, access may be challenging to obtain, but your persistence will pay off when you begin to incorporate analytics data into your work. You may have to start by simply requesting data from the web analytics team. In this situation, it is important to not simply explain what data you want, but why you want them. Explaining the context will help the web analytics team help you because they may think of different or easier approaches, and help build the trust that will lead to you getting access to web analytics tools.

Of course, you may already be engaging in an effort to fold in more knowledge from all of the silos of user research in your organization, such as web analytics, marketing, and customer support. Ideally, there is room in your organization for a variety of centers of expertise, but when these centers work together they achieve even more than they would in isolation.

Mastery is a journey, not a destination. This book will not be all you need to become a web analytics expert, but it will allow you to begin the adventure. You may still need assistance, particularly with regard to technical configuration, but you will have a better idea of what web analytics tools are capable of doing and what to ask for. More importantly, you will know a great deal more about how to shine the light provided by web analytics tools onto UX questions.

PART 1

Introduction to Web Analytics

CHAPTER 2

Web Analytics Approach

INTRODUCTION

As we covered in the Introduction, web analytics consists of tools and the practice of analyzing web analytics data. Tools will continue to change, therefore anything we say about them will have a limited shelf life. The practices and techniques are far more interesting because they are portable and, if not timeless, will change more slowly.

In this chapter, we lay the foundation for the techniques in following chapters. First, we will discuss a model for analyzing web analytics data and then the importance of context. Then we'll briefly cover the importance of making your findings repeatable.

GET TO KNOW YOUR WEBSITE

The first step to using your web analytics tool is to not use it at all and instead spend time getting to know your website. Exploring your website is the best way to understand how its pages fit together to make web analytics data more meaningful. As we can see in Figures 2.1 and 2.2, with a tool like Google Analytics, you see your website as lists of URLs or as page titles—these things may give you clues as to the content of a page, but you don't know for sure what is on those pages without looking. Further, although you can find out whether users moved from one page to another, you can't tell if the link was hard or easy to find, or if there are links that users are not using. You don't know what a page actually looks like without looking.

The big problem is that you're primarily dealing with numeric data about individual pages, with an emphasis on understanding individual pages rather than a user's experience from beginning to end, as he or she moves from page to page.

If you work on the same website all day, every day, understanding how it works won't be a problem, since by the time you've picked up this book, you

	Page	Pageviews ↓	Unique Pageviews	Avg. Time on Page	Entrances	Bounce Rate	% Exit
☐ 1.	/	732	574	00:01:46	530	44.72%	44.67%
☐ 2.	/about/	336	232	00:01:15	48	25.00%	18.15%
☐ 3.	/services/	185	138	00:01:40	25	40.00%	26.49%
☐ 4.	/case-studies/	149	119	00:01:58	20	20.00%	22.82%
☐ 5.	/services/archives/ppc-articles/adwords-budget/	91	87	00:07:13	87	87.36%	87.91%
☐ 6.	/contact/	75	68	00:01:43	18	50.00%	44.00%
☐ 7.	/about/jobs/team-roster/	74	56	00:01:11	0	0.00%	22.97%
☐ 8.	/about/management-team/	74	66	00:01:17	3	100.00%	33.78%
☐ 9.	/services/archives/seo-articles/delivery-methods/	58	55	00:04:05	55	94.55%	94.83%
☐ 10.	/about/jobs/	52	47	00:00:37	3	33.33%	23.08%

FIGURE 2.1

It is difficult to visualize a website just from looking at analytics reports. Most reports display pages by URL.

	Page Title	Pageviews ↓	Unique Pageviews	Avg. Time on Page	Entrances	Bounce Rate	% Exit
☐ 1.	Internet Marketing Company - SEO & Pay Per Click Management Services | Pure Visibility	724	566	00:01:46	522	43.87%	44.06%
☐ 2.	Michigan Internet Marketing Agency - Pure Visibility, Based in Ann Arbor	336	232	00:01:15	48	25.00%	18.15%
☐ 3.	Online Strategy Including SEO and PPC | Pure Visibility	185	138	00:01:40	25	40.00%	26.49%
☐ 4.	Pure Visibility's Online Marketing Clients and Case Studies	149	119	00:01:58	20	20.00%	22.82%
☐ 5.	Setting a Google Adwords Budget	91	87	00:07:13	87	87.36%	87.91%
☐ 6.	Pure Visibility Team Roster: SEO & Paid Search Experts	88	69	00:01:25	1	100.00%	26.14%
☐ 7.	Contact Pure Visibility for Internet Marketing Services | Pure Visibility	75	68	00:01:43	18	50.00%	44.00%
☐ 8.	Co-Founders and Management Team of Pure Visibility	74	66	00:01:17	3	100.00%	33.78%
☐ 9.	Google Adwords Accelerated Delivery and Standard Delivery Methods | Pure Visibility	58	55	00:04:05	55	94.55%	94.83%
☐ 10.	Career Opportunities in Internet Marketing | Pure Visibility	52	47	00:00:37	3	33.33%	23.08%

FIGURE 2.2

More evidence that it is difficult to visualize a website; even when you look at page titles, they still may not tell you much.

will probably have already spent a great deal of time exploring your website to look for potential problem areas. If you are a consultant, this step is vital. A good approach is:

- Find out what the most important user tasks or scenarios are and find out how to do them on the website. Look for places where things can go wrong and where you could get lost (and what those pages are where you find yourself lost). This activity shouldn't be a new experience for you, but the twist is that you're keeping an eye on the URL, which will often be the way you identify pages in analytics data.

- Look up the top 10 or 20 most-visited pages in your analytics tool. Make sure you visit these pages. What's on them? What is each page's purpose?

The things you're looking for as you do this exploration are:

- How does one get to a page?
- What other pages can one navigate to with a single click?
- Are there multiple links to the same page?
- Are there aspects of the website that are not getting tracked by web analytics?

This last bullet point entails exploring the website to see what pages exist, and then verifying that data for those pages actually show up in analytics. It's possible that a page is getting properly tracked but no one is visiting it, but if you look at it over a long enough slice of time, there's a good chance that someone at least accidentally navigated to that page. Explore the website systematically: start at the home page and go through the navigation (and any other way of navigating to a new page) and ensure that those pages appear in the analytics data. Are there more pages that are important to the website? Make sure those appear as well. Are there interactive elements like product configurators or calculators on the website? See if there are any data for those elements, by reaching out to your web analytics or IT team to learn more.

If there are important parts of your website that are not currently tracked, it's better to find out sooner rather than later—particularly before you need to analyze how users interact with them!

There isn't really an end point or a point where you realize you're done with this activity—simply, do it for as long as you feel you have time. In the end, I still end up with analytics in one browser window and the website in another browser window.

DIFFICULT TO READ URLS

In a perfect world, every page of every website would have a human-readable URL. That means a URL that looks like this:

http://www.AwesomePetToys.com/products/toyco/laser_pointer?product_id=2788897

rather than this:

http://www.AwesomePetToys.com/wgg333q2d?f=large&w=12f

A human-readable URL is good for users who encounter the link outside the context of your website, it's good for search engine optimization because search engine crawlers can more easily analyze your website, and it's good for you because when you're looking at analytics data, you'll be able to figure out what a page is about just from looking at the URL. Unfortunately, if you're dealing with an e-commerce website or a website using an old content management system, you may be stuck with hard-to-read URLs. You'll still be able to get your work done, but if you're not afraid to take on regular expressions and some detective work, Chapter 15 discusses how you can create profiles for your analytics data that substitute human-readable names for human-unreadable URLs.

A MODEL OF ANALYSIS

Different questions call for different approaches to analysis, from unfocused and unstructured exploration of the data, to highly structured inquiry intended to address specific questions with concrete answers. Think of these two extremes as either end of an axis (Figure 2.3).

One end of the axis consists of clicking around in the reports or looking over data and seeing what's there. This is where most people start to use web analytics and other tools for visualizing data. You may or may not get interesting insights, but you will walk away knowing more about how people use your website. Keep in mind that it's easy to lose track of time when you don't have an end point or specific goal in mind.

At the other extreme is a completely structured inquiry (like simply looking up how many people viewed a specific page on a specific day), which you will probably not find much use for. Think of it as diving into the data to find a specific piece and ignoring everything else. There may be times when you need a single, specific answer, but typically you will spend your time transforming data and comparing them. Of course, there are times and places for simple measurements, such as tracking key performance indicators (KPIs) as you go through design iterations or a similar situation. And you may find that a simple question can lead to more questions and, before you know it, you're in the middle of a complex analysis.

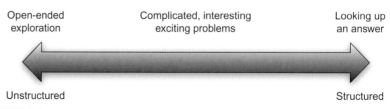

| Open-ended exploration | Complicated, interesting exciting problems | Looking up an answer |

| Unstructured | | Structured |

FIGURE 2.3

Analysis can range from completely open-ended to completely structured. Most UX questions fall between these two poles.

UX work often belongs along the middle of the axis, something we can think of as semi-structured analysis. You should have a question or questions to answer to put boundaries on the time you spend. However, answers are not always as simple as we expect, and in analyzing one area we may serendipitously discover new insights along the way. Semi-structured analysis involves iterations of gathering, transforming, and analyzing data, captured in Figure 2.4.

Pose The Question

Analysis starts with a question, with a gap in your knowledge that you wish to fill. The question sets boundaries on the activity, to let you know when you have accomplished your goal or to help you decide to quit because you are no closer to the goal. You start with the thing you want to learn—a "what" question like "Where do users go after viewing the Our Services page?" or "What pages do users spend the most time on?" or "What are the categories of information needs that drive users to my website?" Alternatively, you may have a "why" question like "Why aren't users clicking on this button" or "Why do so many users go to this page?"

Of course, web analytics is no good at answering "why" questions, so you will need to reframe yours to "what" questions. That will probably mean using analytics to find out what users are currently doing, either to test a theory or to simply give you a starting point for evaluating your website through other means.

Your question will, depending on its scope and focus, decide what data you will gather. Are there particular pages you need data for? A time range that you need to know about? Specific metrics that are relevant? When you have reached the point where you know what data you must gather, you are ready to move on to the next step.

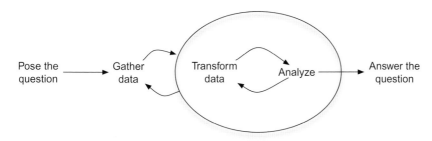

FIGURE 2.4
After posing an analysis question, gathering, transforming, and analyzing data is an iterative process before you can proceed to answering the question.

Gather Data

In this stage you gain access to the data source or sources that will meet your needs and gather the data from the appropriate tools. For a small-scale question using data in Google Analytics, gathering data may be as simple as navigating to the right report. At the other extreme, you may use a script to download thousands of rows of data or get your hands on other sources like a customer relationship management (CRM) system or call-center report.

Transform Data

As with the gather data stage, for a simple inquiry there may be no transformation at all—you're simply looking up a piece of data in a standard report in the interface of your web analytics tool. More likely, though, you will transform the data in some way. You may combine disparate data into a single table, sort or filter through a data set to get the subset that you need, or derive a metric by combining two of the metrics that your web analytics tool produces.

You will probably find Microsoft Excel to be your go-to tool for anything more than simply looking up a number. It offers the ability to assemble disparate data, annotate them, transform them with formulas, and make big data sets manageable through pivot tables. A how-to guide to Excel is outside the scope of this book, although the best way to learn is by doing.

All of this work is to set the stage for the analysis, where you move from the "busy work" to really thinking about the data. In practice, of course, you may do multiple iterations of transformation and analysis.

Analyze

The goal of analysis is think about and interpret the data that you have gathered and transformed. It may be that you can tell a simple story from the data, but it is likely that you will find you have to go back and transform the data further as you find things that you need to clean or the transformation you rendered doesn't quite grant the insight that you need. You may also find that you have to go back to gather more data to complete the picture.

It is easy to spend a great deal of time on analysis, so it's important to know when to stop. This stopping point will vary depending on the question you are answering. In some cases, if you have gathered enough data for a statistically significant result, determining the effectiveness of a design change, that's a good time to stop. In other cases, you may try to describe user behavior and, if you can take a couple of slices of your entire data set and get basically the same result, you can consider that a good stopping point. Lastly, if your goal is to characterize an entire data set like the keywords users searched for, you may wish to stop when you determine that you don't have time to keep gathering more data or if you have stopped learning new things from gathering additional data.

Answer the Question

Finally it is time to tell the story of what you have seen. Obviously, for simple questions with simple, concrete answers, this step can be short. For more complex analyses, you may write a report, some text to accompany the data, create a chart or set of slides, or extensively annotate your spreadsheet. Regardless of how you tell the story, you must tell a story about the data to make them meaningful to others.

Balancing Time and the Need for Certainty

You have to know when to quit. While a simple question (e.g., "What were the top 10 search engine keywords that brought people to the website in April 2013?") may easily yield an answer, for more open-ended questions there may not be a natural end to the analysis.

For example, you may want to know what links users clicked on to leave a particular page on your website. What timeframe do you choose—how far back do you go? Do you look at all the historical data combined or break them up into chunks (such as months) to see how behavior has changed over time?

Perhaps there are 40 links on the page that users can get to. Do you describe how many users click on every one of them or stop with the most popular? Are there any logical groupings to the pages users can get to? With a basic analytics implementation, you won't be able to tell which link users clicked on if more than one link goes to the same page. Do you need to know that level of detail? Is this the only page you care about, or do you want to do the same analysis for multiple pages? Is it enough to look at the data for all visitors, or do you want to segment the data?

One of Pure Visibility's clients, a large childcare provider with about 1,000 centers across the United States, made changes to their five websites: brand new pages to describe each of those childcare centers. These pages rolled out in waves over the course of a few months, with each week bringing a few dozen of the new pages to all of their websites. Pure Visibility was asked whether users were more likely to contact our client to set up a visit to a childcare center after seeing one of the new pages. This was a case where we needed to balance time and the need for certainty, because each individual page only got a small amount of traffic. Answering this question involved pulling data from before and after the new pages came out, multiple times for each separate release date when new batches of pages came out, and repeating the operation for five different websites. In the end, we chose to pull a large enough data sample for us to detect a statistically significant difference in how many users contacted our client, as well as looking at the overall trend in how many users were contacting them.

Getting better answers—gaining additional certainty—is not free. UX professionals are generally familiar with this trade-off as we plan user research activities. With web analytics, the price is typically time.

There is no one-size-fits-all answer on when to stop working on an analysis. It comes down to judging when you have reached a point of diminishing returns. Have you reached a point where you are confident in your answer, are able to make a decision, or no longer learning anything interesting? These may be good times to call it quits.

A good way to approach analysis is to start simple, such as with a high-level version of your question, a narrow slice of time, or just a handful of pages, and quickly determine whether you are on a fruitful path. If you are able to make sense of the data, then expand the scope of your analysis.

SHOWING YOUR WORK

It is essential both for credibility and to make it easier to go back and revisit analyses to show your work. In other words, to supply the data you used or instructions on how to obtain the same data, as well as a record of the transformations you performed.

This doesn't mean actually trying to force stakeholders to review every datum. They should simply be available for situations like the 1 time out of 10 when the executive wants to ask deep, probing questions of your findings, or an analyst with a differing viewpoint challenges your findings.

For simple look-ups, it is usually enough to specify the timeframe you looked at and any filtering or segmentation you may have applied to transform the data. For more complex analyses involving exporting and transforming data, showing your work can involve saving the exported data separate from the spreadsheet where you transformed them, as well as providing instructions for how to recreate the steps you followed. Another good move would be to keep some scrap paper nearby or take notes on your computer as you go. Besides helping others, noting your process may be a lifesaver for yourself.

CONTEXT MATTERS

Bounce rate refers to the portion of visitors that come to a website and then leave before visiting a second page. Imagine you find out that your website has an overall average bounce rate of 56.74%. In a perfect world, every single visitor to your website would be motivated to stay. There will always be people who bounce off the website, though. They may have thought the website looked difficult to use or were turned off by the content, but they may have also been the wrong kind of user, accidentally stumbling upon it or misled by an advertisement. It may be a frequent user who accidentally chose the wrong URL from his or her browser's auto-suggestion feature.

In the end, all you can do is compare data to get context. You can establish a baseline and then see how changes to the website affect that number. You can also split the data into smaller segments, by page or by user, to compare against each other and to the average. Only then can you understand whether a number is good or bad, but even then, it is only in terms of your goals for the website.

Much of this book deals with putting data in context—context meaning understanding data in relation to other, equivalent data, whether across time, between two entities such as pages, or both. We will go into detail discussing ways of splitting up the data to make sense of them. We will focus on comparing pages within the same website or on comparing data from one time period to another time period.

In part, that's because it is nearly impossible to get access to data about other people's websites (particularly if they are a competitor!). Even if you could, comparison would be meaningless because the contexts would be different. Neither website would have the exact same set of users who had been exposed to the same marketing materials, nor would the content or the organization of either website be the same. You can't look to outside benchmarks to provide the context that will tell you if your numbers are "good" or not.

The other reason is related: users on your website act a certain way and, when you look at the data, you can't know whether the website is abysmal or as good as it could possibly get. An ecosystem of factors creates the context. Therefore, you can't make sense of the numbers until you compare them—page to page, or the same pages over time. By seeing that, for example, users spent an average of 50 seconds on all of the pages on your website, it becomes clear that a page with an average time of 1 minute and 20 seconds is well above average.

Data Over Time

One of your major sources of context is the comparison of data over time. There are really two main ways of approaching this:

1. Regular reporting of data
2. Selecting specific time ranges to compare

We discuss regular reporting of data in more detail in Chapter 12, as a way of setting up a culture of reporting. Essentially, you may find it valuable to find specific metrics you want to report on a regular basis, such as weekly or monthly. A culture of reporting means that on a regular basis you report how many visitors to your website buy something or how many start to buy something but give up—things that other parts of your company care about and may want to report on but that reflect the usability of a website.

What you get from regular reporting is the ability to ask, week after week or month after month, "How does this number look in light of the previous numbers?" You get a sense of what a normal value looks like and can make goals for trying to improve your website or find out when some change to the website makes it a lot harder for users to use.

That was the regular reporting of data, the first main approach. The other approach involves deciding what time ranges to compare, typically on an ad hoc basis to answer specific questions. Choosing the right time ranges is, of course, the trick. Unlike the regular reporting way, you will choose time ranges to answer the questions you didn't expect to ask to get the cleanest data you can. It is important to deploy your web analytics tool early rather than when you find out you need the data. That way, you can gather as much baseline data as possible.

You will probably find that there will be a rhythm to how many people visit your website and what they do on it. It will probably vary throughout the day and week, and depending on the type of business or organization, vary by month and throughout the year. Pure Visibility's clients, primarily interested in business-to-business sales, typically see the greatest traffic on Mondays and a steady decline through Sunday. Further, our clients see peaks in visitors at different times of the year as people look for apartments, childcare, or try to spend the remaining budget in their fiscal year.

It's important to know this rhythm from a marketing perspective, since it helps with planning and setting expectations. As a UX professional, you need to be aware that your users' behavior may change from month to month and day to day; at times they may want to gather information and at other times they are ready to buy something from you.

The idea of giving data context by comparing it over time will come into play throughout this book, particularly the ad hoc method, and we'll go into further detail about actually selecting time ranges.

Proportion is Key

Throughout this book, we will tend to focus on proportions rather than absolute numbers as a way to give more context and meaning to the data. For example, you may look at the number of users who make a purchase in comparison to how many users simply came to the website. This particular concept is called *conversion rate* and we will return to it later.

Let's take this example further. Picture an e-commerce website, Awesome PetToys.com, a purveyor of fine toys for pets both common and exotic. In the last month, 100 people came to the website and bought something. The month before, 120 people bought something. Did the website get worse between the months? It's a 17% drop! Now let's add in visitors:

	Visitors to the Website	People Who Bought Something	% of People Who Bought Something
Month 1	5,500	120	2.18%
Month 2	4,500	100	2.22%

When you add in the number of people who came to the website, it turns out that there were fewer in month 2 and, in fact, a slightly greater proportion of those visitors bought something. The actual difference in the proportion of people who bought something is probably meaningless, but the important takeaway is that without knowing how many people are using the website, we lack a key ingredient in measuring whether the website is working for those users.

STATISTICAL SIGNIFICANCE AND STUDENT'S *T*-TEST

A full treatment of statistical concepts is outside the scope of this book, and it is still possible to do practical work with web analytics without expertise on the subject. Nonetheless, it would be worthwhile to brush up on the concepts of confidence intervals and statistical significance, a way of assessing whether the observed difference between samples is simply due to chance.

When you take a sample of a whole population of people, such as the users who visit your website within a certain time period, you observe some aspect of their behavior, like how long they spend on your website or how many of them fill out a form on your website. A confidence interval is a calculation of how high or low that figure may be for the entire population. You have probably come across this concept when you see survey results presented with a margin of error of, say, $\pm 2\%$. Statistical significance is when you take the confidence intervals for two different populations and see if they overlap; if they don't, you can be reasonably confident that the difference you observed isn't due to chance—it is statistically significant.

We will do this with the two-sample *t*-test for comparing measurements of time, and for everything else, the $N - 1$ two-proportion test, which is a more accurate approach to compare completion rates, conversion rates, and anything else where a user either did or didn't do something. Fortunately, calculators, spreadsheets, and the generosity of people who have made tools available online make these calculations less daunting.

We will put these topics to use in Chapter 11. For a much better treatment than is possible here, Sauro and Lewis' *Quantifying the User Experience* (2012) is an excellent resource; introductory statistics books will also cover the concepts used in this book.

SOMETIMES THE DATA CONTRADICT YOU

It's going to happen sometimes—web analytics data will appear to contradict something you found through another method like usability testing. Chapter 10, where we discuss tying web analytics data into other usability methods, deals with resolving the contradiction in greater detail. I mention it here because it's another case where context matters.

Short of some sort of configuration problem, the data in your web analytics tool are true, but that doesn't automatically mean that your contradictory finding is false. If you went out and interviewed a series of users to find out how they researched industrial incinerators and most interviewees told you they wanted to read about energy efficiency, there could be multiple reasons why analytics shows that hardly anyone is going to the energy-efficiency page:

- The interviewees know energy efficiency should be important, and wanted to look responsible in front of you.
- Users can't find the page about energy efficiency.
- Users think they've found the information somewhere else.

Nothing changes the fact that people aren't going to this hypothetical energy-efficiency page for industrial incinerators. The important thing is that you simply don't disregard the finding from your interviews, but rather try to understand it in a new way.

Sometimes the Answer is "No"

There will also be times when you don't find the answer to your question or can't tell a story about the data you see. For example, you may have created a segment that just shows visitors who searched for the name of one of your products and you want to compare them to all visitors to see the differences in how they interact with the pages of your website. You may find that there is no significant difference in the amount of time they spend on pages or the bounce rate.

Even when you find that a data set isn't as interesting as you had hoped or that you can't support a theory, you have still learned something that you didn't know before. You have closed off a fruitless avenue of inquiry.

Make Your Findings Repeatable

It is essential that you make it possible for others to recreate your findings. It's a matter of ensuring accuracy as well as protecting you and your team's credibility. The more complex an analysis, the more data you pull and assemble, the more that can go wrong.

For this reason, keep a record of the steps you took during an analysis. The record can be in a separate document, in line with the data (e.g., in the same spreadsheet as your data), or even a piece of scrap paper. If you export data from your web analytics tool, save those exports and make them available to whoever checks your work, as well as archived for future reference. The most important information to save is what date ranges you are working with and the specific metrics and dimensions you used.

When working with spreadsheets to manipulate data, try to use formulas and references as much as possible rather than copying and pasting numbers from cell to cell. Doing so will make it much easier for someone else to figure out how you transformed the data, as well as check the specific methods you used.

KEY TAKEAWAYS

- Analyses can range from completely unstructured to rigidly structured. Much of the questions UX professionals pose will fall between these two ends of the axis.
- The steps of analysis are:
  - Pose a question that you want to answer.
  - Gather the data you will need.
  - Transform the data into the form that will answer your question.
  - Analyze the data. What story emerges from the data?
  - Answer the question by taking the story you have pieced together and applying it to the question you posed.
- It will often be necessary to balance the need for greater certainty, clarity, or proof against the need to manage how much time you spend in analysis.
- Always keep a record of where you obtained data and how you transformed them. It may otherwise be hard to retrace your footsteps.
- Web analytics tools are a poor way to understand how your website's pages look and fit together—it's important to also have first-hand experience of what it's like to use your website.
- Context is essential for understanding any of the data because no number, in isolation, is meaningful. Adding context means:
  - Comparing data between pages or between users of the same website.
  - Comparing data over time.
  - Looking at proportions rather than raw numbers.
- Sometimes web analytics data will appear to contradict findings from other user research methods. Don't automatically discard your finding, but try to find a new way to understand it or add nuance.
- Even when you do not find a conclusive answer or must discard a theory, you still know more than you did before you started.

CHAPTER 3

How Web Analytics Works

INTRODUCTION

A basic understanding of how web analytics tools work is important for understanding their limitations and for interpreting the data you get.

There are two basic ways you can learn about user activity on websites: log files and page tagging. Log files keep track of what pages load upon each web page request and allow you to take a deep dive into a rich data set, but they can be challenging to use and deploy. Page tagging is less accurate than log files, but there are usually fewer obstacles to getting started with the process and when using page tagging tools. Within the category of page tagging, you will find tools that allow you to analyze how users move from page to page and tools for analyzing what they actually do on each page. This book mainly draws on Google Analytics for examples, which falls into the category of page tagging.

LOG FILE ANALYSIS

One of the two approaches to web analytics is log file analysis using tools like AWStats and Sawmill. It is worth understanding how this approach differs from page tagging, and while log file analysis is outside the scope of this book, the concepts covered in this book transfer well. Web servers keep records of transactions. Every time they get a request, whether it is from a browser or a search engine crawler, it gets recorded in the log and doesn't require that the user have JavaScript enabled, which is a weakness of page tagging tools. On the other hand, if the user accesses a cached version of a page rather than getting it from the server, the log doesn't record the transaction. The result is that the data are imperfect in different ways.

Why aren't we analyzing log files? Partly, it's because page tagging tools are well marketed and actually quite easy to use, relatively speaking. The other reason is that it may be far more challenging and expensive to install a log file analysis tool than to set up a page tagging tool. Log files are huge, and it can be challenging for IT departments to share them. Also, they may periodically

```
<!DOCTYPE html PUBLIC "-//W3C//DTD XHTML 1.0 Transitional//EN" "http://www.w3.org/TR/xhtml1/DTD/xhtml1-transitional.dtd">
<html xmlns="http://www.w3.org/1999/xhtml" dir="ltr" lang="en-US">

    <title>Page Title</title>

<script type="text/javascript">

  var _gaq = _gaq || [];
  _gaq.push(['_setAccount', 'UA-XXXXXX-1']);
  _gaq.push(['_trackPageview']);

  (function() {
    var ga = document.createElement('script'); ga.type = 'text/javascript'; ga.async = true;
    ga.src = ('https:' == document.location.protocol ? 'https://ssl' : 'http://www') + '.google-analytics.com/ga.js';
    var s = document.getElementsByTagName('script')[0]; s.parentNode.insertBefore(ga, s);
  })();

</script>

</head>

<body>
```

FIGURE 3.1

An example of Google Analytics' tracking code. This small amount of code is what makes it work. Google Analytics will generate the appropriate code for your own website.

purge them, making it impossible to get much historical data. Installing the appropriate software and configuring databases appropriately may simply be beyond the IT capabilities of an organization. With a page tagging tool, you add a few lines of JavaScript to the pages of your website, which you may be able to do through the content management system that powers your website rather than manually changing every page. Based on your level of expertise or the amount of resources available to you, there's a good chance that it will simply be easier to get started using a page tagging tool. On the other hand, some kinds of highly interactive websites, such as those that make heavy use of AJAX, may be much harder to track with a page tagging tool than with log files—they would require extensive additional tagging of page elements, whereas log files, by their nature, simply track every request to the server.

PAGE TAGGING

The page tagging method works by adding a small piece of JavaScript code to all of the pages on your website that you want to track (Figure 3.1). When a user's browser loads a page, it opens up the HTML file and starts interpreting the code. When it hits the JavaScript code, it will send the following data to a database:

- What page just got loaded
- When it was loaded

- Where the user just came from (in terms of search engine or a link from another website)
- IP address
- Technical details like the user's browser, operating system, screen resolution, and colors

It also puts a cookie on the user's computer that will let the analytics tool know whether it's already recorded data from that user. From this small amount of data, web analytics tools are able to provide a rich set of information about user activity. By combining data about when pages were viewed with anonymous data on who viewed them, these tools can map out the sequence of pages that users viewed during their visit.

With page tagging solutions, there are two main categories: tools for tracking activity as users move from page to page, and tools for tracking activity on pages. Google Analytics falls mainly in the "move from page to page" category, as does Webtrends and Omniture (although they have capabilities for measuring on-page behavior).

GOOGLE ANALYTICS ASYNCHRONOUS TRACKING CODE

If you start looking at the source code on other people's websites, trying to find Google Analytics tracking code, sometimes you'll see it at the bottom of the page before the </body> tag and sometimes at the top of the page before the </head> tag. What you're seeing is technology in transition. Back in the "old" days of 2008, a page waiting to load a script tag would hold up the rest of the page load, so industry best practice was to put it at the bottom of your HTML. Having the code at the bottom does no harm to the end user, but lowers accuracy—when tracking code is placed at the bottom of a page, any time the user stops loading the page before it reaches the bottom, that page isn't tracked. There were many requests for development of a tag that could be at the top of the page and would also not slow down page loads. A couple of years ago, Google Analytics did just that, introducing a version of their tracking code (asynchronous code) that runs in the background while the page continues to load. That means it can go at the top of the page. This new code makes Google Analytics more accurate (sometimes much more accurate, depending on the website), but not everyone is using it yet, which is why you will still sometimes find tracking codes at the bottom of pages. If you're working on a website with the old version of the code or with the new code at the bottom of the page (which is surprisingly common), send the word out about the new code and try to get it changed and/or moved up to the top.

Cookies

A cookie is a piece of data that a website stores on users' computers. They are used to keep track of things like user preferences, what the user was doing on the website the last time he or she visited, and to keep track of whether a user is currently logged on to a website or not.

Web analytics tools use cookies to track whether a user has visited a website before and how the user originally got to the website (e.g., through a search engine). As the user moves from page to page, the cookie lets analytics know that these pageviews are all part of the same visit. If the user does not load a page on the website for a certain period of time, the visit ends.

Accuracy

The data you get from page tagging web analytics tools are not 100% accurate. The tools do, however, provide you with data that are good enough to work with, because they are internally consistent and the amount of error compared to the real amount of traffic is consistent.

The problem is that there is no perfect way to collect data about users' actions. Because page tagging tools rely on JavaScript, if a user's browser has JavaScript disabled, the tool won't gather any data. If users have installed a browser plug-in to prevent analytics tools from tracking their actions or activated privacy mode, then you won't be able to gather any data about them. Also, sometimes the Internet or the analytics tracking script just doesn't work properly and data don't get collected.

What makes web analytics useful is that the data are consistently accurate to within 10% of actual traffic numbers. Consistency lets you measure trends over time and make actionable decisions based on data.

We are left, then, with just a minor and somewhat philosophical point: the data in your web analytics tool are not a definitive statement of what really happened, but rather just what you can measure about what really happened. If you read that 10,467 people visited your homepage in a single week, that's simply how many visitors the tool recorded. Another web analytics tool (you can run more than one on the same website) would give you a slightly different number, a log file analysis would produce a slightly different number, and if you had perfect knowledge, you would know that the actual number was slightly different. If accuracy is critical, such as counting how many sales you received or how many people registered for an account, you should go to a more appropriate tool (like a CRM tool) as your source for "reality."

SMARTPHONES

You will be able to gather analytics data from users with smartphones such as Apple's iPhone. Smartphones have JavaScript-enabled browsers that can run JavaScript. However, you will probably not be able to get data about how people with feature phones (i.e., phones that don't have JavaScript-enabled browsers) use your website. Depending on your users, lack of JavaScript capability could be a trivial concern or a huge problem—the United States has relatively few feature phones accessing websites, whereas developing countries see a great deal of usage.

Accounts and Profiles

In Google Analytics, each website has its own analytics account and each account has one or more profiles (Figure 3.2). Other web analytics tools use different models for organizing data, and if you are using one of them, you can safely move on to the next section.

The *account* is the repository of data. Each account has its own unique identifier (e.g., Pure Visibility's Google Analytics account is UA-461660) that ensures the tracking code sends data to the correct place.

A *profile* is the way the data are actually displayed to you. A profile may just present you with all the data in the account, but at the very least you will probably be working with a profile that filters out the IP address of the place you work so you don't skew the data. You can set up profiles to transform the data further, such as isolating parts of a larger website or rewriting URLs to cluster similar pages for easier analysis. Chapter 15 goes into greater detail on how profiles work.

This book focuses on Google Analytics for examples, but it is not the only web analytics tool that organizes data into profiles. This is a common and useful feature for organizing data into meaningful chunks.

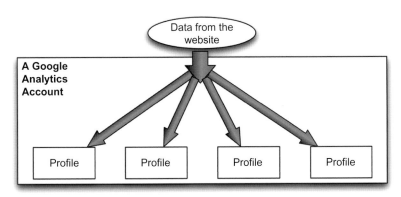

FIGURE 3.2

Data about website usage flow into a web analytics tool and then into one or more profiles. In Google Analytics, an account receives the data and contains one or more profiles.

INSTALLATION

This book doesn't go deep into the subject of setup and configuration—the concern is more with practical use of tools, and most readers will be in situations where other people are responsible for implementation. It may be helpful, though, to understand the basic steps of setting up web analytics. The general outline is that installation consists of three basic stages:

1. Create an account.
2. Set up profiles and filters.
3. Generate the tracking code to install on your website and install it.

These steps will vary from tool to tool; with Google Analytics, they are done without intervention from Google. Other tools will require interacting with the vendor for the first two steps.

In practice, steps 2 and 3 can be anything but simple and there may be multiple iterations of profile configuration. Setting up filters, which is the way you determine what data do and do not get captured, has the potential to be a tricky and time-consuming operation. It may involve things like finding IP addresses that your company uses so you can filter out your own visits. Generating tracking code entails putting together the JavaScript that has to go on every page or writing code to track interactive features on your website.

Click Analytics

There are also tools for analyzing user behavior on a page itself rather than movement between pages. They can capture where specifically users click (e.g., fields on a form or on a part of a page that look clickable but aren't), where they move the mouse, what keys they press, and how long users spend looking at the top of a page before scrolling down—basically, they let you make recordings of a user's session. You can view these data in aggregate—for example, by looking at a page of your website overlaid with a dot for everywhere that users clicked. Some tools even offer you the ability to play back individual user sessions as if you were standing over the user's shoulder.

These tools let you answer questions like these:

- In what order do users fill out fields in a form?
- Are there fields that take a long time for users to fill out?
- Where do users click on things that aren't clickable?
- On a clickable object, where exactly do users click?

Much like a page tagging analytics tool, click analytics tools involve inserting a snippet of JavaScript onto the pages you want to track.

Click analytics products, such as Tealeaf, CrazyEgg, and ClickTale, to name a few at the time of writing, are worth exploring if you want to gather more evidence about user actions on pages. Chapter 12 will delve further into click analytics tools and analysis.

METRICS AND DIMENSIONS

Metrics and dimensions are key concepts in web analytics. Metrics are numeric measurements of various aspects of users' behavior, like how long they spend viewing a page or how many times users viewed a page.

Dimensions are the categories that user data may be grouped into, such as what browser they used or what keyword they searched for. Dimensions describe different attributes of users, their computers, how they got to your website, or even parts of your website that users visit, which you can use to divide your users into segments. When dimensions are paired with metrics, you can learn things like how many users use each kind of browser, how many views each page receives, and how many visits came from Texas versus New York last Thursday.

Let's take a look at a metric and a dimension to try to unpack this relationship. We will cover them in greater detail later, but a kind of metric is the pageview and a kind of dimension is the URL of a page. Every time a user loads a page in his or her browser, web analytics counts it as a pageview.

One can simply count up all of the pageviews that a website receives—that is, every time every single page on a website was loaded in a user's browser. However, the pageviews metric becomes more useful when paired with the page dimension. You can count how many pageviews each individual page of your website received. You can count how many pageviews a group of pages received, such as the "About Us" section of your website. The page dimension gives you a way to divide all of the pageviews that web analytics measured into meaningful, useful segments.

Another possible pair is the average time on website metric and the mobile dimension. The mobile dimension only has two possible values—yes or no—based on whether or not the user visited the website using a mobile device like a phone or a tablet. Average time on website is the average amount of time that a group of users spent on your website. You can find out the average amount of time that all of your users spent on your website, but when you combine this metric with the mobile dimension, you can see the average amount of time that mobile users spent on your website and compare it to the average amount of time desktop computer users spent on your website. Again, the mobile dimension is just one possible way of segmenting metric data.

The term *metric* is widely used in web analytics tools, but *dimension* is Google's terminology. The concept of a dimension is used in other tools, though (e.g., you have *elements* in Omniture), and overall you will find that the specific metrics and dimensions in this chapter exist in other analytics tools. They simply may vary in how easy they are to get to and what they are labeled.

The best way to understand these concepts better is to spend a bit of time seeing them in action. Later in this chapter, we will return to the concept of dimensions in the section "Interacting with Data in Google Analytics." For now, let's start with metrics, with an example of a report from Google Analytics (Figure 3.3). This is the "Visitors Overview" report, which gives you high-level data about the users coming to your website, in the sense that these values are sums and averages for all of the visitors to the website. The "Visitors Overview" report has a large graph that shows a specific, selectable metric over time, and then high-level metrics about the visitors to your website.

Visits

A visit is a single time that a person comes to a website, clicks around and views some pages, and then leaves. By itself, visits isn't a very useful metric, but much of this book involves slicing the total number of visitors into smaller segments according to how those visitors behave on the website, so the visits metric will come up repeatedly.

THE LIMITS OF TRACKING VISITS

Analytics tools can't get a perfect measurement of how long a visit lasts, because the tools can't actually tell when a user leaves the website they are tracking (see the "Average Visit Duration" section for more information). In Google Analytics, a visit ends when the user hasn't viewed any pages for 30 minutes (these 30 minutes are excluded from any calculations of how long the user spent on the website). If the user comes back to the same website later, it is a new visit—even if the user goes to the website, leaves it open in their browser for several hours without touching it, and then starts using the website again.

Unique Visitors (Metric)

If a user starts a new session on a website, analytics counts that as another visit. Unique visitors is a way of capturing how many individuals came to a website and whether they visit multiple times or just once.

A visitor is only unique within whatever timeframe you've selected—it doesn't reflect whether that user visited before or after the dates that you are analyzing. Analytics tools judge whether or not a visitor is unique by the presence of a cookie, so there's no way of knowing whether the same person is

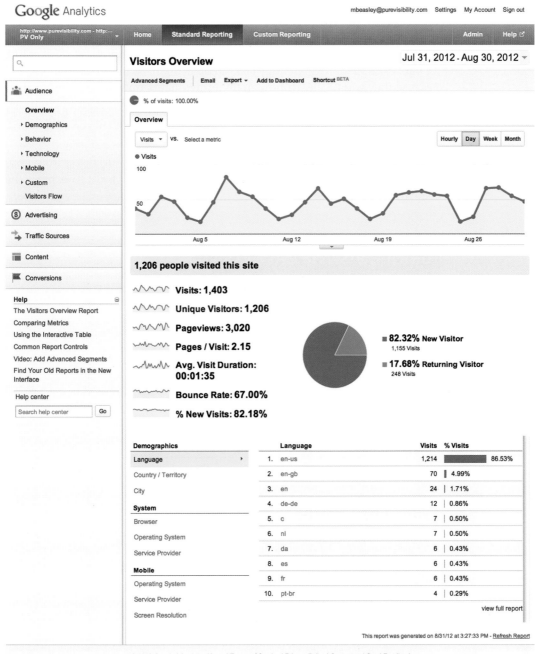

FIGURE 3.3
The "Visitors Overview" report, which shows high-level metrics for your entire website.

using the computer or if multiple people are. If a single person uses a desktop computer and then visits a website from his or her phone, he or she gets counted again as a unique visitor. This point is particularly important, as users increasingly access the same website through multiple devices, often as part of a single overarching task. People often focus on unique visitors because they want to learn how many individual people are coming to their website; however, its limitations make it better suited to using it in combination with other metrics rather than as a single, somewhat misleading, measurement of visitors to a website.

Google Analytics explicitly uses the label "unique visitors" to better differentiate it from "visits." You will also find "visitors" in other tools to express the same thing as "unique visitors."

UNIQUE VISITOR CAVEATS

Unique visitors falls under the category of "nice to know" but usually appears more useful than it actually is. Even though stakeholders may be very curious to learn what the real number of visitors is, knowing this number generally doesn't lead to any different decisions than the regular visits metric. More importantly, "unique" is relative to the time you're looking at. A visitor may be unique for the week you're looking at, but actually came to your website five times in the previous week. If you look at unique visitors one week at a time, that one user will get counted as one unique visit in both weeks. If you change your time range to cover both weeks, those unique visits don't get added together; rather, that user just shows up as one unique visit. You will get more value from investigating the behavior of new versus returning visitors, and perhaps, among those returning visitors, those that return frequently and those that do not (depending, of course, on who your users are).

Pageviews (Metric)

A pageview is a single time that a user went to a page. If the user goes to a page more than once during his or her visit, it's a separate pageview each time. In Figure 3.4, we can see that the user went to six pages total, repeating one of them. Each one counts as a separate pageview.

In Figure 3.4, if the person was the only person to use the website, all of the pages would have just one pageview except /widgets/, which would have two pageviews. The most obvious use of this metric is to get a relative measure of what pages people are visiting and which ones they're not. Comparing the pageviews of different pages will help you find out what pages are popular or unpopular with users. When you make design changes to your website, one of your goals may be to get more people to a particular page—that is, increase pageviews.

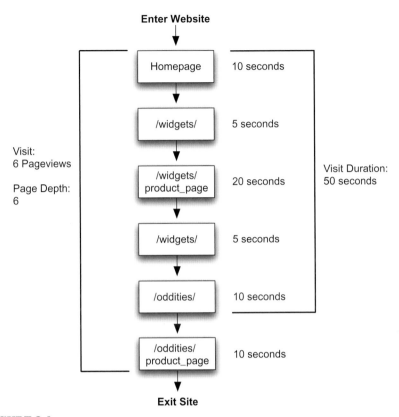

Enter Website

Homepage	10 seconds
/widgets/	5 seconds
/widgets/ product_page	20 seconds
/widgets/	5 seconds
/oddities/	10 seconds
/oddities/ product_page	10 seconds

Visit:
6 Pageviews

Page Depth:
6

Visit Duration:
50 seconds

Exit Site

FIGURE 3.4

This diagram shows the relationship between pageviews, visits, and visit duration. A visit consists of one or more pageviews. The amount of time between each pageview is added together to calculate the visit duration.

Pages/Visit (Metric)

Pages/visit and page depth both capture the number of pages that users go to during their visit. If they visit the same page multiple times, each additional pageview is counted.

As with many other metrics, there is nothing intrinsically good about high or low numbers, but in a practical sense, high numbers are usually good because they usually reflect users taking the time to explore your website and/or do stuff. It is often useful to compare this metric across different segments of users or over time.

Average Visit Duration

Average visit duration is the amount of time that a user spends on your website. As previously discussed, any time that the user spends on the last page he or she views isn't counted, which also means that users who bounce from the website have a visit duration of 0.

As we dive deeper into analytics data, it is common to compare two or more populations, usually as a proxy for how engaging or "sticky" a website is. When segmenting users in Google Analytics, you can do it according to visit duration, such as filtering out users whose visit duration was less than 45 seconds long, for example.

Bounce Rate (Metric)

The bounce rate of a page or a group of pages is the number of users who entered a website on a page and left without visiting any other pages, divided by the total number of users who entered the website on that page. It only counts users who start their visit on a page and excludes anyone who navigated from another page on the website. It's useful to keep this in mind, because the bounce rate may be calculated based on a very small number of visitors, if it is a page or group of pages that is deep within a website.

A low bounce rate is generally a good thing. A high bounce rate may be fine if the purpose of a page is to show the user some information and then send him or her on his or her way without doing anything, but that situation may not come up very much. As with other metrics, "high" and "low" are relative to other pages on your website (although in my experience, bounce rates lower than 30% are quite low).

% New Visits (Metric)

The % new visits, for a given set of users, is the number of users who have never been to the website before divided by the total number of users. In Google Analytics, "new" means they haven't visited within the last two years. Unfortunately, this metric doesn't reflect people who are using a different computer or even a different browser or who clear their cookies.

The % new visits metric can be useful as a way to describe users who you are analyzing or as a way to measure success if you are attempting to get users to come back to your website after their initial visit.

VISITOR TYPE (DIMENSION)

A closely related dimension is visitor type. Users are classified as either "new" or "returning" based on whether or not their browser has a cookie from this website from the past two years.

Using These Metrics

In isolation, these metrics won't answer particularly interesting questions. They serve more as jumping-off points for deeper inquiry—it's when we dig into other reports and compare these metrics over time and segment them according to users' behavior, whether according to a single dimension or a combination of dimensions, and filtering by the values captured as metrics, that we are able to gain the deepest insights.

INTERACTING WITH DATA IN GOOGLE ANALYTICS

These metrics and others become more meaningful when we split them up according to different dimensions (and, in later chapters, combinations of dimensions)—that is, basic segmentation. To see segmentation in action, we turn to an example of a typical report in Google Analytics. If you click on Content in the side navigation, then Site Content, and then All Pages, you will reach the "All Pages" report. We will return to this report in Chapter 7, but for now, we look at this report to learn more about interacting with data within the tool (in later chapters we will export data and work with them). Interacting with tables of data is one of the most important and common activities you will engage in when working with web analytics, and this section will give you a sense of the power you have to manipulate data.

Again, we see a big chart at the top of the report that displays a metric over time (days, weeks, months, and, in some reports, hours). It can display any of the metrics that you see in the table in the lower half of Figure 3.5.

Below the large chart, there are averages or sums for all of the metrics in the report, for all of the data in the entire time period selected—not just the data visible in the table.

The table is where we encounter a dimension in use to divide up metrics. In this case, the dimension is page, with each row showing the various metrics' data for just that page. We can see in Figure 3.5 that the average time on page for the various pages ranges from 33 seconds (/about/jobs/) to 3 minutes and 52 seconds (/services/archives/seo-articles/delivery-methods/), but in this report, above the table, we can see that the average amount of time that users spend looking at pages for the entire website is 1 minute 24 seconds.

The rest of this chapter deals with interacting with the data in the table itself, which will be a common activity in Google Analytics because so much of the data are displayed in a tabular format. You will spend a great deal of time looking at data that are divided up across a single dimension (and, later in this chapter, two dimensions in the same table), and the main difference between many reports is what dimension it uses to segment the data.

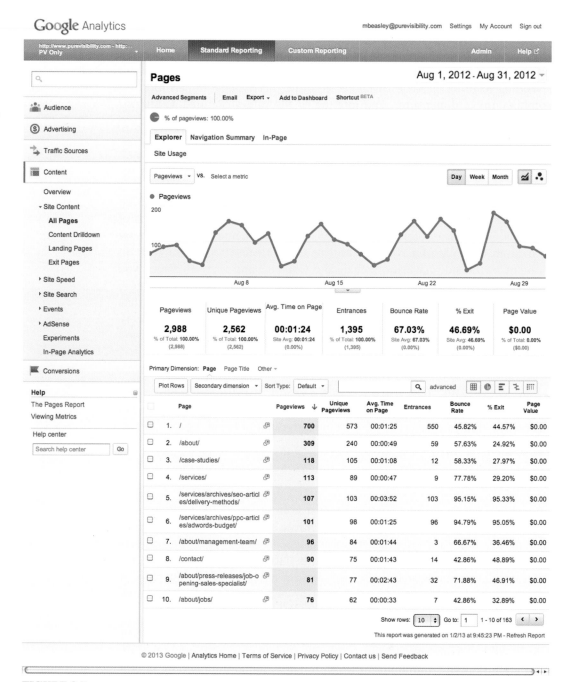

FIGURE 3.5

An example of the "All Pages" report, a typical report in Google Analytics from an interaction perspective.

Plot Rows

There is a checkbox on the far left side of every row of data. You can check one or more boxes and then click on the Plot Rows button to change the big chart so that instead of displaying a line for all data combined, it also shows lines for the rows you have selected. In Figure 3.5, the chart shows the sum of all pageviews every day. You could select just the homepage and the /about/ page (rows 1 and 2 of the table) and display how many pageviews those pages receive per day, as in Figure 3.6. It can be particularly helpful to do so to find out if a page follows the same overall trend as the rest of the website, or if it moves different, such as having a sudden surge of pageviews.

Secondary Dimension

By default, the table takes a single dimension, such as all the pages that users may view, and displays a row for each value. The Secondary Dimension button lets you add another dimension column to the table. When you add another dimension to a table you go to a finer level of granularity with your data because you are now segmenting it according to two dimensions. For example, instead of just looking at usage data for pages on your website, you could then divide the data for each page into whether the user was new or returning (Figure 3.7).

Sort Type

By default, tables are sorted according to some metric (often, visits or pageviews), typically in descending order. In the example of Figure 3.5, the data are sorted starting with the page with the most pageviews, the home page, and then the next most viewed page, and so on. If you are comparing two time ranges, it sorts according to the data from the more recent time range, as seen in Figure 3.8.

When comparing time ranges, you can choose two other sort types from the Sort Type dropdown menu. One is Absolute Change, which sorts the rows according to the size of the difference between the two time ranges. You can see in Figure 3.9 that whereas the homepage had the most pageviews (as shown in Figure 3.5), the page /about/press-releases/job-opening-sales-specialist/ had the greatest growth in pageviews when comparing August to May. Sorting tables by Absolute Change often fills the top rows of a table with data that are not very useful, as in the case of Figure 3.9, where the top 10 pages are rarely viewed compared to other pages in the website. This situation is where Advanced Search can be helpful—you can use it to filter out any pages with fewer than 100 pageviews, for example.

Another sorting feature that is occasionally useful is dropdown option Weighted Sort. Weighted Sort is only rarely available in Google Analytics and

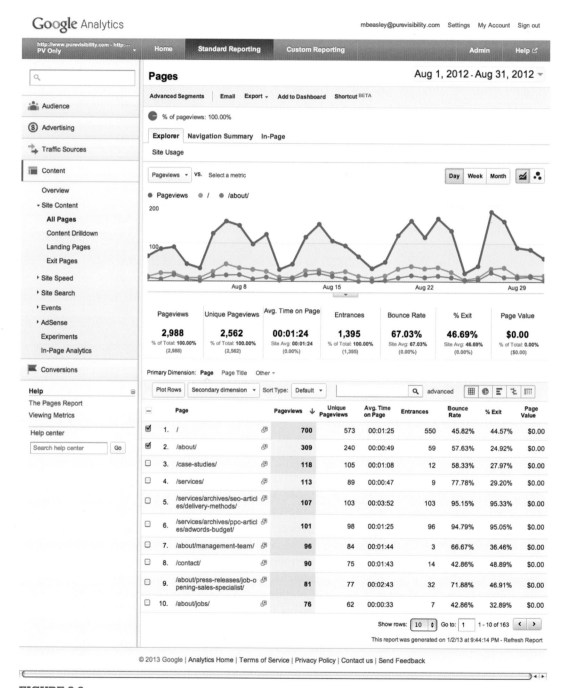

FIGURE 3.6

The report from Figure 3.5, but with only data from rows 1 and 2, the homepage and /about/ page, displayed in the graph. This was done by selecting them using the checkboxes on the left side of the table and clicking on the Plot Rows button.

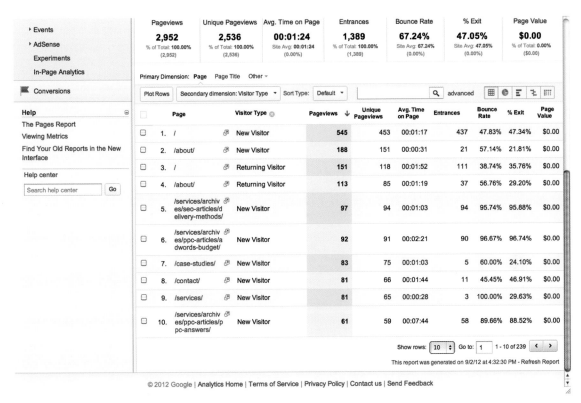

FIGURE 3.7
The data from Figure 3.5, but with a secondary dimension added to divide data about pages according to whether the users were new to the website or returning.

is a sorting algorithm that balances the degree of change in two values against the size of those values.

Search

There are two types of search available: simple and advanced. The simple search lets you enter a string of characters, and then it shows only the rows of data where that string appears. If you were to use simple search for the report in Figure 3.5, you could search for "services" and it would only show data for the pages that include "services" in the URL. Performing a search will also change the data above the table that shows sums and averages (Figure 3.10).

Advanced search is, unsurprisingly, more advanced. It lets you filter the table according to metrics and dimensions that aren't explicitly exposed in the table and combine multiple filters using AND and OR. This feature works much like advanced segments, which we will cover in Chapter 9.

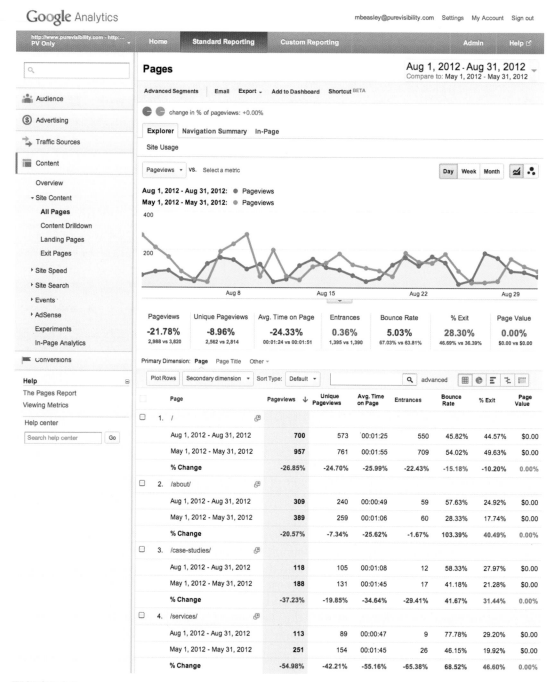

FIGURE 3.8
The data from Figure 3.5, compared to data from an earlier month. Note that the data are sorted in order of pageviews from the more recent month.

☐	6.	/services/archives/ppc-articl ⊕ es/adwords-budget/						
		Aug 1, 2012 - Aug 31, 2012	101	98	00:01:25	96	94.79%	95.05%	$0.00
		May 1, 2012 - May 31, 2012	93	90	00:04:20	90	91.11%	91.40%	$0.00
		% Change	8.60%	8.89%	-67.51%	6.67%	4.04%	4.00%	0.00%
☐	7.	/about/management-team/ ⊕						
		Aug 1, 2012 - Aug 31, 2012	96	84	00:01:44	3	66.67%	36.46%	$0.00
		May 1, 2012 - May 31, 2012	71	61	00:01:27	2	100.00%	33.80%	$0.00
		% Change	35.21%	37.70%	18.93%	50.00%	-33.33%	7.86%	0.00%
☐	8.	/contact/ ⊕						
		Aug 1, 2012 - Aug 31, 2012	90	75	00:01:43	14	42.86%	48.89%	$0.00
		May 1, 2012 - May 31, 2012	75	67	00:02:29	13	69.23%	44.00%	$0.00
		% Change	20.00%	11.94%	-31.16%	7.69%	-38.10%	11.11%	0.00%
☐	9.	/about/press-releases/job-o ⊕ pening-sales-specialist/						
		Aug 1, 2012 - Aug 31, 2012	81	77	00:02:43	32	71.88%	46.91%	$0.00
		May 1, 2012 - May 31, 2012	2	2	00:00:33	0	0.00%	50.00%	$0.00
		% Change	3,950.00%	3,750.00%	392.95%	∞%	∞%	-6.17%	0.00%
☐	10.	/about/jobs/ ⊕						
		Aug 1, 2012 - Aug 31, 2012	76	62	00:00:33	7	42.86%	32.89%	$0.00
		May 1, 2012 - May 31, 2012	63	53	00:00:29	3	66.67%	23.81%	$0.00
		% Change	20.63%	16.98%	13.72%	133.33%	-35.71%	38.16%	0.00%

Show rows: 10 ⬍   Go to: 1   1 - 10 of 226 ‹ ›

This report was generated on 1/2/13 at 9:58:57 PM - Refresh Report

FIGURE 3.8   (Continued)

Beyond Tables

There are other ways to display data besides the humble table, available through the buttons in the upper right corner.

Percentage

You can take a single metric from the table and show not just the actual value (like how many visits came from each kind of mobile device), but also what portion of all visits each row represents, along with a pie chart to visualize the relative amounts of each row. For a more effective way of visually comparing values, you can select the next button, Performance.

FIGURE 3.9

The data from Figure 3.5, sorted according to the Absolute Change in page views from May to August. This sorting results in the top 10 rows of the table being filled with rarely viewed pages.

☐ 5.	/about/jobs/analysts-day/							
	Aug 1, 2012 - Aug 31, 2012	19	15	00:01:07	1	0.00%	15.79%	$0.00
	May 1, 2012 - May 31, 2012	0	0	00:00:00	0	0.00%	0.00%	$0.00
	% Change	∞%	∞%	∞%	∞%	0.00%	∞%	0.00%
☐ 6.	/case-studies/b2b-internet-mark eting/							
	Aug 1, 2012 - Aug 31, 2012	18	15	00:02:21	3	33.33%	16.67%	$0.00
	May 1, 2012 - May 31, 2012	0	0	00:00:00	0	0.00%	0.00%	$0.00
	% Change	∞%	∞%	∞%	∞%	∞%	∞%	0.00%
☐ 7.	/services/archives/ppc-articles/p pc-answers/							
	Aug 1, 2012 - Aug 31, 2012	65	62	00:06:46	61	88.52%	87.69%	$0.00
	May 1, 2012 - May 31, 2012	48	43	00:05:50	43	90.70%	87.50%	$0.00
	% Change	35.42%	44.19%	15.98%	41.86%	-2.40%	0.22%	0.00%
☐ 8.	/services/analytics/omniture-site -catalyst/							
	Aug 1, 2012 - Aug 31, 2012	16	16	00:01:26	14	92.86%	81.25%	$0.00
	May 1, 2012 - May 31, 2012	0	0	00:00:00	0	0.00%	0.00%	$0.00
	% Change	∞%	∞%	∞%	∞%	∞%	∞%	0.00%
☐ 9.	/contact/							
	Aug 1, 2012 - Aug 31, 2012	90	75	00:01:43	14	42.86%	48.89%	$0.00
	May 1, 2012 - May 31, 2012	75	67	00:02:29	13	69.23%	44.00%	$0.00
	% Change	20.00%	11.94%	-31.16%	7.69%	-38.10%	11.11%	0.00%
☐ 10.	/services/archives/seo-articles/s ame-results/							
	Aug 1, 2012 - Aug 31, 2012	15	14	00:00:03	14	92.86%	93.33%	$0.00
	May 1, 2012 - May 31, 2012	0	0	00:00:00	0	0.00%	0.00%	$0.00
	% Change	∞%	∞%	∞%	∞%	∞%	∞%	0.00%

Show rows: 10 ⟳ Go to: 1 1 - 10 of 226 ‹ ›

This report was generated on 1/3/13 at 8:58:24 AM - Refresh Report

FIGURE 3.9   (Continued)

Performance

The Performance option is just like Percentage, except instead of a pie chart, it uses a vertical bar graph.

Comparison

The Comparison feature lets you compare a specific metric to the website average, on a row-by-row basis. For the example in Figure 3.11, we see the same data as in Figure 3.5, but comparing the average time on page for each individual page for the average time on page for the website as a whole.

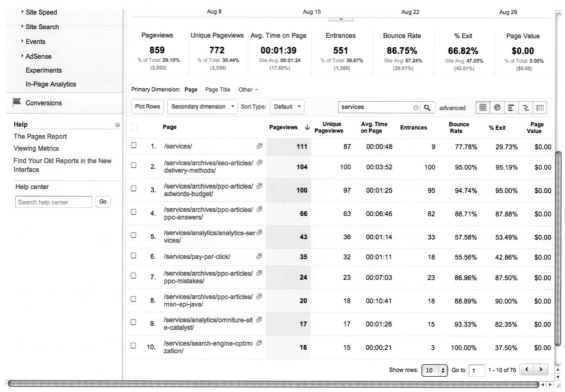

FIGURE 3.10

When you perform a search to filter what data appear in the table, the sums and averages above the table also change. Compare this screenshot to Figure 3.5.

Term Cloud

Only available for certain reports like search keywords, the Term Cloud creates a word cloud. Each row of the table may be a single word, and the size of the word is determined by whatever metric you choose. The usefulness of this report will probably be determined by how useful you find word clouds.

Pivot

Lastly, there is Pivot, a complex and powerful way to interact with data. Pivot lets you show data in a pivot table, which lets you take a dimension and turn it from a row to a column. In the mobile devices example, you would have a row for each kind of mobile device, and then you could select another dimension, such as browser type or whether the user is new or returning, and make that a column. Then, within each column, you could show multiple metrics like pageviews or average time on page. The end result would be the ability to show, for each page, the total number of pageviews and average

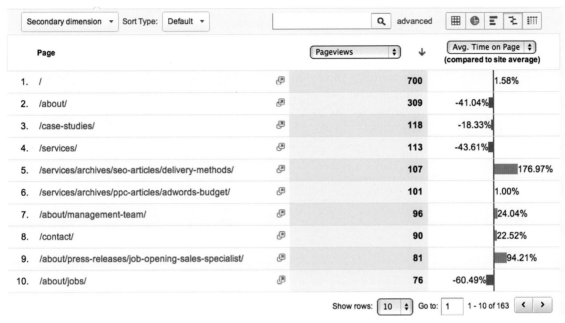

FIGURE 3.11
The data from Figure 3.5, but changed from the Data (Table) view to the Comparison view, displaying a comparison between the average time on page for each page to the overall website average time on page.

time on page, the count of pageviews from new visitors and their average time on page, and the count of pageviews from returning visitors and their average time on page. This feature is complicated and powerful. Although we will not use it in this book, it is important to be aware of it if you use Google Analytics.

KEY TAKEAWAYS

- There are two basic approaches to web analytics: page tagging and log files.
- Page tagging works by adding code to every page of the website that executes when the browser processes the page. For Google Analytics, this code sends:
  - What page was loaded and when
  - Where the user came from
  - IP address
  - Browser and device
- Page tagging tools use a cookie to determine if each pageview is part of the same session, and whether the user has been to the website before.

- Perfect data are impossible because not every user has JavaScript enabled and because sometimes the Internet just doesn't work, but web analytics data from page tagging tools are reliable enough for analyzing trends.
- A metric is an aspect of user behavior that can be measured and expressed as a number, such as how many pages the user views.
- A dimension is an attribute of a user or the user's visit that can be used to categorize the user, such as whether the user is new to the website or returning.

CHAPTER 4

Goals

INTRODUCTION

"What is the UX team doing for this business?" One of the attractive things about web analytics is that it can tie together a story of how people get to a website, interact with a website, and do something that leads to the website generating money for its owner. This chapter discusses the latter. The ultimate purpose of this chapter is to describe how you can show that UX work relates to your organization's success by measuring things that matter to the organization's stakeholders. More concretely, this chapter is about measuring how many people fill up their shopping cart and buy something, sign up for an account, download a whitepaper, watch an important video, fill out an application, or otherwise do something that you really want users to do on your website. The reports discussed in this chapter tell you what portion of your visitors complete these actions that you care about and let you explore what pages they visited before doing so.

When web analytics is used in a marketing context, goals measure the effectiveness of marketing campaigns at getting visitors to take some action that generates revenue for the organization. There are good resources out there for tying specific monetary values to website activity (to answer questions like "How much is it worth to get a user to sign up for an account?"), but the focus of this chapter is less on measuring how much money a website generates as it is on measuring whether or not a website is successful, a subtle but important twist. Success includes making money, but also encompasses actions on the website that aren't directly tied to money, as well as things that will never make money but do fulfill the purpose of the website.

Before we go further, though, we have to define goals and conversions.

WHAT ARE GOALS AND CONVERSIONS?

Two important concepts as we dive into web analytics are the *goal* and the *conversion*, which mean basically the same thing, yet coexist, getting used interchangeably.

CONTENTS

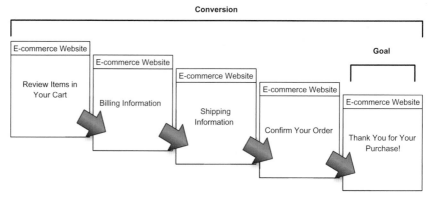

FIGURE 4.1

You can see that the goal is the specific end point, when you know that a user has succeeded at a task. The conversion is the entire act of initiating the action leading to the goal and actually getting to the goal. In practice, these terms get used somewhat interchangeably.

A *conversion* is some kind of action that you want users to take on your website. This term comes from marketing, where it describes a prospective customer taking an action that signals his or her interest in your product or service. In terms of a website, conversion means contacting the sales team, directly buying something, or signing up to download a whitepaper, for example.

Web analytics takes this concept and extends it so you can measure not only how many people take an action that is directly related to sales, but anything that signals that a user is interested in what you're selling or engaged with your website, rather than a casual visitor. You could measure how many people stay on the website for a certain amount of time, interact with a free financial calculator, or download a PDF that doesn't ask for their personal information, for example.

With web analytics, you measure these user actions by choosing a *goal*—a concrete end point or "finish line" that shows that users converted (Figure 4.1). This could mean measuring how many people reach a certain page (e.g., the confirmation page at the end of a shopping cart checkout), how many people click on a link to download a PDF, or how many users spend two minutes on the website.

GOAL CONVERSION RATE (METRIC)

Goal conversion rate is the portion of selected users who have taken a given action. *Selected users* can mean the entire population of people who have come to a website, or a smaller portion who you have selected. This metric is valuable for measuring online marketing, but when you make design changes intended to make it easier to complete a goal or to get users to do so, you will compare this metric over time to see if you have increased it.

> ## GOAL COMPLETIONS (METRIC)
>
> *Goal completions* is simply the count of how many times users took whatever action constitutes a goal. For goals with multiple steps, like an e-commerce checkout process, there is another metric, *goal starts*, that captures how many times users reached the first step in that goal.

Unfortunate Colliding Terms

In this book, we discuss two uses of the term *goal* with slightly different meanings. In usability, a goal is something that a user sets out to do with an interface, something that drives him or her to take action. Web analytics' use of the term focuses more on what the business wants the user to do—you can think of this usage as kind of like "scoring a goal" in the sports sense. In a perfect world, this business-centric definition of a goal would align perfectly with the actual goals users have.

Of course, a goal can also appear in usability as something you are trying to attain through your design work, like a completion rate of 90% or a task time of under two minutes. For the sake of clarity, we will refer to this as a *design objective*.

All Websites Should Have Goals

For the most part, we will use the term *business*, but the concepts in this chapter (and throughout the book) apply to any kind of organization that may have a website, such as nonprofit organizations, universities, small businesses, and large businesses. For the sake of brevity, we'll stick with *business*, which also ignores the matter of whether you are working on your own organization's website or you are a consultant.

Everybody who has a website should have at least one goal to measure how well the website is serving its users, even if that goal doesn't perfectly capture the whole picture. Later in this chapter, we'll dive into selecting analytics goals.

Why Do Goals Matter for User Experience?

Simply, goals matter for user experience because we must ensure that our work produces value for the business—that we are in alignment with what the organization cares about. Of course, conscientious UX professionals will always strive to work on things that are valuable from a business perspective. Goals create the KPIs that we can look at and communicate about regularly and capture what we learn from our discovery process.

What you can do right away is go in and find out what goals are already configured in your analytics tool (if you didn't do it yourself). Finding out what is there may help confirm your own discoveries about what user actions on the website are valuable to your organization, may help you find new priorities that you were unaware of, or may help you find out how known user goals translate into concrete onsite actions. Typically, any goals you find configured in your web analytics tool will be oriented toward a marketing viewpoint, measuring user actions that signal that marketing efforts are working. You will have to determine how well these marketing-oriented analytics goals overlap with the UX-oriented goals you will ultimately choose.

Nothing beats getting out and talking to various stakeholders, though. This discovery process should be a two-way conversation. While you are discovering what actions other business stakeholders want users to take, you also have the opportunity to propose actions that relate to high-level business goals that you can measure and improve.

After finding out or identifying what things are valuable to your company, analytics goals help you show the value of your UX work. At a basic level, they give you a rationale for any efforts that are focused on goals. Even better, you can put numbers to how many people have taken these actions and perhaps even link that number to revenue. In this situation, you could even go so far as to estimate how much additional revenue your improvements to the website generated. Even without the kind of business analysis that connects goals to money, you can still show how many more people converted because of your work. Chapter 11 goes into this topic more.

CONVERSION RATE

Measuring the number of people who convert (i.e., the number of users who reach a goal) is interesting, and when you're counting the number of purchases on your website or the number of leads the sales team gets, it's an important and relevant thing to measure. However, just a count of conversions is a little contextless.

Conversion rate is the number of conversions divided by the number of visitors. If 10,000 users come to your website in a month and 150 of them sign up or download a whitepaper or whatever it is that you care about, you have a conversion rate of 1.5%. This metric matters because the number of visitors to your website is going to go up and down, depending on market conditions, the time of the year, and whatever marketing efforts are sending them to the website. If you were only looking at the number of conversions, it would look like your website was tanking horribly when, in fact, people were just staying off the Internet because it was a holiday.

Typically, when you make changes to a website, it is with an eye toward improving the conversion rate—that is, making it easier for more users to convert, or persuading more users to convert.

WHY DO YOU NEED TO TREAT GOALS DIFFERENTLY?

You can measure any of these user actions, like making a purchase, filling out a form, or downloading a brochure, through the appropriate report in your analytics tool. However, designating a goal confers a special status on that action, which basically just makes it more convenient to measure in your analytics tool. Rather than digging through the report that shows all the pages all people visited, for example, you can just go to the conversions report and immediately see how many people reached the thank-you page after the sign-up form.

Goals are meant to create KPIs. Instead of trying to pay attention to everything that can be measured, the idea of a KPI is that you can choose a handful of metrics that can give you a high-level measurement of how well your business is meeting its goals—the "headlines." One of the purposes of the Conversions section of Google Analytics is to let you go straight to the KPIs. It is a way of saying that these metrics are the most important way of measuring whether your website is successful. After all, it is only possible to pay attention to so many things, and if you are regularly monitoring your analytics data, these reports will help you keep an eye on what matters.

GOAL REPORTS IN GOOGLE ANALYTICS

The most important part of the goals reports is the conversion rate, which you can find in Google Analytics in the "Overview" report (Figure 4.2). This report is functionally similar to much of the rest of the Google Analytics interface—there is a large graph that can be changed to show different metrics, and then below that the sum or average of various metrics for the selected time period.

One important aspect of this report is that it defaults to showing all goals. If you have more than one goal, it at first shows you the sum of all conversions and the average conversion rate. To look at any individual goal (assuming you have more than one configured for your website), you must first select it from the dropdown menu above the large graph.

There are four metrics that appear below the large graph:

- Goal Completions: How many times the goal was reached during the selected time period. A user may complete the same goal more than once,

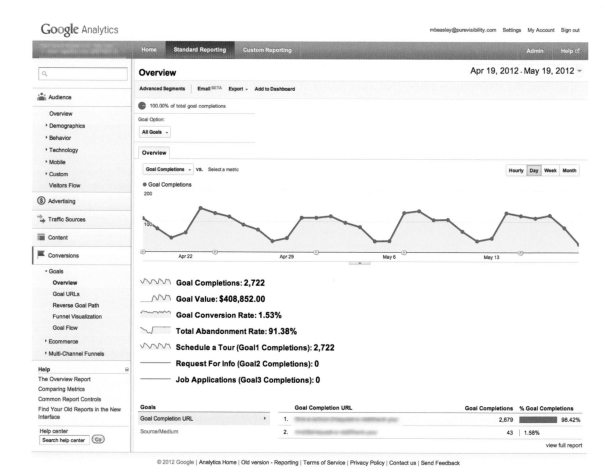

FIGURE 4.2
An example of the "Overview" report.

either in the same visit or multiple visits. This number is nice to know, but because it is dependent on how many users actually visit the website, it is not as meaningful as the conversion rate.

- Goal Value: With enough insight into your company's sales process, it is possible to calculate a monetary value for each time a user reaches a goal. This metric is more useful for marketing analysis than UX analysis, and if you don't configure it, it will just read 0.
- Goal Conversion Rate: The conversion rate for the selected time period for either all goals or the single goal you have selected.
- Goal Abandonment Rate: The portion of users who begin to convert but do not finish. This metric is meaningful for funnel transaction goals,

covered later in this chapter. For destination-only, on-page action, or engagement goals, it will simply read 0 because there is no way to start the conversion without completing it. Most goals you encounter will not have an abandonment rate.

There are two main purposes you will probably put this report to. The first is to look at the conversion rate over time to see how it has changed, typically to determine the effects of some kind of design change. The second is to specify one or two time ranges and look at the overall conversion rate for those time ranges. To use the graph to explore changes in conversion rate over time:

- Select a specific goal if you have more than one configured.
- Change the large graph from Goal Completions to Goal Conversion Rate.
- Either select a single time range or select two time ranges.

It may be difficult to see fine changes due to the scale of the chart—exporting the data and graphing them in another tool like Excel is potentially a useful approach to detecting fine changes. You may see that one line is not consistently above the other, but rather that they cross repeatedly. This can be a sign that any increase or decrease in performance is slight or that there is no real difference between the two conversion rates. Another pattern that you may encounter is a point of divergence, where one line pulls away from another. This is a situation where it is important to look for context (e.g., changes to the website) to explain this divergence—does the divergence line up with a design change that you already know about, or are the causes a mystery?

It is best to compare one time range to a similar time range in the past rather than look at just one time range (see the difference between Figures 4.3 and 4.4). That's because you may find that the conversion rate changes over time due to conditions beyond your control (i.e., outside of the website). There may be seasonality to your business, with time periods when you have an influx of visitors who are just "window shopping" and time periods when users are more ready to convert, such as researching campgrounds during the winter and actually booking a visit during the summer. When you compare two time ranges, you can see if a change in conversion rate has historical precedent—if it follows a historical trend, runs counter to the trend, or magnifies a trend. Of course, there will be times when there is no practical way to compare two time periods. You may be analyzing a completely new functionality or your website may be undergoing successive changes that render it impossible to cleanly compare recent performance to historical performance.

This approach is useful for quickly identifying points in time when the conversion rate changed. It can be useful for showing how successive changes to a website affected users or to provide a useful visual for when you report on how users reacted to your design. However, this approach is not useful for

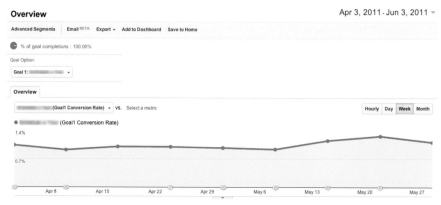

FIGURE 4.3
One way to look at conversion rate data is as one continuous range of dates. There were changes on May 4 that improved the conversion rate.

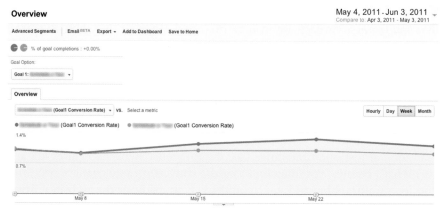

FIGURE 4.4
Another way to view the data is to compare time ranges. This figure shows the same time range as Figure 4.3, but broken in the middle and stacked on top of each other. The conversion rate diverges after May 4, with the blue line representing May 4–June 3. It is hard to tell from the chart alone whether the difference in the conversion rate is meaningful or the product of chance; to better answer this question in a more statistically oriented way, it would be better to select time ranges and compare the overall conversion rate (this gets at the second main use of the "Overview" report).

providing specific numbers, such as "The conversion rate for October 2012 was 1.64%, 5% higher than the 1.56% conversion rate for September 2012."

The second main use of the "Overview" report is to pull specific conversion rate numbers for selected time periods. You would take this approach if you want to specifically quantify how much a conversion rate has changed from one time period to another. Say you made changes to your website that rolled out on October 1, and a month has passed. To quantify how the conversion rate has changed, you could select two time ranges: October 1–31 and September 1–30 (or August 31–September 30). When you scroll down below the large graph to the conversion rate, it will show you the average conversion rate for both time ranges and the difference between them.

This approach is not sensitive to day-to-day or week-to-week variations in the conversion rate because it is simply the average of all days across the time periods you are looking at. The best approach is to look at both the graph and the averages to form a fuller picture.

Further, we're currently only looking at the average conversion rate among all visitors to the website, regardless of who they are and what they've come to the website to do. If you are trying to measure the conversion rate for a goal that's only relevant to a small portion of visitors, you may find it hard to see a change because the conversion rate will be calculated with a large denominator.

Imagine your website is www.example.com, an example that should be familiar by now, selling widgets online. The website gets 5,000 visitors every month. Of those users, only 2,000 of them would buy the enterprise widget, your high-end product. Just for the sake of this example, imagine you can reliably tell them apart from all the other users.

Segment	Number of Users in Segment	Number of Users Who Bought the Enterprise Widget	Conversion Rate
All visitors	5,000	40	0.8%
Target users	2,000	40	2.0%

Remember, these are the same 40 users who actually bought the enterprise widget in both segments.

After you make a change to improve the conversion rate, you gather another month of data. Again, for the sake of the example, you get 5,000 visitors a month and 40% of them are likely to buy the enterprise widgets. This month, though, 60 people buy them instead of 40!

Segment	Number of Users in Segment	Number of Users Who Bought the Enterprise Widget	Conversion Rate
All visitors	5,000	60	1.2%
Target users	2,000	60	3.0%

In this example there was a huge improvement in the conversion rate. In practice, you may see even smaller improvements, making it even harder to find when you look at all users rather than a more targeted subset.

When it is time to report on the efficacy of design changes, if it possible to meaningfully segment out a group of target users, you should report on how the conversion rate changed for this segment while also explaining that you are measuring that specific segment rather than all users.

Goal URLs

Whether or not the "Goal URLs" report (Figure 4.5) is useful depends on how your website works. This report shows you the specific pages where people completed a conversion. Why would you need to see this information?

If you have only one goal page per goal, then you probably don't need this report. If you want people to register for an account on your website, and everyone who fills out the form reaches www.example.com/registration/thank-you, then the "Goal URLs" report will only show this one URL.

However, say you have 40 different whitepapers on your website that users can download after filling out a form. Any time they fill out the form, they end up on a page such as:

- www.example.com/products/health-widgets/whitepaper? widget_efficiency&form=thank-you
- www.example.com/products/pharmaceutical-widgets/whitepaper? widget_safety&form=thank-you

You may have set up just one goal to measure any time the user downloads a whitepaper (any page containing "form = thank-you"). The "Goal URLs" report would show you how many users reached each individual goal page.

Once you understand what it is showing you, the report is simple. You select a specific goal or all goals, and the table displays how many goal completions there were for each goal URL.

Reverse Goal Path

The "Reverse Goal Path" report (Figure 4.6) shows what page users completed a goal on, just like the Goal URLs report, as well as the three previous pages users visited. It can show you the ends of all of the paths that users take to converting. Depending on how your website is built, you may gain insight from seeing the pages that users viewed before converting or simply find that the paths they take as they navigate your website are too diverse to draw meaning from.

The diversity of possible paths users may take through a website is a common problem in showing click paths—unless a website is highly linear, you will

FIGURE 4.5
An example of the "Goal URLs" report.

find that there is great variety in the sequence of pages users visit. It may be interesting to see the variety of paths that users have taken, but the "Reverse Goal Path" report will really only be useful if there is a limited set of paths that users can take, where you can still get useful information out of seeing the last three pages they visit.

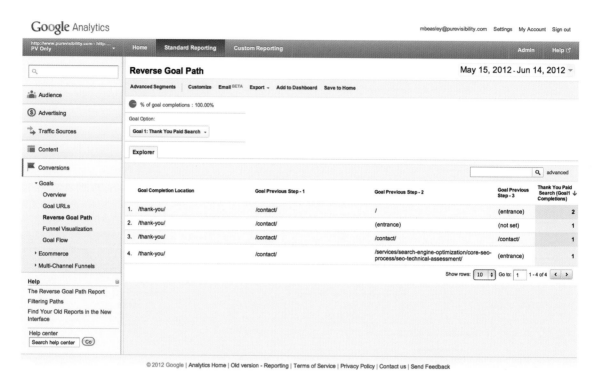

FIGURE 4.6

An example of the "Reverse Goal Path" report.

Funnel Visualization Report

The "Funnel Visualization" report (Figure 4.7) is useful any time you have a goal that consists of a sequence of pages, such as the checkout process on an e-commerce website or a multistep registration process. At every step of the process, some amount of users will give up, or abandon, the process. This report shows you how many users follow the steps along the funnel, as well as where they go to if they exit and where they come from if it is possible to enter the funnel in the middle.

You may be surprised at where users come from when they enter the funnel in midstream, so it would be worth exploring how it is possible to do so by trying to replicate that navigation on the website. Looking at the pages that users exit to may give you insight into the unresolved needs users still have. In the case of the "Request a Visit" form, about 25% of users are simply leaving the website, indicating that they were not convinced or motivated enough to proceed. About 10% went back to look at the "Search Results" again, indicating indecision about what school to select, that they did not like what they

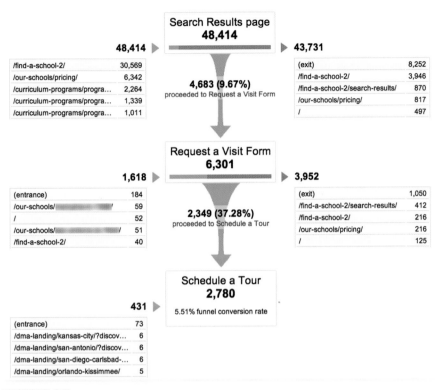

FIGURE 4.7

This screenshot shows the process of searching for a childcare center and filling out a form to schedule a tour. The path from "Search Results" to "Request a Visit" to "Schedule a Tour" does not have to be linear, but it is a common enough path that it was worth setting up the goal in this way. We can see that relatively few users make it from "Search Results" to "Request a Visit," but then a larger portion go from "Request a Visit" to "Schedule a Tour." Along the way, users enter the funnel from the left and exit on the right.

saw on the "Request a Visit" form, or that they did not know what to expect when they clicked on "Request a Visit." About 5% started the search process over again and went to look at tuition information.

Ultimately, you may not find all of the information about how users entered or exited the funnel actionable, but simply being able to see how many users proceed from one step of the funnel to another gives you the ability to measure the effectiveness of changes to pages inside the funnel.

Goal Flow

This report is essentially the "Funnel Visualization" report, but with the ability to show how many users entered the funnel according to a handful of dimensions like medium, browser version, or country. Segmenting users according to these dimensions is really only useful for user research purposes because you can characterize the users who do convert, such as according to what browser they use.

E-commerce

This book will only cover the e-commerce-specific aspects of analytics in passing. You can use data about purchasing behavior to segment data in other reports or to characterize the purchasing behavior of users who you have segmented according to other aspects of their behavior (see Chapter 9). You may also find these reports useful if you want to measure the effectiveness of efforts to increase the number of users who make purchases, increase how many items users purchase in a single visit, or increase the number of purchases for specific items.

Here are metrics that you find in these reports that may be useful:

- E-commerce Conversion Rate: This is just a conversion rate, but specifically for people who have purchased something (if you have configured a goal measuring how many people complete the purchasing process, it should show the same number).
- Transactions: How many orders were placed, as opposed to how many individual items were purchased.
- Revenue: The value of all of the items purchased.
- Average Value: The average value of each order (i.e., Revenue divided by Transactions).
- Unique Purchases: How many individual users placed orders.
- Quantity: The number of individual items sold.

There are also two dimensions—product and product category—that describe what users have purchased on your website. You can use these dimensions to segment users according to what they have purchased, which is useful if this is a relevant way to differentiate your users.

Multichannel Funnels

The idea behind the "Multichannel Funnels" report is that users may come to your website multiple times before they convert, using different mediums, such as a search engine or a link from another website. They may learn of your website from a friend's post on Facebook, remember your website a week later and look it up in Google, and then a week later go directly to your website and buy something. Historically, Google Analytics (and web analytics tools in general) would attribute that conversion to the last way the user reached your website, typing in the URL directly, rather than recognizing that the user learned about your website through social media and researched your website using a search engine. From a marketing perspective, it is exciting to learn more about how multiple online marketing efforts contribute to getting a user to convert.

Exploring these reports may help you write a more realistic story of how a user interacts with your website through understanding the most common ways that users interact with your website multiple times. Unfortunately, it may be hard to determine what action you would take based on the information in these reports.

Note also the unfortunate use of the term *channel* in this section of Google Analytics instead of *medium* as in other reports; these terms are interchangeable.

WHEN DO YOU USE THESE REPORTS?

A big reason you would reach for the conversion reports is to understand how conversion rates for one or more goals have changed over time. You may do so to regularly report on the conversion rate to watch for changes. Otherwise, it means comparing two time ranges to look at how changes to the website, marketing efforts outside the website, or in users themselves have influenced the conversion rate. Some example questions you could answer are:

- How did a complete redesign of the website change the conversion rate?
- A new page with customer testimonials was added to the website. How much did the conversion rate increase?
- Usability testing lead to several fixes to the shopping cart checkout process. How much did it improve the conversion rate and abandonment at every step of the checkout process?

Chapter 15 will go into greater detail on the topic of ongoing reporting. Briefly, there are two main reasons to monitor the conversion rate on a regular basis. First, to watch for changes to the website that you did not know about (but may have some accountability for). Second, and more important, to provide you with a steady data stream to help you discuss the effectiveness of user experience in your organization.

Of course, you may also turn to these reports to answer one-off information needs, such as comparing the results of a usability test to how people dropped out of a shopping cart checkout.

FINDING THE RIGHT THINGS TO MEASURE AS KEY PERFORMANCE INDICATORS

The process of choosing goals to measure the usability of your website is useful even when you're not dealing with web analytics. After all, even though user experience encompasses improving the user's experience in every way, even ways that don't directly affect the bottom line, you still, at some point, have to talk to the people in charge and show that your work is good for the business.

Before going any further, it is a good idea to look for any goals that may already be set up in your web analytics tool or to research what, if any, metrics the management at your organization state are important. This information is valuable input, although any goals you find already set up in web analytics will not necessarily be useful ways to describe the usability of your website.

Incompleteness may take the form of ignoring important actions on the website that can be measured. Lack of clarity may come from simply not knowing the specifics of what can be measured. Uselessness may come from too much knowledge of the specifics of what analytics can measure, and focusing on metrics that are not meaningful in isolation (e.g., bounce rate). Sometimes, you'll find out that the KPIs management is using simply don't tell you anything about whether a user successfully used your website.

You and the rest of the organization still have to speak to the metrics that management cares about (although if you have a web metrics team, they will probably take responsibility for doing so). The point of this section, and an important activity for user experience in general, is to explore the underlying questions and concerns that management is trying to express but may not be able to articulate as effective KPIs. The rest of this chapter discusses concepts that are generally applicable to web analytics tools rather than just Google Analytics, which we have used as an example of a tool. In this section, we attempt to use generic terminology for these concepts.

What Should You Measure?

The basic steps to choosing what to measure in analytics are a series of questions that build on each other:

1. What is the purpose of this company/organization?
2. How does the website fit in with this purpose?
3. What does the company/organization want users to do on the website?
4. What specific, measurable behavior shows that users took that action?

What the list doesn't explicitly call out is: "What does the user want to do?" This question matters, and is actually pretty central to the success of a business. It doesn't appear in this list, though, because that question is more relevant when figuring out what to build rather than measuring what people are doing now. If you get to the third question and find that you've got a mismatch between what the business wants and what you've learned about your users, then it's time to fight for a redesign.

What Is the Purpose of the Company/Organization?

You're just trying to measure what people are doing on the website, so why start all the way back here? In a perfect world, everything a business does flows from its purpose or mission. Netflix wants to connect people with the entertainment they desire in an easy way. eBay wants to empower people to sell goods online. The University of Michigan wants to educate people and conduct research. "Make money" shouldn't be the mission—rather, making money should arise from whatever goal a business has.

The real reason to ask this question is to set up the next question. It is the foundation for making sure that a website is trying to get people to do the right things from the business' perspective. And it should be a pretty easy question to answer. Otherwise, you've got bigger problems than this book can solve.

How Does the Website Fit in with This Purpose?

This question is a little bit harder than the last one. You may work on a website that sells things directly to customers online, or a lead-generation website that tries to get information from a user to start a conversation between the user and your sales team. On the other hand, you may have a website geared toward getting users to read content online, for the purpose of generating ad revenue, getting subscriptions, or simply educating people or keeping them from calling for phone support. Your website may also do more than one of these high-level activities.

A website doesn't necessarily support everything that a business wants to do. Amazon, eBay, and Craigslist mainly advance their goals through their websites, but GE, Intel, and the University of Michigan have lots of things they want to do and their websites only support some of those goals directly. Intel, for example, has support for their chips and information on where to buy their products, but when Apple decided to start using Intel's chips, they probably didn't go on the Intel website and order a bunch of chips. So what subset of your company's goals does the website actually support? Maybe it is all of them, but either way, the clarity on what not to worry about is essential for the next question.

What Does the Company/Organization Want Users To Do on the Website?

You asked the previous question to figure out what you *don't* need to worry about on the website. Now, among the things that you want the website to accomplish, what exactly do you want users to do?

This question is where business goals and user goals meet—and they had better meet, or else you've got some big problems. It could be easy to answer this question. The answer could be "buy something on the website" or "call us up and talk to a sales rep" or "sign up for an account." If the answer is less concrete, though, you've got to find a way to make it concrete by coming up with an action that tells you whether or not a user was successful, one that lets both you and the user know.

The answer or answers you come up with should be something you can use when you write scenarios to describe user behavior or tasks for usability testing—clearly defined tasks with clearly defined end points.

EXAMPLE OF GOAL SELECTION: A MADE-UP E-COMMERCE WEBSITE

Let's look at a simple example for goal selection. Imagine there is a business called AwesomePetToys.com, with a website of the same name. They sell high-end pet toys directly to consumers and wholesale to businesses like veterinarians' offices, and have no physical stores. Their website functions much like a typical e-commerce website, with product pages, search and browse functionality, recommendations, a wish list, and a shopping cart and checkout process.

1. What is the purpose of this company/organization? The purpose is simple: sell the highest-quality pet toys to the most discriminating pet owners. To do so, an important part of AwesomePetToys.com's business is actually selling pet toys online. Also important is to evaluate how satisfied pet owners are with their toys and to always look for new products to add.

2. How does the website fit in with this purpose? The answer should seem obvious: the website exists so AwesomePetToys.com can sell pet toys online. More interesting is the matter of what the website will not support. Is it an appropriate tool for inspecting their pet toys and finding new products? It has nothing to do with inspecting pet toys, and a great deal of the process of finding new pet toys probably happens offline. Perhaps, though, the website could find a way for the creators of high-quality pet toys to locate AwesomePetToys.com and recommend their product.

3. What does the company/organization want users to do on the website? Let's come up with some concrete actions:
   - Buy pet toys.
   - Add toys to a wish list.
   - Submit a pet toy for consideration as a product.

4. What specific, measurable behavior shows that users took that action? Now we will translate the bullets from the last question into specific actions:
   - Put pet toys in the shopping cart and purchase them.
   - Add toys to a wish list.
   - Submit a form where one can describe one's pet toy.

Obviously, on a real e-commerce website, these would not be the only things we would want users to successfully be able to do. For example, AwesomePetToys.com would need to provide some kind of support for customers, and it would probably be possible to define specific actions that users should be able to successfully complete. Although we have distilled AwesomePetToys.com's features down to a handful of actions that users can take, these actions are actually the culmination of other activities, like searching for a kind of pet toy, browsing pet toys, reading about pet toys, and so on. The goals that we have selected here are the end points of these actions—improving all of these other areas of the website should ultimately improve the number of users who complete these goals.

EXAMPLE OF GOAL SELECTION: UNIVERSITY OF MICHIGAN SCHOOL OF INFORMATION

The University of Michigan School of Information (www. si.umich.edu, shown in Figure 4.8) is a great example of an organization with diverse business goals, and it's nice to use a nonprofit organization as a point of discussion.

1. What is the purpose of this company/organization? According to their website, the University of Michigan School of Information's (UMSI) mission is "We create knowledge so people can use information and technology to build a better world. We educate socially engaged information professionals." This translates to education and research. More specifically, it means educating graduate and undergraduate students, attracting Ph.D. students and faculty, and having all of those people create new knowledge. Educating students decomposes further into some important

activities: attracting new students, supporting their education, and providing services that they need like course schedules. It is also important to note that although their purpose is not to make money, UMSI requires money to operate and raises it from student tuition, grants, and donations.

2. How does the website fit in with this purpose? When you start to unpack their purpose, it turns out it has many parts. While their website may have information about UMSI's various activities, practically speaking, the website will largely support the education of students and getting funding through donations. Attracting talented professors and getting grants are critical activities, but they involve a much smaller pool of candidates with a much more personal touch. The high-level goal of educating students entails

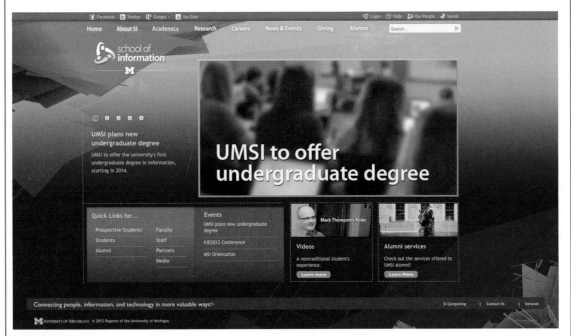

FIGURE 4.8
The University of Michigan School of Information homepage in June 2012.

introducing the school and enticing students to apply and helping them stay enrolled by helping them find interesting events to go to and providing necessary services like course and graduation information.

3. What does the company/organization want users to do on the website? Some obvious choices emerge from the last couple of questions. Let's focus on the mission to attract students:

   - Contact the school about applying (it doesn't appear to be possible right now to apply online; in fact, it's kind of difficult to figure out what you are supposed to do if you wish to apply).
   - Access course descriptions (actually registering for courses takes place in a separate university-wide system).
   - Contact student groups (as part of having a more rich student life; there are several student groups geared toward different interests).

4. What specific, measurable behavior shows that users took that action? The specific, measurable actions should follow from the items we identified in the previous question:

   - Send an email to the admissions office.
   - View pages describing specific classes.
   - Send an email to individual student groups.

Ultimately, these goals are just a subset of all the goals that UMSI may choose after conducting a more in-depth discovery session with actual stakeholders. Here, we don't pursue other areas that feasibly could be supported by the website, like attracting and actually taking donations through the website, or attracting staff or faculty and actually having them apply online. At the time of writing, the website is not geared toward tracking these three goals; rather than providing ways to contact admissions or student groups in a trackable way, the website displays email addresses. All course descriptions are presented on a single page, making it challenging to find out if users were interested in reading course descriptions for any particular class.

Of course, I do not work for UMSI and the preceding analysis is largely conjecture meant to show the thorough process. It's also important to note that web analytics can only measure a portion of the website's effectiveness as a tool for driving people to apply to the program, etc., in conjunction with the rest of the school's marketing efforts. A more comprehensive approach would be to combine web analytics data with data from other sources, such as the system that records how many applications the school has received.

What Specific, Measurable Behavior Shows that Users Took that Action?

This question extends the previous question just a bit. "What do you want users to do on your website?" asks the question from a human perspective. "What specific, measurable behavior shows that users took that action?" is the analytics perspective.

Typically, you find a page on your website that users would only reach if they had intentionally performed the action. This is the confirmation page at the end of a shopping cart checkout, or the thank-you page after you submit a form. It could be an amount of time that you use as a proxy for measuring how engaged someone is with your website. It could be whether users click on a link to download something.

After you've settled on what behavior will let your analytics tool know that users completed an action, you are ready to start setting up goals. I'll get into that more later.

The next section digs into choosing measurable behavior in more detail.

Do Users Want To Do These Things?

If you reached the end of this process and came up with an action that you can't see users actually wanting to do, then there is a misalignment somewhere. Indeed, UX professionals are often called upon to resolve tension between user goals and business goals. We come from the position of having done research on users and having evidence of what they want to do.

Of course, a business may have good reasons for wanting users to do something. An example is the whitepaper, a common artifact on the Internet. A whitepaper is a document a business produces to provide knowledge to the reader while also advertising the business' expertise. Sometimes you see businesses making whitepapers freely downloadable, but often you have to give up information like your name and email address, and perhaps more, before you can download the whitepaper. It is the business' way of getting you to do something that you don't want to do—give up your personal information.

If your stakeholders want users to do something they would normally not want to do, then it is up to you to work on resolving that tension. You may ask questions like: "Why would they want to do that? What can we provide them in return? How can we explain to users why they should take this action?"

WHAT CAN YOU MEASURE ON A WEBSITE THAT CAN CONSTITUTE A GOAL?

Regardless of the web analytics tool you use, there are three basic categories of behavior you can measure as goals.

The basic, common thing that most people use to measure whether users have reached the goal is whether they reach a specific page that they would only reach if they had meant to perform that action. In most cases, your job is just to identify that page, or to get your developers to build that page.

It's also possible that an important user action on your website is when they interact with some kind of advanced widget, like a financial calculator or an image editing application. Unless you're comfortable with coding, you'll probably need some help measuring this kind of behavior. We will cover measurement of more complex interactions (i.e., ones that don't result in new pageviews) later in this book.

Lastly, it is technically feasible to measure how many people stay on your website for a certain amount of time or who visit a certain amount of pages.

Let us explore these three kinds of behavior in greater detail. The following sections are agnostic with regard to the web analytics tool you use; as such, terminology in this section may not always match what you see in your web analytics tool.

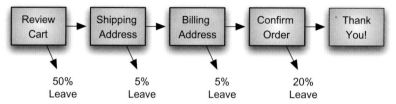

FIGURE 4.9

A made-up diagram of a shopping cart checkout. The first page, Review Cart, marks the start of the funnel and the last page, Thank You!, marks the end of the transaction. When the user reaches the Thank You! page it is counted as a goal.

Reaching a Specific Page

Historically, measuring whether users have reached a specific page has been the most commonly used method of counting goals. The idea is to pick a specific page of the website with a unique URL that a user could not reach by accident, and counting every user who was able to reach that page as a goal, or conversion. There are two variations on this idea that are applicable to common web analytics tools.

Funnel Transactions

We touched on the idea of a funnel earlier in this chapter when looking at Google Analytics funnel visualization. This concept is used in other tools. Funnel transactions are when there are a series of steps—pages—that a user visits before completing the transaction, such as in Figure 4.9. The idea here isn't to just measure how many users complete a process, but also how many make it through each step of the process. It's the visualization of a pool of users starting a transaction and fewer and fewer making it to each step that gives this goal its name.

An e-commerce checkout process and signing up for an account are two common examples. This is also an easy kind of user action to measure with web analytics. As long as there is an end point to a transaction—typically a confirmation or thank-you page—your analytics tool can count how many people bought something.

There are two parts to the funnel transaction goal. The first is the end point, and if you just measure how many people reach that, you can start to approximate how successfully people can complete the transaction. However, in a multistep transaction, things can go wrong at every step. The second part of a funnel transaction goal is identifying the pages that users pass through, often including a specific beginning point. Identifying each step of the goal in your web analytics tool lets you identify how many users reach the first page, the second page, and so on, and find out if there are places where a lot of users drop out of the funnel.

People interested in analytics from more of a marketing perspective with an e-commerce website can have their analytics tools set up to measure how much money each customer spent per transaction. They measure the success of their marketing efforts not just in terms of how many people complete transactions, but also through the average size of each transaction (either in a monetary sense or in the amount of items bought, or both). If you have a usability goal related to customers being able to buy a certain amount of items, it is functionality that will probably require the assistance of a developer to implement additional code on your website.

Destination Only

The destination-only goal is similar to the funnel transaction, both conceptually and in terms of how you set up a destination-only goal. Both are triggered when the user reaches a page. The difference is that the destination-only goal doesn't take place over several pages. It actually takes place over two: the page where the user decides to take action and the destination page (Figure 4.10).

Some examples are a "Contact Us" form followed by the confirmation page or the "Sign Up for Our Whitepaper" form followed by the page that lets users download the whitepaper. First, there is a page where the user decides whether or not to take action, and then a page that shows he or she must have taken that action. Although you can choose any pair of pages, if you don't pick one where the user almost certainly deliberately chose to take action, then you'll measure the people who succeeded at a task along with the people who accidentally accomplished it. That's why forms (even as short as a couple of fields) are common choices and a link in the middle of a page is not.

On-Page Action

Without additional tracking code, Google Analytics only measures when a user reaches a new page. It is, however, possible to add code that will notify the analytics server when the user interacts with something on a page, such as clicking on a button, playing a video for a certain amount of time, or opening or interacting with a lightbox-style dialog box. In Google Analytics, tracking these on-page actions is called *event tracking*.

Chapter 12 goes into greater detail on how this method works. The important thing to remember is that practically any interaction that the user has with the website can be measured as a goal. However, these on-page actions

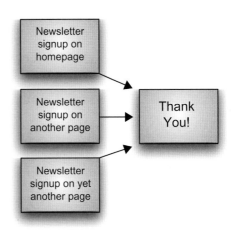

FIGURE 4.10
Destination-only goals involve just two pages. Although your website may have only one page that leads the user to the goal page (Thank You!), you can also set it up so it doesn't matter where the user came from.

require additional tracking code to be installed on the website and, of course, it is important to only count user actions that indicate that they have succeeded at accomplishing a task

Engagement

This last kind of goal simply refers to people staying on the website beyond a certain amount of time, or visiting more than a certain number of pages. The idea behind engagement goals is that if users stay on your website long enough, it's because they are engaged with your website. You can, perhaps, see the flaw in this reasoning.

Web analytics doesn't give you any insight into users' minds; it follows that you would have no idea, based on analytics data alone, why users stuck around on your website for so long. Consequently, there isn't a great deal of value in this kind of goal—users may have stayed on your website for a long time because they found it delightful, or they may have hated it but really needed to use it to accomplish some goal.

The engagement goal is listed here for the sake of completeness, but it is most likely not going to be useful for any kind of UX analysis.

GOING BEYOND THE WEBSITE

Unfortunately, at this time you can't measure every important user action with web analytics. Depending on your company or organization, you may be successful when you get users to pick up the phone and call you, prevent them from having to call you to ask questions, or when they interact with a third-party registration system that won't let you add analytics tracking code. The real world is full of situations where you have to go outside analytics to measure the successfulness of your website.

Finding and integrating these data sources is beyond the scope of this book, but I encourage you to be on the lookout for other ways that your organization records data about users' interactions and to try to build relationships with the people who can supply those data.

BEYOND MAKING MONEY

A goal doesn't have to be tied to making money, although that is the most common usage. A goal just has to be something that, if users perform that action on the website, you know the website is being successful. It doesn't even have to be the only way that you know your website is successfully serving users—the idea of a KPI is that you can't keep your eyes on *every* metric because then you would just drown in data. The important thing is that there is agreement that a goal is a relevant choice.

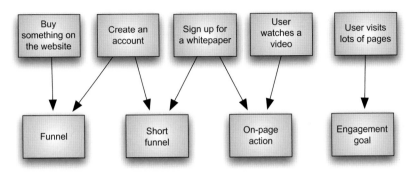

FIGURE 4.11
Some examples of actions on a website mapped to the kinds of goals that can be measured.

TYING IT TOGETHER

It is possible to measure a wide range of user activity as a goal, whether with Google Analytics or other web analytics tools. The main takeaway from this last section of the chapter is that if you have identified an action as showing that users have intentionally completed a task that is important, you can find a way to measure it in your web analytics tool.

Figure 4.11 shows some examples of user actions mapped to goals. Two of these examples map to two different implementations. In the case of "create an account," it depends on whether there are multiple pages that the user goes through to complete the task. For some websites, creating an account or similar features take the user through multiple pages, where the user may drop out at any point. On the other hand, simple forms may consist of a form on one page and a thank-you page.

Signing up for a whitepaper is another example of a user filling out a form. The reason it may fall into either a destination-only or on-page action is based on implementation. If it is a form that leads the user to a unique thank-you page, it would be destination only. On the other hand, some websites are built in such a way that the user is not taken to a new page, in which case it would be necessary to add some additional tracking code to monitor when users fill out the form. Of course, it is possible to set up this specific example of signing up to download a whitepaper as a multipage funnel, but users would have to really want that whitepaper before they would complete a long sign-up process. There may also be good business reasons to make a whitepaper available with a single click rather than having users give away their personal information, but the intentionality of this action is more questionable because some amount of users will click on the link accidentally.

The funnel goal usually involves tasks that fit into a traditional idea about usability—the task is well-defined, has a beginning and an end, and can be tested fairly well in a lab. To put it another way: a usability test participant doesn't really need to buy something for you to get value out of testing a shopping cart checkout process. On the other hand, other kinds of goals that involve much shorter interactions may measure tasks that are not that hard for users to complete and unlikely to be improved dramatically.

These goals (and to an extent, funnel goals as well) can represent three things:

- How effectively the website is delivering on its business goals.
- A high-level measure of the persuasiveness and credibility of the website.
- A high-level indicator of how usable the website is.

The latter two points are important for goal selection. The entire experience of using a website matters. Our work to improve websites' user experience, if not measured directly by a specific goal, should ultimately affect how many users complete a goal.

KEY TAKEAWAYS

- A web analytics *goal* is an action that you want users to take on your website that lets you know that they have successfully completed a task or are engaged with the website.
- Selecting goals in web analytics is an important part of measuring the effectiveness of a website from an online marketing perspective, and where those goals are aligned with real user tasks, they help us measure the quality of the website user experience at a high level.
- The *conversion rate* is the amount of users who reached a goal divided by all of the users in a population, such as all users of a website or a segment of those users.
- The basic process of figuring out what actions on your website to measure as goals is:
  - What is the purpose of this company/organization?
  - How does the website fit in with this purpose?
  - What does the company/organization want users to do on the website?
  - What specific, measurable behavior shows that users took that action?
- You can measure practically any action that users can take as a goal. Some high-level categories are:
  - Reaching a specific page
  - On-page action
  - Engagement

Learning about Users through
Web Analytics

CHAPTER 5

Learning about Users

INTRODUCTION

Web analytics lets you learn about some aspects of your website's users, an activity called visitor analysis. As UX professionals, we usually study technological aspects of users to the extent that it affects how they use websites (or whatever interface you're working on). Web analytics gives you insight into some of these technological aspects, like:

- Where are they from, geographically
- Their browser and operating system
- Screen resolution
- Whether they use a mobile device and what kind

A big challenge in the area of learning about your users from web analytics is finding actionable information. The data can resolve questions like "How many users will we hurt if we optimize the website for a width of 1280?" or "How many users do we abandon if we don't accommodate mobile users?" However, these questions aren't very challenging. One problem is that you have data about all of the visitors who come to your website, but you will have a hard time isolating which data tell you about your target users and which do not. Nonetheless, we can use web analytics to get an overview of the technological and demographic aspects of users—what we will call the visitor analysis.

Through analyzing how they came to the website, we can also learn about the information needs that drove users to the website. The main vehicle for doing so is analyzing the keywords that users searched for that brought them to the website. Not every user gets to your website through a search engine, however, and although we can learn the most from them, we can still gain some insights through the users who don't come in through search engines, such as users who click on links on other websites. Chapter 6 will spend more time analyzing referral visitors.

CONTENTS

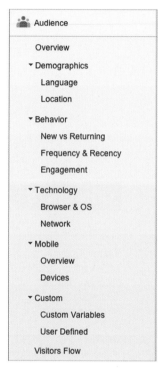

FIGURE 5.1

The Audience menu in
Google Analytics.

This chapter covers exploratory data analysis of visitor data—that is, characterizing the data to describe and categorize your population of users and looking for patterns.

VISITOR ANALYSIS

The relevant reports in Google Analytics for this chapter are in the Audience menu (Figure 5.1). These reports provide information about visitors, which can be an interesting source of data that describe the visitors to your website, but the metrics and dimensions in these reports become useful when you use segmentation to filter other reports according to visitor characteristics.

Short of answering specific, close-ended questions (e.g., "How many of our users use the Chrome browser?"), the kind of analyses you will do will be exploratory in nature—analyzing the data to summarize their characteristics and playing with data to see what patterns emerge. Diving into the data to see what is there is a productive exercise, but it is important to balance the time you spend. Over time, you will also develop a sense of when to stop analyzing.

The data available in these reports cover behavioral and technological aspects, as well as the physical location of users. The data cover the full spectrum of your website's users rather than just our target users. When we develop personas, we give them specific traits; these reports force us to recognize that our users are actually quite diverse, using all sorts of browser versions, varying in how frequently they visit the website, and so on. There are few metrics or dimensions where *most* users fit into a single category.

Of course, web analytics cannot tell you anything about *why* users do anything. The visitors reports will not give you any insight into users' minds, nor into other demographic aspects such as gender, age, and so on.

Many of the reports in the Audience menu are fairly self-explanatory, so we will cover them briefly. Of course, you can find these data in other analytics tools.

Demographics—Location

Web analytics tools can use IP addresses to do a pretty good measurement of where a user is located, down to the level of city (although sometimes not that fine-grained, depending on the country). If geography really matters for the users you want to analyze, then this report can tell you how many users come from different locations.

COUNTRY, REGION, METRO, AND CITY (DIMENSIONS)

These dimensions tell you where users are located in a geographic sense. Analytics tools determine users' locations based on their IP addresses, which means that the data are pretty good but not perfect.

As with other dimensions, the geographic dimensions can help you learn about your website's users or segment them in case geography is an important distinction for different kinds of users.

Unfortunately, region and city do a poor job of capturing the metropolitan area a user lives in (in the United States, at least). Take the example of New York City: it is the most populous city in the United States, but it is only one part of the economically and culturally united New York metropolitan area, which consists of three states and hundreds of communities. The Region dimension would capture the entire states of New York, New Jersey, and Connecticut, whereas the City dimension would only capture one of the cities at a time. In the world of marketing, a designated market area (DMA) signifies an area with social, economic, and political ties. The Metro dimension classifies users according to which DMA they come from. Currently, this feature is only available for the United States; anyone outside the United States is classified as "(not set)."

Behavior—New vs. Returning

A returning visitor is one who has been to your website before and a new visitor is one who has not. Chapter 3 dealt with the definition and limitations of these concepts in greater detail.

There are two places to look for these data in Google Analytics—first, you can see the % new visits in the "Overview," which is the first report you see when you access a profile. This is the average percentage of new visitors for the whole website for the selected time period.

Second, there is the "New vs. Returning" report, which presents you with the percentage of new visitors again, but also lets you compare new visitors and returning visitors with regard to bounce rate, conversion rate, pages per visit, and more.

Simply knowing how many users are new or returning can be interesting, but probably isn't going to be extremely useful unless there is a business reason for trying to increase the portion of one group or the other. When we get to the section on segmentation in Chapter 9, we'll discuss a way to make this metric and many others far more useful in exploring user behavior.

Behavior—Frequency & Recency

"Frequency & Recency" is the report in Google Analytics that tells you how often users come to your website and how recent their last visit was. There are two sections to this report: Count of Visits breaks down all of the visitors for a selected time period and tells you how many visited the website once, twice, three times, and so on; and Days Since Last Visit describes how many days have passed since each user's last visit to the website.

If a defining trait of a group of users is that they come to your website frequently, then this report, taken alone, will tell you how many users currently behave that way. When you describe your users with personas, you can write realistic behavior with regard to how often your persona comes to your website. Learning about how often users come to your website can have implications for content strategy or whether to gear your design for novice or expert users.

DAYS SINCE LAST VISIT (METRIC)

You can go beyond simply learning how many visitors have been to your website before and break down how recently they visited. As with other metrics related to how users get to the website, it can be useful for simply learning more about the people coming to your website, as well as for segmenting your users if your research has shown this characteristic to be relevant. For example, you could segment data to only show users who visited your website the previous day or earlier on the same day to find out what frequently returning visitors do on your website.

Behavior—Engagement

The "Engagement" report also has two sections: Visit Duration and Page Depth. This report provides more detail on the metrics average time on website and average page depth, breaking down how many users fit into different time ranges (such as 0–10 seconds, 11–30 seconds, and so on) or how many users visited one, two, three, four, etc. pages. Looking at the breakdown can be useful if you want to see the variance for those averages or otherwise just better characterize how often your users come to your website. You will probably find that visit duration and page depth skew low, with most people visiting few pages and not spending very long on your website.

PAGE DEPTH (DIMENSION)

Pages per visit is used to express the average number of pages per visit for multiple users, whereas page depth is a dimension used to categorize users according to whether they only visited one page, two pages, three pages, and so on. It is obviously conceptually similar to pages per visit, but as a dimension, it is used to break data into segments.

When you want to segment according to how many pages users visited in Google Analytics, you would use page depth, such as filtering out anyone who visited fewer than three pages on the website.

Technology—Browser & OS

For user experience, the main use of these reports is probably to settle disputes about who to optimize your website for. You can learn about what browser and operating system (OS) your users have, and what specific version they use. These reports will tell you what screen resolutions your users have on their devices. In the past, these data would help you answer questions like: "How many people do we lose if we optimize our website for an 800 × 600 resolution?" or "How many users will be affected if we don't support any browser except Internet Explorer?"

If you are working on a website with highly advanced functionality where the users' technological capabilities are important, then the "Browser & OS" report is something that you will find useful. You may also find the breakdown of specific mobile devices in the –"Devices" report under "Mobile" useful, where you could separate iPhones from Android phones, for example.

Mobile—Overview

There are two reports under "Mobile" in Google Analytics. "Devices," as just mentioned, breaks down the specific mobile devices that users may use. The other report, "Overview," tells you whether the users visit your website using a mobile device in the simplest terms possible: "yes" or "no." A user is counted as using a mobile device if he or she is using a phone or a tablet. If your website doesn't do a good job of supporting users with mobile devices, this report can help you make the case for doing so. You will probably find that mobile user share has grown rapidly over the last few years.

MOBILE (DIMENSION)

For every user, "Mobile" is set to either "yes" or "no" depending on whether or not a user uses a mobile device. You can use this dimension to find out how many users are on a desktop computer and how many are on some kind of mobile device (and you will probably find that the proportion of mobile users is growing every year). When we get to Chapter 9, we will unlock the real power of this dimension to allow us to analyze how mobile users' behavior differs from desktop users.

Custom (As in Custom Variables)

In the Audience menu, there will also be a couple of reports that are useless without additional code being added to your website. Beyond the data that Google Analytics automatically record, you can create additional dimensions that let you segment users (which will come into play when we get to Chapter 9). For example, if your website has a login, you can add code to your website that will tell analytics whether a given user has ever logged in to your website or not. You could potentially separate users who have put an item in their shopping cart or commented on an article sometime during their session from those who have not.

To do any of these things, you will either need the help of a developer or have some programming skills yourself. That's because there's no pregenerated code for feeding these data to Google Analytics; rather, you will have to create the code that speaks to analytics yourself. The functionality of custom variables also overlaps with event tracking, which is a way of tracking user actions that don't result in a new page being loaded. Chapter 14 covers custom variables and event tracking in further detail. Before 2010, Google Analytics allowed its users to set up a single user-defined segment before replacing it with the ability to set up more than one custom variable. The "User Defined" report is there to support people still using the old method of creating their own custom segment.

KEY TAKEAWAYS

- You can use web analytics to learn about the device users use to access your website, how often they come to your website, and where they are located geographically.
- These data cover the full range of your website's users, a different approach from the specificity we create with personas. We can use these data to categorize and characterize our users and look for patterns.

CHAPTER 6

Traffic Analysis: Learning How Users Got to Your Website

INTRODUCTION

Where a user came from may tell you about what he or she is on your website to do. Traffic analysis involves looking at the sources and mediums that brought users to your website. As discussed in Chapter 3, a *source* is the specific place that a user came from, such as from the Google search engine, following a link on Widgets.com or on a social media website like Twitter, or by directly typing your website's URL into the browser. A *medium* is a derived category containing one or more sources of the same type, like "organic search" being the medium that contains multiple sources like Google and Bing.

Traffic analysis, like visitor analysis, is also very much an exploratory, pattern-finding activity. You are more likely to look to these data to find questions to ask—through further analysis of web analytics data or other methods like usability testing—such as how well your website supports users who come in with a specific information need or what information is interesting and/or relevant to users who come in with a certain stated need. It is rarer that you approach these data to answer focused questions, which are more likely to come from marketing.

SOURCE AND MEDIUM (DIMENSIONS)

Source and medium are essential dimensions for reporting for online marketing efforts. A source is the specific place a user came from. In Google Analytics, it is either a URL or, if the user typed the URL into his or her browser or followed a bookmark, the tag "(direct)".

You probably won't use source very much, unless you are interested in the behavior of users who come from a particular source (e.g., everybody who follows a link to your website from another, specific website).

Medium is derived from source. Rather than telling you the specific place a user came from, medium tells you the category of the source he or she used

CONTENTS

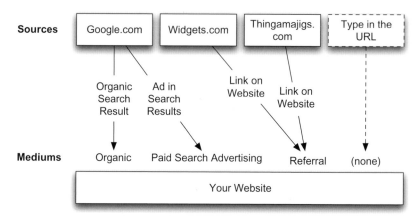

FIGURE 6.1

The source is the specific place a user came from to get to your website, such as Google or Thingamajigs.com. Sources get categorized into mediums like organic (e.g., Google, Bing, Yahoo!) or referral (e.g., Thingamajigs.com and AwesomePetToys.com).

to get to the website (Figure 6.1). There are four default mediums in Google Analytics:

1. *Organic.* People who used a search engine to find your website but did not click on one of the ads.
2. *Referral.* People who clicked on a link from another website.
3. *(none).* The "direct" visitors who either typed your website's URL into their browser or who bookmarked the website in the past.
4. *CPC.* People that arrived through "cost per click" (often referred to as "pay per click") advertising, such as from Google or Bing's advertising networks. You may not see it if your organization is not engaged in this form of advertising.

The users who get grouped under organic and referral will have some website listed as their source—typically Google or Bing for organic, and referral could be any website that links to yours.

Depending on your organization's online marketing efforts, you may have more values listed under medium, as mediums can be added to incoming visits through URL tags to organize various marketing campaigns. We describe this in more detail later in the chapter.

As with other dimensions discussed in this chapter, medium can help you characterize how your users are getting to the website. You will almost certainly find that users who come in through different mediums interact with your website differently, and Chapter 9 will help you analyze these differences.

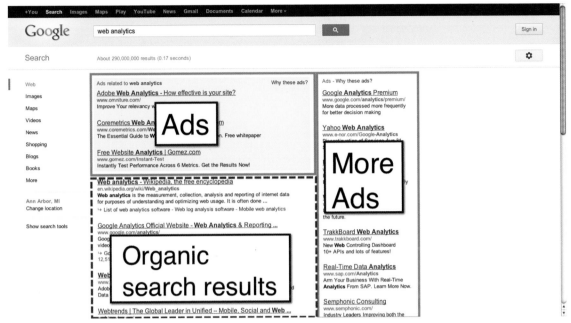

FIGURE 6.2
Paid search results and organic search results on the Google search engine results page. Some searches produce more ads than others. There is clearly a great deal of money to be made off of web analytics.

ORGANIC SEARCH

Search comes in two flavors: organic and paid (Figure 6.2). Organic refers to the search results that are generated by the search engine's ranking algorithm and appear prominently in the center of the search engine results page. Paid search refers to the ads that people can place in search engines. Both organic and paid keywords can provide insight into users and web analytics tools can distinguish between them, allowing you to analyze them separately.

In Google Analytics, the "Organic Search Traffic" report (Figure 6.3) can show you how people express their information needs and how many users, in a selected timeframe, expressed that information need.

KEYWORD (DIMENSION)

One of the most powerful things you can learn from web analytics is what people who visited your website searched for in a search engine. This dimension gives you insight into what information needs your users have and the different ways they express those needs.

The keyword dimension only captures the search queries that actually brought users to your website; it doesn't tell you anything about the things people searched for that didn't bring them to your website.

FIGURE 6.3
The "Organic Search Traffic" report for Pure Visibility, covering a year of data. In the next few pages, we will dig deeper into these data.

This report is good for discovering how users express their information needs and how common those expressions are. You can browse through the list in decreasing order of how many people searched for each keyword, or use the search functionality above the table to look up specific keywords and find out how common they are. The other table options, like Performance, can also tell you what portion of your organic visitors searched for a particular keyword.

The frequency of keywords that brought users to your website will probably fit the shape of the by-now-ubiquitous long tail, or Zipf distribution, as shown in Figure 6.4. This concept was popularized by Chris Anderson in 2004, discussing Amazon and Netflix. The basic idea is that users search for a few keywords a lot of the time, and a lot of keywords very few times. You will probably find that a large portion of your organic visits come from very few keywords, and you will have hundreds or thousands of keywords that only one or two people searched for.

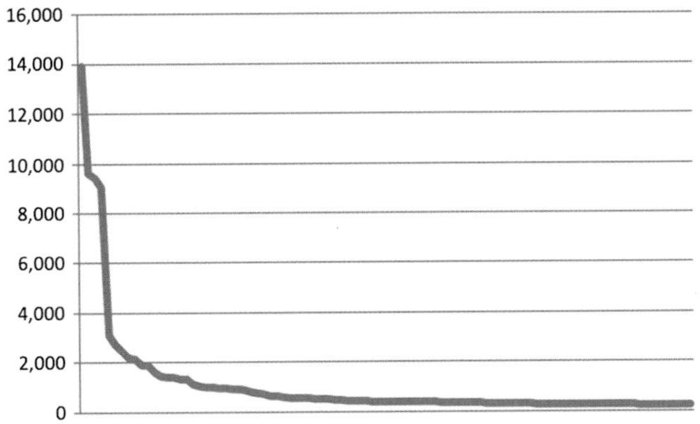

FIGURE 6.4

The basic shape of the long tail of search, with a "head" where very few keywords are searched for many times, and the majority of keywords are searched for very few times. Not pictured here are 45,000 additional keywords that received fewer than 100 searches each. This is a Zipf distribution and it's pretty common in the realm of things that people search for, words that people use in day-to-day life, and even the popularity of websites.

Unfortunately, web analytics tools present search queries in the form of a huge, difficult-to-understand mess. In Figure 6.3, we can see that the second, third, and fourth most frequent keywords are actually variations of the same phrase: "pure visibility." Every variation in spelling or reordering of words is treated as a separate keyword, which can mask how often users search for the same basic concept. Getting value from this mess requires compromising the effort you put in through manipulating the data by hand or regular expressions against the degree of accuracy you hope to get. The search query analysis lies on the extreme end of effort. After we discuss that technique, we'll go over a "discount" approach.

Why Analyze Keywords?

Analyzing keywords gives you insight into things that users search for and the ways they express those information needs. From there, you can start to ask how well your website addresses those information needs: Do you have information that will help them? Where on the website is that information? Understanding what people are searching for may have information architecture implications, possibly affecting how you build your website's navigation.

You can look at the words people use. Do they match the way you describe your products or services? You may learn that users talk about you in ways that you didn't expect. On the other hand, the keyword data only reflect what language search engines see on your website. If your website uses different words than your users do, then the people who actually find your website are the ones who use those unusual words. If you have conducted other kinds of user research, and the language they use isn't represented in the keyword data, it means that your website is out of alignment with their language.

It's important to understand that search engine keyword data only show you the people who chose your website after performing a search for which your website appears. That means that the keyword data aren't representative of the entire population of your potential users (although search engines do make available data on how many people do search for any keyword you can think of). In fact, the number of users coming to your website for a given keyword won't just be a product of how many have that information need, but will also be affected by how well your website ranks in search results for that keyword. This limitation means that you should not make firm conclusions about how many users come to the website with various information needs based on keyword data alone, and be aware that you have users and potential users who express themselves in ways that don't match your website. You can only form conclusions about the current users of your website, which is still a valuable thing to be able to do. Despite being unable to find out what keywords users who didn't visit your website searched for, you will still be able to discover unexpected keywords, and you can still analyze website usage metrics to compare users who expressed different kinds of needs with their keywords.

This approach to analyzing search engine keyword data can also apply to analyzing website search data. Website search data are an amazing opportunity to get insight into what users want to learn about and do on your website, unfiltered by how well search engines understand what your website is about. These two data sources complement each other (and *should* complement each other, since it doesn't really make sense to try to combine them).

SEARCH TERM (DIMENSION)

Web analytics can provide you access to data about what people search for within your website. These website search data can tell you about what topics your users are interested in and how they express those interests.

The search term and an associated metric, total unique searches, tells you how users have expressed their information needs. Just by looking at the way users search for what they need and the relative numbers of users who enter each search term can provide you with interesting information. Of course, it is possible to do even further analysis.

SEARCH ENGINES AND SEARCH ENGINE OPTIMIZATION

Search engine optimization (SEO) practitioners also study the keyword data in web analytics and go further, researching what relevant searches a website didn't appear for. When it comes to learning about users, search engine optimization and user experience have a lot to offer each other.

Besides keyword research, another aspect of search engine optimization is ensuring that search engines understand websites properly. Search engines like Google have software that visit websites, following links on pages to discover where they lead and how pages are related to each other, and interpreting the content of pages to try to understand what the page and the website as a whole are about. While the goal of search engines is to find pages people would consider the most useful, the software that crawls websites can't understand what pages are about or what is useful content and what is not as effectively as a human.

That's where search engine optimization comes in—removing barriers to showing search engines what websites are really about. Removing the barriers ranges from simple activities like ensuring the proper use of HTML tags, to aligning the content on pages so each page is about a single concept, to large-scale projects like adjusting the hierarchy of pages on a website to mimic search engines' taxonomies of concepts.

SEARCH QUERY ANALYSIS

The search query analysis is an exploratory exercise that analyzes the keywords that brought users to your website, to group those keywords into categories and characterize those categories in terms of size and usage metrics like bounce rate and conversion rate. The gist of the search query analysis is that you take all of the data about what users searched for in a certain time period and export it. After you export it, you can consolidate variations and then begin to group the phrases into clusters according to what users were trying to express. In this way, you can get a more accurate account of how many users express different information needs and insight into how you can do a better job of segmenting the data according to the variety of searches users make within a category.

The following description focuses on search engine keywords, but it can be applied to website search data as well—you will simply obtain the data from different reports and have different metrics associated with the data, like how many users refine their search, how many pages they view after performing a search, and how many simply leave after performing a search.

	A	B	C	D	E	F
1	# ----------------					
2	# PV Only					
3	# Organic Search Traffic					
4	# 20110704-20120703					
5	# ----------------					
6						
7	Keyword	Visits	Pages / Visit	Avg. Visit Du	% New Visits	Bounce Rate
8	(not provide	2,822	2.12	0:01:35	80.01%	66.90%
9	pure visibility	811	3.35	0:02:30	58.20%	38.59%
10	purevisibility	84	3.79	0:03:50	52.38%	30.95%
11	pure visibility	53	3.7	0:02:28	64.15%	32.08%
12	google adwo	48	1.5	0:00:25	100.00%	81.25%
13	msn api	43	1.12	0:00:05	100.00%	90.70%
14	internet mar	37	2	0:00:32	86.49%	59.46%
15	accelerated c	33	1.15	0:00:45	90.91%	84.85%
16	pay per click	33	2.24	0:01:43	100.00%	57.58%
17	seo answers	32	1.56	0:00:55	100.00%	75.00%
18	pure visabilit	30	3.73	0:01:50	80.00%	26.67%
19	internet mar	28	4.36	0:02:18	67.86%	21.43%
20	seo ann arbo	28	3.25	0:03:03	57.14%	25.00%
21	pure visibility	27	2.96	0:02:45	59.26%	48.15%
22	purevisibility	25	3.08	0:02:44	84.00%	40.00%
23	internet+ma	24	3.71	0:04:50	4.17%	29.17%
24	linda girard	23	2.52	0:01:12	78.26%	78.26%
25	search marke	22	4.36	0:06:25	59.09%	54.55%
26	pay per click	21	2.52	0:03:00	90.48%	42.86%
27	pure visibility	21	2.52	0:01:41	80.95%	38.10%
28	online marke	20	1.45	0:00:27	5.00%	90.00%
29	java msn api	19	1	0:00:00	73.68%	100.00%
30	pure visibility	19	3.47	0:01:24	31.58%	52.63%
31	ann arbor se	18	4.11	0:03:19	77.78%	22.22%
32	adwords bud	17	1.41	0:04:50	70.59%	76.47%
33	average ppc	17	1	0:00:00	64.71%	100.00%
34	internal navi	17	1.47	0:00:30	100.00%	88.24%
35	ysm panama	17	1.06	0:01:24	5.88%	94.12%
36	pure visibility	16	4.25	0:02:52	87.50%	25.00%

FIGURE 6.5

A spreadsheet exported from Google Analytics containing keyword data. It shows just the website usage data; goal data must be exported separately and then copied and pasted.

Exporting the Data

The first step is to choose a timeframe—a timeframe where you expect users have behaved normally, or behaved in a way that you're curious about if there is a seasonal aspect to your business, such as a time when people enroll for classes or do Christmas shopping.

If you're using Google Analytics, you should keep this timeframe short, such as two weeks or a month, depending on how many visitors come to your website. These tools aren't built for exporting keyword data. Google Analytics will only let you export 5,000 rows of data at a time, which means you must either export page after page of data, or select a very small time range, export all of the keyword data, and then move on to the next narrow time range. Further, Google Analytics won't let you export website usage data and goal data simultaneously; you will have to export those data separately and then paste them together, as in Figures 6.5 and 6.6. However you approach it, it's going to hurt to export a large data set, but you should try to choose the longest timeframe that you can balanced against the amount of data you will have to work with.

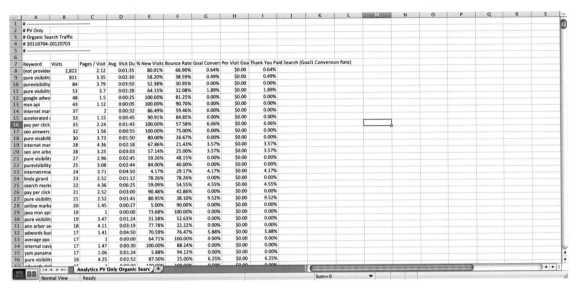

FIGURE 6.6
The same spreadsheet, but with goal data pasted in.

HACKING THE URL

At the time of writing, it is possible to display and export more than 50,000 rows of data at the same time in Google Analytics. The first step is to change a report to show more than the default 10 rows of data, such as 25 rows of data. Then, search the URL for this string: explorer-table.rowCount%3D25. Change the "25" to whatever round number you want, like 10,000, 50,000, or 100,000; however, the higher the number you use, the more slowly Google Analytics will respond, and at some point it will stop responding entirely.

It is possible to find third-party tools to automate the download from Google Analytics, such as Google-Analytics-export-to-csv (http://www.keplarllp.com/blog/2012/01/introducing-google-analytics-export-to-csv-a-fast-simple-way-to-get-your-google-analytics-data-into-your-favourite-analytics-programme). The only drawback is that they use the Google Analytics API, which limits how much data one can request from the system per day. If you try to export too much data (e.g., a whole year's worth) you will have to do it in batches over multiple days.

However, there is a good chance you will be able to export a month of keyword data. You will probably end up with a spreadsheet, like in Figure 6.5. If you exported multiple spreadsheets, you can combine them by simply taking all of the rows of data from one sheet and pasting them into the bottom of another spreadsheet.

Create Candidate Categories

Next, you start to come up with the categories you'll put the keywords into. Your list will be provisional; it is almost guaranteed that you will end up revising your list as you learn more about keywords.

Categorization is an unstructured activity that you can do either in your exported data or in your web analytics tool's interface. In this activity, your professional judgment comes into play. You're looking for themes and patterns. What keywords reflect the same basic information need? Are there different levels of specificity in the need? Does the language reflect expert or novice users? Is there a time or seasonal component?

If you have read Lou Rosenfeld's great book *Site Search Analytics*, this activity should seem familiar. However, the emphasis of categorization is grouping synonymous keywords, and to find ways to compress the variations in keywords together into meaningful categories. How high level versus how specific those categories should be will be a reflection of your domain and what questions you want to answer. Start forming categories and then see if more queries fit the distinctions you have just made. You may be able to draw upon previous user research activities or even work that your website's SEO team has done.

Here is a list of the categories that I put together for Pure Visibility's website:

- Not provided
- PPC information
- Branded (Pure Visibility)
- Miscellaneous
- SEO information
- Internet marketing services
- SEO services
- Specific person
- PPC services
- General marketing services
- Workshops
- Internet marketing information
- Jobs
- Analytics information
- Social media information
- UX information
- Analytics services

- Book (*Internet Marketing Start to Finish*)
- UX services
- General marketing services
- Social media services
- Web design services

The first, not provided, reflects a change that Google made in 2011 that hides the keyword of anyone using Google while also logged in to a Google account, such as Gmail. Depending on one's users, not provided may obscure a large portion of keywords. Unfortunately, there is no way to learn more about what is in this category.

Searches for "Pure Visibility" or some variation of the name comprises another large category. If you work with a company that makes and/or sells products, you may find that users search for your company name as well as product names. Whether to put all of these users into one category or break them apart comes down to how different these users may behave. Three members of the Pure Visibility team also wrote a book on Internet marketing, which I have broken out into a separate category.

For other topics, like paid search advertising (pay per click), search engine optimization, and user experience, I created categories for informational searches and for users who seemed to have searched for service providers. This distinction is common. In the case of informational searches, some examples were "setting ad words budgets" or "characteristics of effective landing page." On the other hand, search for services specifically mentioned a provider, such as "SEO marketing companies," or a location, like "SEO companies in Michigan."

The end product from this stage is a list of candidate categories and a guide to how to classify search queries into those categories. The category guide can take the form of a list of example words for each category that will help you identify its keywords, and optimally a set of regular expressions you can use to segment data in analytics (or to use in a script that will process the keyword data for you, if you are able to do that).

Processing the Data

There are two ways to approach processing the data: by hand or by writing some kind of script that will do it for you. Since automation requires the same conceptual steps, we'll focus on doing this work by hand in this chapter, and you can use the steps as pseudocode if you choose to script it.

By now, you should have a large spreadsheet containing your list of keywords and the data associated with each keyword. The basic activity that you do next is to add a column and begin categorizing each keyword, as in Figure 6.7.

Category	Keyword	Visits	Pages / Vi	Avg. Visit	% New Vi	Bounce R	Goal Conv	Per Visit	Thank You	aid Search (Goal1 Conversion Rate)
Pure Visibility	pure visibility	811	3.35	0:02:30	58.20%	38.59%	0.49%	$0.00	0.49%	
Pure Visibility	purevisibility	84	3.79	0:03:50	52.38%	30.95%	0.00%	$0.00	0.00%	
Pure Visibility	pure visibility ann arbor	53	3.7	0:02:28	64.15%	32.08%	1.89%	$0.00	1.89%	
Pure Visibility	pure visability	30	3.73	0:01:50	80.00%	26.67%	0.00%	$0.00	0.00%	
Pure Visibility	pure visibility, inc.	27	2.96	0:02:45	59.26%	48.15%	0.00%	$0.00	0.00%	
Pure Visibility	purevisibility.com	25	3.08	0:02:44	84.00%	40.00%	0.00%	$0.00	0.00%	
Pure Visibility	pure visibility michigan	21	2.52	0:01:41	80.95%	38.10%	9.52%	$0.00	9.52%	
Pure Visibility	pure visibility ann arbor mi	16	4.25	0:02:52	87.50%	25.00%	6.25%	$0.00	6.25%	
Pure Visibility	pure visibility inc	11	2.45	0:01:15	90.91%	54.55%	0.00%	$0.00	0.00%	
Pure Visibility	pure visibility ann arbor michigan	10	2.4	0:00:42	70.00%	30.00%	0.00%	$0.00	0.00%	
Pure Visibility	purevisibility+consultant	10	11.4	0:16:58	0.00%	40.00%	10.00%	$0.00	10.00%	
Miscellaneous	pure marketing	9	2.22	0:00:14	88.89%	77.78%	0.00%	$0.00	0.00%	
Pure Visibility	pure visiblity	8	2.38	0:00:28	75.00%	50.00%	0.00%	$0.00	0.00%	
Pure Visibility	pure+visibility	7	5.57	0:20:53	14.29%	28.57%	0.00%	$0.00	0.00%	
Pure Visibility	purevisibilty	7	1.86	0:00:14	0.00%	57.14%	0.00%	$0.00	0.00%	
Person	barbra wells pure visibility	6	1.5	0:05:30	0.00%	66.67%	0.00%	$0.00	0.00%	
Pure Visibility	http://purevisibility.com	6	2	0:00:31	100.00%	50.00%	0.00%	$0.00	0.00%	
Pure Visibility	http://purevisibility.com/	6	1.5	0:01:15	66.67%	66.67%	0.00%	$0.00	0.00%	
Pure Visibility	pure visibility, ann arbor	6	2.67	0:01:14	16.67%	0.00%	0.00%	$0.00	0.00%	
Pure Visibility	pure visiblity	6	3.5	0:02:00	33.33%	33.33%	0.00%	$0.00	0.00%	
Person	catherine juon pure visibility	5	4.4	0:02:59	60.00%	20.00%	0.00%	$0.00	0.00%	
Person	linda girard pure visibility	5	1.8	0:00:06	100.00%	40.00%	0.00%	$0.00	0.00%	
Jobs	pure visibility careers	5	1.8	0:02:01	20.00%	20.00%	0.00%	$0.00	0.00%	
Pure Visibility	pure visibility, inc	5	1.2	0:00:03	100.00%	80.00%	0.00%	$0.00	0.00%	
Miscellaneous	pure	4	1	0:00:00	75.00%	100.00%	0.00%	$0.00	0.00%	
Miscellaneous	pure made in heaven	4	1.25	0:02:42	75.00%	75.00%	0.00%	$0.00	0.00%	
Pure Visibility	pure visiblity	4	1.5	0:00:24	25.00%	75.00%	0.00%	$0.00	0.00%	
SEO service	pure visibility seo	4	5	0:02:26	75.00%	50.00%	0.00%	$0.00	0.00%	
Pure Visibility	purevisibility klout	4	2.25	0:07:32	0.00%	50.00%	0.00%	$0.00	0.00%	
Pure Visibility	www.purevisibility.com	4	3	0:01:22	100.00%	25.00%	0.00%	$0.00	0.00%	
Pure Visibility	and arbor pure visibility	3	1.33	0:07:41	33.33%	66.67%	0.00%	$0.00	0.00%	
Person	brent bowles pure visibility	3	2.67	0:10:51	0.00%	33.33%	0.00%	$0.00	0.00%	
Internet Marke	pure internet marketing	3	1.67	0:00:35	100.00%	66.67%	0.00%	$0.00	0.00%	
Pure Visibility	pure visibility inc.	3	1	0:00:00	100.00%	100.00%	0.00%	$0.00	0.00%	
Jobs	pure visiblity project manager	3	1.67	0:02:36	0.00%	66.67%	0.00%	$0.00	0.00%	

Analytics PV Only Organic Searc +

Normal View   Filter Mode   Sum = 0

FIGURE 6.7

At this point, I have removed the top rows of the spreadsheet so the column headers are in the first row, and added a Category column. Through using Excel's Filter functionality, I gradually whittle down the list of uncategorized keywords.

You should use whatever filtering functionality you have in your spreadsheet tool (such as Microsoft Excel) to iteratively search for a specific string, using the filtering rules you came up with in the previous step, and then categorize all of those keywords at once. This process can be time consuming to do by hand, but one advantage you have over creating a script is that you can handle exceptions or difficult-to-classify keywords.

What about keywords that seem like they could fit into more than one category? In the case of one of Pure Visibility's clients, one of our categories was for branded searches (like "Tutor Time") and another category was for variations on "daycare" or "childcare." Unsurprisingly, people searched for "Tutor Time daycare."

You can put a keyword into more than one category. You may have a reason for maintaining exclusivity in your categories, but since the goal of this activity is to characterize the search behavior of users, you should organize the data in the way that best describes users. The simplest way to put a keyword in multiple categories is to simply duplicate that row of data and assign one category to one row and a different category to another row. It is best that you use this ability with caution, though, because once you start duplicating keywords, you will probably end up duplicating hundreds of words.

Instead, is there a root concept that takes precedence? In the case of the "Tutor Time daycare," we chose to classify it as a branded search because we were interested in exploring the behavior of people who weren't specifically expressing an interest in the brand. We could have also put this keyword into two categories or classified it under "daycare." Also consider whether you have encountered a new category. In the end, whether to duplicate will be a judgment call.

If exclusivity is important to you, create a hierarchy, or sequence, for your categories, to decide which ones have precedence over others. If you approach categorization programmatically, you will have to determine the order of precedence (even if you do make it possible to put something into multiple categories).

TIPS

Filtering the Spreadsheet

After I have all the data in my Excel spreadsheet, I select all of the columns of data and turn on Filter. From there, I repeatedly filter the Keyword column to show all of the keywords that have some bit of text in common, in the hope that they will all have the same category. At the same time, I filter the Category column so it only shows blank cells. Every time I do something to refresh the filters, it hides the rows that I've already categorized.

The Miscellaneous Category

You won't be able to get away from the Miscellaneous category. The Internet is a sufficiently weird place that even if you carefully scrutinize every keyword that brought users to your website, there will be times when you find the meaning completely inscrutable.

In the case of the Pure Visibility example, Miscellaneous is where I put people who seemed to be researching our clients, people looking for Internet service providers, and people searching for things like "Google's core values" and "laptop and donut."

It may be disappointing to see the size of your Miscellaneous category (in the case of Pure Visibility, I put 6.8% of users into that category), but coming up with better classifications for these weird searches would be time consuming and give you little value.

A Subject Matter Expert Is Helpful

If you are not an expert in the topic or topics of the website you're analyzing, it would be helpful to have some kind of subject matter expert on hand to answer questions or, better yet, review your work. A subject matter expert is particularly helpful when you encounter keywords where the user searched for a very specific aspect of some topic, like a particular paid search or SEO tactic.

Do a Second Pass

After you've categorized everything, you should go through your categories and make sure you didn't make any typos or inconsistent terminology. If you take on this project over the course of several hours, it's bound to happen.

Give Up on Perfection

As with everything analytics related, perfection is practically unattainable. You will miscategorize things. You will second guess yourself about a classification. If you do the categorization programmatically, there will be errors. Perfection, going over the data again and again until you're certain about every classification, is not worth the time it would take. When to stop is ultimately a judgment call; an obvious point is when you start to run out of time, or when you no longer find things to reclassify when you scan the most frequently searched phrases in each category.

After you have applied categories to all of the rows of data, it's time to add a few columns:

- Pages (Visits × Pages/Visit)
- Duration (Visits × Average Visit Duration)
- New Visits (Visits × % New Visits)
- Bounces (Visits × Bounce Rate)
- A column for each goal to count conversions (Visits × Conversion Rate)

You add these columns so that you can correctly calculate average visit duration, % new visits, etc. When we move on to creating a pivot table, we have the option to average these data, but it won't weight them correctly—that is, if 100 visitors have a bounce rate of 50% and 10 visitors have a bounce rate of 80%, the bounce rate for all 110 visitors isn't 65%, it's 53% because there are so many visitors with the lower bounce rate. By calculating pages, duration, etc., we can use the pivot table to take the sum of these new metrics by category and then transform them back into properly weighted averages and percentages.

Lastly, select all of the columns of data and create a pivot table.

Analyzing the Data Again

Populate the pivot table (Figure 6.8) with your categories as the row labels, and then show the values for the following items:

- Visits
- Pages
- Duration
- New visits
- Bounces
- Count of conversions for any goals you have in your analytics account

With the exception of visits, these are the new columns that you created in the data. Make sure you show the sum of these values rather than the count. The next step is to calculate the pages per visit, average visit duration, etc. You can add these columns right next to the pivot table.

There is one more column to add to the data: the portion of visitors who fit into these categories (% of Visits in Figure 6.8). This is the number of visits in a category divided by the total number of visits from the original data. If you duplicated rows during the processing phase to put a keyword in more than one category, then you need to go back to the original data and find out what the total number of visits was. From there, you can copy all of the data shown in Figure 6.7 and paste it into a new spreadsheet and continue your analysis. The following paragraphs describe some approaches to analyzing the data.

Row Labels	Values Sum of Visits	Sum of Pages	Sum of Duration	Sum of New Visits	Sum of Bounces	Sum of Conversions	Pages/Visit	Avg Duration	% New Visits	Bounce Rate	Conv. Rate	% of visits
(not provided)	2823	5983.64	2927.102894	2258.8822	1888.918	18.0608	2.12	0:53:06	80.02%	66.91%	0.64%	34.13%
analytics info	71	109.98	81872.03287	61.9998	57.0001	0	1.55	3:03:12	87.32%	80.28%	0.00%	0.86%
analytics service	15	28	16082.00874	10	9	0	1.87	3:12:50	66.67%	60.00%	0.00%	0.18%
Book	14	24	13158.00752	9.0002	9.0002	0	1.71	20:35:04	64.29%	64.29%	0.00%	0.17%
Internet Marketing info	86	149.02	90644.06372	78.0001	63.9998	2	1.73	0:01:04	90.70%	74.42%	2.33%	1.04%
Internet Marketing Service	349	1105.95	157896.5764	252.0033	164.0021	8.0016	3.17	10:13:02	72.21%	46.99%	2.29%	4.22%
Jobs	85	184.92	57018.11206	44.0002	50	0	2.18	19:13:54	51.76%	58.82%	0.00%	1.03%
Marketing Agency	4	5	2924.001435	4	3	0	1.25	0:00:31	100.00%	75.00%	0.00%	0.05%
Marketing info	1	1	1462	1	1	0	1.00	0:00:00	100.00%	100.00%	0.00%	0.01%
Marketing services	144	358.9	112574.1612	125.0001	76.9997	1	2.49	18:21:37	86.81%	53.47%	0.69%	1.74%
Miscellaneous	554	849.94	631584.3209	511	450.0014	2	1.53	1:03:13	92.24%	81.23%	0.36%	6.70%
Person	184	457.96	163744.2143	111.9997	86.0004	0	2.49	21:56:28	60.87%	46.74%	0.00%	2.22%
PPC info	1475	1835.96	1419602.513	1367.9999	1315.0017	1.9996	1.24	10:37:02	92.75%	89.15%	0.14%	17.83%
PPC services	169	392.84	121346.1861	159.0007	96.0021	4.9998	2.32	0:35:40	94.08%	56.81%	2.96%	2.04%
Pure Visibility	1460	4755.99	327490.6301	838.0011	581.9681	9.9748	3.26	7:24:27	57.40%	39.86%	0.68%	17.65%
SEO info	442	603.9	494156.2379	400.9997	361.9997	0	1.37	0:00:47	90.72%	81.90%	0.00%	5.34%
SEO services	235	787.94	197370.3891	186.9994	80.9998	5.9996	3.35	20:58:33	79.57%	34.47%	2.55%	2.84%
social media info	25	33	33626.0069	23	21	0	1.32	0:58:00	92.00%	84.00%	0.00%	0.30%
social media services	4	11	4386.001458	3	1	0	2.75	12:00:31	75.00%	25.00%	0.00%	0.05%
UX info	20	29	26316.01244	17	16	0	1.45	19:12:54	85.00%	80.00%	0.00%	0.24%
UX services	9	24	13158.01399	8	5	0	2.67	0:02:14	88.89%	55.56%	0.00%	0.11%
Web design service	3	18	4386.00515	3	0	0	6.00	0:02:28	100.00%	0.00%	0.00%	0.04%
Workshops	100	212.01	115498.1142	82	61.9999	0	2.12	23:32:51	82.00%	62.00%	0.00%	1.21%
(blank)												
Grand Total	8272	17961.95	4089222.713	6555.8864	5399.893	54.0362						

FIGURE 6.8

The pivot table showing, for each category, the sum of visits, pages viewed during those visits, and so on. Next to the pivot table are the calculated values of pages per visit, average visit duration, and so on.

Sort the list by different metrics to find which categories have the highest values, which have the lowest, and which have metrics that deviate the most from average. What are the highest values for things like bounce rate (in the case of search engine keywords) or search exit (in the case of website search)? If you have goals set up, which categories have the highest conversion rates and which have the lowest? Which categories of search engine keywords produced the most pages per visit and which produced the fewest? Which website searches lead to the most refinements (i.e., users immediately entering a new search)? In some cases, you may be able to think of obvious explanations, but this line of inquiry can produce interested questions for you to follow up on by exploring the website further and through user research.

What are the relative sizes of the categories? As mentioned earlier, the number of searches for a given keyword will be influenced by your website's rank in search engines. How well does the size of the categories match other research you have on what your users need? If there are fewer users coming to your website for a category of keyword than you expect, it may indicate that you're not matching the users' language.

With website search data, you can look at whether users are searching for things that are not on your website or using language that does not match your current website. Even search engine keyword data may produce this kind of insight, such as when users search for a longer phrase that includes a word or concept that can be found on your website. A side benefit of this work is that you have a data set that can help you build robust filters for segmenting analytics data and can get a sense of how much of a population you are able to capture with your filter. This segmentation will allow you to explore other reports in your analytics tool, just looking at one of the groups of users you discovered with the search query analysis.

Basic Keyword Analysis

Comprehensively analyzing keywords can be time consuming—it could easily take 20–30 hours of analysis time to do it by hand, and easily that much to write a script. In the next section of this chapter, we cover basic (or "discount") keyword analysis. The moves are practically the same, but the focus will be on the head terms rather than the breadth of keywords that users searched for. For that reason, we'll focus more on how this approach differs.

Export the Data

The difference here is in choosing a time range. With the search query analysis, a drawback of choosing large time ranges is that increasingly large data sets are increasingly unmanageable. You won't face this constraint since you will instead focus on the head terms, so choose a large time range. Alternatively, if there are seasonal variations to what users want, choose a subset of the year to explore those seasonal variations.

You can poke around in the analytics interface and still see patterns and gain insight, but as with the search query, you will probably want to export the data to a spreadsheet so you can make notes. Next, export those data to a spreadsheet. Twenty-five keywords is a good amount to start with.

Categorize the Keywords

As with the search query analysis, add a column and begin describing the keywords with category names. Since you're working with relatively few keywords, you can take more time to go beyond simple category names to engage more deeply with the things people searched for and tease out nuances.

A good approach would be to search for these keywords yourself. Does your website still appear? What page in your website appears and how does this search engine result look? Even though the search engine results page isn't part of your website, it's still part of your users' experience, and it is possible to change the page title and preview that appears for your website in search results. What other pages show up? Although search engines are not perfect, they do a really good job of matching search results to what people search for, so looking at search results is a good way to understand what a particular query means. Of course, you could see what search results you get for every keyword in the search query analysis, but it would get very time consuming to do it for more than a sample.

Compare Metrics

As with the search query analysis, you can add columns to the spreadsheet to show what portion of total users and total keywords each row represents. Website usage metrics such as pages per visit and time on website can give you clues about how well your website actually serves people with different information needs. Basically, the approach described in the search query analysis, once you've categorized the keywords and combined metrics, applies to analysis of just the head terms.

REFERRAL TRAFFIC

There may be other websites on the Internet that link to yours. If a user clicks on one of those links and follows it to your website, he or she gets counted as a referral visitor. The main thing you know about referral visitors is where they came from—not just what website, but also the specific page on that website. This information can potentially give you some insight into what they were doing just before they came to your website. Depending on the purpose of your website, referral may be a significant source of users, particularly as social media has exploded over the past few years as a way users share information with each other.

These data allow you to do some detective work to find out the context of the links to your website and what users might have been doing or what goals they had in mind when they clicked on the link to your website. A website may belong to an organization that has some sort of relationship with yours, such as a company that sells your company's products or a list of top university programs that points to your university's website. You may be able to infer what the user was doing; users who followed a link from Wikipedia were probably researching a topic, whereas a visitor from a social media website may have been following a friend's recommendation that a specific piece of content was an interesting read.

Analyzing referral data is an exploratory exercise. There is often a great deal of diversity in the sources that send users to your website, with a few websites that each send many users, and many websites that each send a few users. For a high-level perspective on how the behavior of these users differs based on how they got to your website, you can look at website usage metrics like pages per visit or average visit duration, as shown in Figures 6.9 and 6.10. Chapter 7 covers the interpretation of these metrics. You can also

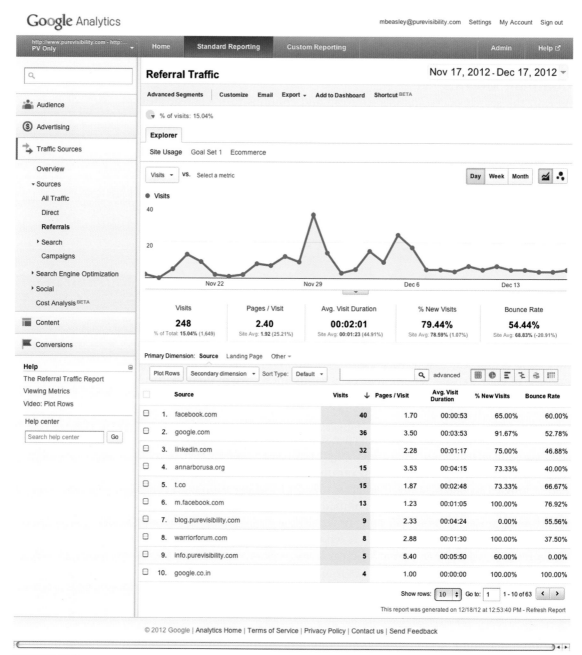

FIGURE 6.9

The "Referral Traffic" report, showing how many users came from various websites that linked to the Pure Visibility website, and website usage metrics for those users.

FIGURE 6.10

The "Referral Traffic" report again, but after clicking on one of the websites to show the specific pages that sent people to the Pure Visibility website. This report lets you explore the specific context users were in when they encountered a link to your website.

compare conversion rate for the goals you have set up on your website (as per Chapter 4) across referral sources and to your website as a whole to get a sense of how motivated users are to take these actions based on where they come from. In Chapter 9, we cover the subject of segmentation. This ability lets you isolate users who came from specific sources and then look at just the data for those users in other web analytics reports, letting you further explore how the behavior of users coming from one website varies from users coming from another website.

Obviously, any conclusions about what the referral website indicates about users will be assumptions. In the end, it is possible that you can't form any conclusions based on the referral website. If a user came from a link in your company's Facebook page, then it's very likely that they didn't have a specific task in mind and were just browsing. On the other hand, if users came from another website that lists your company as a vendor, those users may be interested in finding out if you can provide that same service for them. It would be a good idea to visit the websites that users came from and find the context of that link to your website. Doing so may give you clues about what needs users may have in mind when they clicked on the link. Pay attention to where on your website that link sends them.

Does this landing page actually support the need that you have inferred? If not, you may wish to make changes to your website or to request that the other website change where they're sending users on your website (after all, *your* users' experience extends to the *other* websites that send users your way).

DIRECT TRAFFIC

You can learn almost nothing about the motivations that drove direct visitors. You know that they know (or guessed) the URL of your website and either typed it in, used a bookmark, or clicked on a link in an email. You can also see what page they landed on. This information opens up some possibilities for data segmentation depending on what pages they landed on.

There are two trends that complicate direct traffic and make it more inscrutable. One is the ability of modern web browsers to autocomplete URLs that the user has previously visited. This feature may suggest precisely the website that the user had in mind, but it may also suggest a website that the user visited long ago and forgot about. The other trend is toward people using search engines to find websites that they've already visited before—they may know the brand name or the name of the website, but rather than trying to guess the URL based on it, they simply search again. Over the past few years, we have seen the share of direct traffic decline for our clients at Pure Visibility, and believe it to be related.

The result is that you may have people showing up as direct visitors who didn't remember your website, and users who would have been direct, but instead show up as organic or pay per click.

PAID SEARCH KEYWORDS

If your company is engaged in paid search advertising, you will have another source of keyword data. You can mix these data in with the organic keyword data, or view each separately.

Anything you did with a basic keyword analysis or the search query analysis you can do with paid keywords. However, in Google Analytics, you must remember something important about the data: when you go to Traffic Sources→Sources→Search→Paid Report, by default it doesn't show you the actual things users searched for. It shows you what keywords the users' searches actually matched.

When you manage paid search advertising, you choose keywords that you want to bid on to have an ad appear. You don't have to guess every permutation of the users' keywords, though. You can set different levels of exactness, so, for example, you could have an ad show up even if people misspell your company's name, or have the same ad appear whether people just type in your company's name or type in your company's name as well as a few extra words.

Keyword data from a paid search advertising campaign gives you access to a source of keywords that may already be clustered in the same way you would approach the search query analysis. On the other hand, depending on how your campaigns are managed, the buckets that your paid search management person came up with may not help you. This is something you will have to explore for yourself. You can see the actual keywords that users entered by changing the primary dimension from keyword to matched search query.

It's important to remember that the users who enter your website through paid search are probably different from the users who enter through an organic search; to start with, they are people who are willing to click on ads or who can't distinguish ads from other search results. They are also a segment of users who your business selects rather than users who select you. The amount of users who come in through different keywords don't simply reflect how many people actually search for a particular concept. They are how many people search for a concept that you are willing to pay for, which will influence the number of users in each keyword "bucket" and may even have ramifications for their behavior once they get to your website.

MORE MEDIUMS

It's possible to set up more mediums beside organic, referral, and (none). We've already mentioned CPC, and other mediums may appear if your company engages in other forms of online advertising. It's even possible to write links to your website that mark visitors with a specific medium. An example would be the links in an email newsletter being written to classify those users as coming from the "email" medium rather than a referral or directly.

Customizing mediums is done through adding parameters to the end of the URL, such as http://www.widgets.com/?utm_source=newsletter&utm_medium=email&utm_campaign=july. As you can see, you can specify the source and even other fields that have more of a marketing focus.

Why do this? It is mainly useful for measuring the efficacy of marketing campaigns, and there aren't any corresponding reports for these mediums as there are for organic, paid search, or referrals. You may find these custom mediums useful for segmentation.

KEY TAKEAWAYS

- You can use web analytics to learn about the device users use to access your website, how often they come to your website, and where they are located geographically.
- These data cover the full range of your website's users, a different approach from the specificity we create with personas. We can use these data to categorize and characterize our users and look for patterns.
- Although web analytics can't tell you about why users behave as they do, you can look at where they came from (such as from another website) or what they searched for to infer their goals.
- Keyword analysis consists of these general steps:
  - Selecting data to analyze from some time range.
  - Interpreting and categorizing the keywords to form semantically meaningful groups.
  - Analyzing metrics to see how many users searched for each category and how their usage metrics (like time on website) differ.
- Some approaches to analyzing website usage from keyword analysis are:
  - Looking for keyword categories that have the highest value for a metric.
  - Finding the lowest value for a given metric.
  - Looking for values that deviate the most from the average for that metric.
  - Compare the relative number of users in your keyword categories to what you have learned about users' needs through other research methods.
  - Find words and phrases that do not match your website's terminology or that are for concepts your website does not cover.
- Keyword analysis can have implications for the language you use on your website, the content that you create for the website, and how you organize the navigation.
- If users followed a link from another website to get to yours, it may be possible to infer possible motivations based on the context of that website.

CHAPTER 7

Analyzing How People Use Your Content

INTRODUCTION

Content analysis will give you oblique insights into how users interact with the pages on your website. You can find out where they go and how long they stay there, what pages people enter your website on, and from which pages they exit your website. You must complete the story by making inferences based on your professional judgment or by learning firsthand from users through other user research methods.

When you start to dig into data about pages, you can discover startling things, confirm your assumptions, and see how changes to your website affect users' behavior.

The first part of this chapter covers the site content reports in Google Analytics as a way to provide a practical framework for digging into the metrics you will find in most web analytics tools like bounce rate, time on page, pageviews, and so on, and the implications of different patterns. The focus of the first section of this chapter is on how users interact with individual pages. We then move on to click-path analysis, where you analyze how users have moved from page to page on your website.

WEBSITE CONTENT REPORTS

The "All Pages" report in Google Analytics, shown in Figure 7.1, will be your primary place for looking at page-level metrics. It seems to be called this name to differentiate it from other reports that just focus on landing pages and exit pages.

When you first reach this report, it starts in Explorer mode, the mode where you interact with tables of data. We will delve into "Navigation Summary" and "In-Page Analytics" reports, accessible near the top of the page, later in the chapter. In the lower half of the page, you see the by-now-familiar table of data, with page set as the primary dimension and the pages sorted by pageviews.

CONTENTS

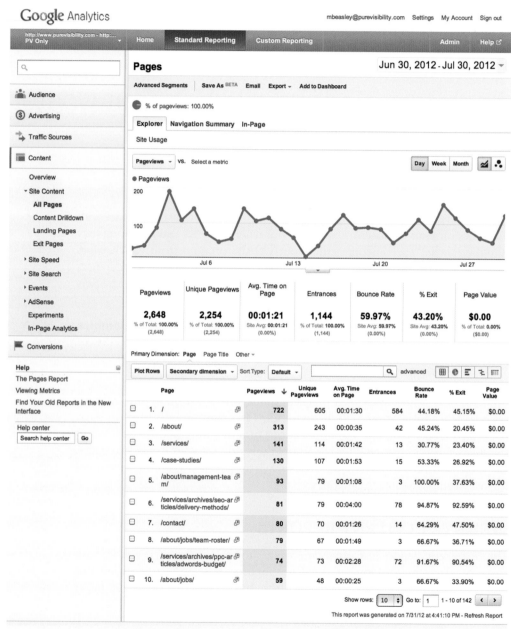

FIGURE 7.1

An example of Google Analytics' "All Pages" report, currently showing page-level metrics for the 10 most-viewed pages on the Pure Visibility website.

You can approach the data with specific questions in mind or for open-ended exploration. Specific questions are usually along the lines of "How long do users spend looking at the laser pointer product page?" or "How does the average time on page for the article on keyword optimization and the article on link-building compare?" It's also possible to compare an entire class of page (e.g., all product pages on an e-commerce website) to other pages, and we will get to that later in this section.

Whether you are investigating specific pages or doing open-ended exploration, you are looking for the same basic patterns:

- The highest values for a metric
- The lowest values for a metric
- Pages that have metrics that deviate from the average value

The following are patterns that you may encounter.

PAGE (DIMENSION)

A page is a single page of your website, identified, in Google Analytics, by the URI. The URI is the uniform resource identifier, or the part of a URL that tells you where a page is within a website. If you have http://www.example.com/widgets/product_page.html, the URI is /widgets/product_page.html.

You will use this dimension a great deal because it tells you what page you're looking at. It may take a while to adjust to looking at URIs, but that's one of the reasons it's important to give websites human-readable URLs (see the "Difficult to Read URLs" sidebar in Chapter 2). If you are using another tool like Omniture, part of installing web analytics on the website is coming up with a naming scheme for all of the pages so they have meaningful, human-readable names.

High Pageviews/Low Pageviews

As discussed in Chapter 3, a pageview is a single time a page was viewed by a user, and it counts each time the user views a page if he or she goes to it multiple times in the same session.

Let's look more closely at Figure 7.1. We can see a fairly typical distribution of pageviews—the homepage is the most viewed page, followed by pages that appear in the main navigation like /about and /services/. Rows 6 and 9 are notable, though, in that they are pages deep on the website that are among the most-viewed pages.

It may be interesting to find out why so many users are going to those pages. There are two main reasons why users go to these pages: the pages are enticing to users (either appropriately or not) or the pages are a landing page for many users (i.e., the first page users view upon entering your website). You would start by going to the website and actually looking at these pages for clues; it may become quickly apparent that a page is a good fit for your users' needs.

It could be the case that these pages are particularly easy to find (maybe there's a link to them on the homepage) or they have a particularly enticing link label. You may be able to get some clues through click-path analysis. It could also be the case that users just really want to read this content and find it (perhaps in spite of the website's design).

Look at the entrances metric in comparison to pageviews and unique pageviews. The higher that entrances is in proportion to either of these other two metrics, the more people are entering your website through this page. A high proportion of entrances to unique pageviews simply indicates that many of the users who reach this page do so by landing on it. A high proportion of entrances to pageviews indicates that users are landing on a page and then not returning. Pair that with looking at average time on page and you can start to see a story about how users may land on a page and spend a great deal of time on the page before moving off, landing on a page and then leaving quickly and never coming back, and so on.

Another place where you can get an idea of how often users are landing on a page in Google Analytics is the "Landing Pages" report. In cases where a page gets viewed frequently because users are landing on it, it is worth discovering where those users are coming from. In Google Analytics, you can do so by adding a secondary dimension to the "All Pages" or "Landing Pages" report for medium (to find out how they find the page), source (to find out what websites may link to this page), or keyword (to find out what information needs users have when they find this page).

It is very important to not overlook how large the portion of pageviews coming from entrances is. Users landing on a page will probably interact differently with that page than users who reached it by navigating from another page on your website. Learning how they found that page can give you insight into their motivations.

You may also find out that pages you believe to be important are not ranked as highly as you would expect. The reasons why users *aren't* visiting a page basically come down to the opposite of why they do visit pages: difficult to find in the website, poor information scent on the links that lead to the content, or users may just not be interested in the information.

You can infer reasons why users do or do not visit pages and even test design changes intended to drive more people to a page (for more about testing changes, see Chapter 11). In the end, though, your best way to learn why users do what they do is, unsurprisingly, studying them directly. You may wish to construct usability test tasks that involve finding certain pages or touching on what information they actually need to accomplish a task during the course of an interview.

DOES A PAGEVIEW INDICATE INTEREST IN A SUBJECT?

Analytics answers "what" and not "why," so pageview data provides clues about whether a page appealed to users, but these data are not sufficient in isolation. That's because, for example, users may go to a page because they want to, but they may also go there by mistake or because they are forced to in order to get to something they really want.

Metrics like average time on page can shed some light on whether a pageview is intentional or not. The higher it is, the more likely it is that many users stuck around and did *something* on the page. At the end of the day analytics is the "smoke" that guides the UX investigator to look for the "fire" of user goals. That fire must still be identified through traditional UX methods.

Pageviews are Much Higher than Unique Pageviews

Pageviews will (almost) always be higher than unique pageviews, reflecting how users may go back to a page they already visited. If the amount of pageviews for a given page is significantly higher than unique pageviews in comparison to other pages on your website, it may be worth investigating why that is.

Unfortunately, there is no absolute rule on what is significantly higher. If you find that pageviews are 40–50% higher than unique pageviews or more, it may be a sign that something notable is going on with that page.

It could be the case that users are intentionally going back to this page (as in the case of navigational hubs or pages that are frequently updated with new content), but it may reflect a navigational problem (e.g., if the links to the page are labeled differently in different places or if users are flailing when trying to find some other page). Of course, context matters, and if many other pages have a similar ratio, it may just be the nature of your users and website that they frequently revisit pages.

A common term for users repeatedly and briefly returning to a page is *pogo-sticking*. Some pages simply serve as navigational hubs, pages that users return to multiple times during their visit as they explore difference paths. In this situation, pogo-sticking is reasonable behavior. Otherwise, when pageviews is high compared to unique pageviews, it is worth exploring what pages people come from to get to a page and what pages people go to afterward. You may uncover a confusing relationship between two pages, such as unclear navigation labels or controls that unexpectedly take users to another page.

In the case of users pogo-sticking on the results on a search results page (sometimes known as *thrashing*), it may mean that your website search must be improved. Exploring how users move through your website is called click-path analysis, which Chapter 8 will explore further.

Low Time on Page

There is no objective standard of high or low or good or bad. You can be pretty sure that users spending fewer than 10 seconds on a page aren't doing very much. A minute is a long time and two minutes is an eternity for the Internet. Of course, context matters, and you may have a page where you can get a lot done in 10 seconds or where a minute is a relatively small amount of time.

As a result, time on page is only low in comparison to other pages or to the average for the website as a whole. A low average time on page indicates that most users going to a page aren't taking time to read content or interact with a page. Reasons for low average time on page could include:

- The content of the page doesn't match what users thought they were going to get.
- The content isn't very interesting or is poorly written.
- There isn't a lot of content on a page.
- The page is very well organized and users can quickly satisfy their goals.
- The purpose of the page is to direct users to other pages, like a search results page.

At this point, your knowledge of what the website is like comes into play, or where you have to look to user research to understand why they are spending so little time on the page.

If you find that a page has a low time on page combined with a high pageview to unique pageview ratio, that's a good sign that users are flailing on your website—moving quickly from page to page, trying to find something.

Comparing time on page to the overall average for the entire website can be problematic because there will be a diversity of times on page based on the roles different pages play, such as forms, articles, product descriptions, or search results pages. It is more informative to compare a page's average time on page to the average for other pages with similar designs or roles within the website, as we will discuss later in this chapter.

FILTERING OUT RARELY VIEWED PAGES IN GOOGLE ANALYTICS

Say you want to sort according to time on page to find out which pages had the lowest or highest average time on page. You sort the list and, all of a sudden, you see pages you didn't even know existed, with one or two pageviews each, and extreme times on page like one second or 30 minutes! When you sort by any metric other than pageviews and unique pageviews, you will find that the extreme values of these metrics often consist of rarely viewed pages.

If you want to ignore these rarely viewed pages and instead focus on more common ones, you can use Google Analytics' advanced filtering (right next to the search box above the explorer table) or even filtering in Microsoft Excel to hide rarely viewed pages. Just pick some arbitrary cutoff point like 100 pageviews, and then show only pages with greater than 100 pageviews. Often, this filtering will make the table much more useful to interact with.

TIME ON PAGE AND AVERAGE TIME ON PAGE (METRICS)

Average time on page is the average of the amount of time that visitors spent on a given page for a selected time period. It is specifically the average of the length of every pageview that a page got for a selected time period. There are two pages not included in this average:

1. Single-page visits ("bounces").
2. The final page in a multipage session.

The reason these are both excluded is the same: there's no way to know how long a visitor actually spent on the last page in a session before leaving the website or closing the browser tab. In the grand scheme of things these exclusions do not affect the value of the metric, since the trends are consistent across all sessions, and "bounce" events require a different analysis anyway.

There is nothing intrinsically good about a long average time on page or a short one. Rather, context matters—navigation hubs that exist merely to direct users to other pages should probably have short average time on page, whereas you would want users to spend a lot of time on pages that are full of content and meant to be engaging. You will probably find the average time on page to be disappointingly low, reflecting how users skim rather than read website copy.

There is, unsurprisingly, a metric called time on page, and every pageview has a time on page. You won't encounter it when interacting with the content reports in Google Analytics, but it will come up when we look at segmentation.

High Time on Page

All we know about pages with a high time on page is that users are spending time on the page doing *something*. Some possibilities are:

- Actually reading a lot of content.
- Watching one or more videos.
- Waiting for a file to download or upload.
- Filling out a lengthy form.
- Using some interactive part of the page, like a calculator, photo editor, or visual portfolio creator.
- Trying really hard to figure out how to use the page.

Again, the context of the page itself matters—if the only thing on a page is a complicated interactive widget, then people are probably interacting with it. A high time on page probably isn't a bad thing, but usability testing may show that the page is crucial yet frustrating, so users are tending to spend a great deal of time on the page against their will.

TABBED BROWSING

Users may also leave a page open while opening other pages in other tabs in their browser. When they open a new page, the analytics tool counts them as having gone to a new page, even though the old one is still open in a browser window—their time on the old page doesn't increase. If they go back to the tab with the old page later and click on a link, it will look as though they went from whatever page they loaded most recently. You could end up with a situation where users navigate from page to page in ways that seem to be impossible! Using a strategy of opening links in new tabs may indicate that a user does not trust your website and they don't want to lose their place, or the behavior may simply be idiosyncratic to the user. Unfortunately, tabbed browsing is difficult to detect using web analytics and other user research methods are better suited to studying this behavior.

High Entrances to Unique Pageviews Ratio

Entrances is most informative when compared to unique pageviews. Unique pageviews show many actual users viewed a page at least once within the selected time period, and entrances shows for how many of those users this page was the first one they viewed. There's nothing really good or bad about finding out that a page is a common entry point or rarely an entry point, but it may affect how you evaluate the effectiveness of the page or incorporate it into usability test tasks. If most of the unique pageviews for a page are entrances, that means that it is a page where users commonly enter the website; as such, it should support the tasks that bring users to the website and make it easier for users to figure out where they are on the website and what the website is all about.

We will discuss landing pages later in this chapter, in the section on the "Landing Pages" report.

TROUBLESHOOTING ANALYTICS

There is also a chance that a high entrances to unique pageviews ratio indicates an analytics configuration problem, most likely one where some pages on your website are not being tracked by your analytics tool. When users click on links on these nontracked pages, they will show up as entrances. Diagnosing analytics configuration problems is largely a bigger topic than this book can deal with, but a quick thing to check in this situation is the source of all of these entrances. If the source for many of these entrances is your own website, it is a clue that there may be pages on your website that aren't tracked.

High Bounce Rate

As discussed in Chapter 3, the bounce rate is the portion of people who exited the website without visiting any other pages, within the subset of people who landed on a page (i.e., the entrances). Generally speaking, you want bounce rate to be low—or, at least, a low bounce rate will seldom signal a problem.

A high bounce rate probably indicates that, for whatever reason, users are not satisfied with the page in some way. It could mean that it doesn't fulfill their needs as far as providing information or fulfilling whatever goal they have in mind. It could be that they found the design of the page completely inscrutable and they gave up and moved on. On the other hand, it could mean that the page design is fine but it shows up in search results when users search for something unrelated to what the page is actually about. It may mean that somebody else's website links to you, but misleads users about what they'll get from your website. These are the sort of problems that you may have to address with the help of people outside your UX team.

It may also be the case that a page with a high bounce rate somehow meets users' needs so quickly that they don't need to explore your website any further. For example, a product page may answer the question of how expensive a product is, and then they leave. An FAQ page may, in fact, have answers to questions that users frequently ask, removing any necessity to explore your website further. To remove this ambiguity about whether a user who bounces was satisfied or dissatisfied, when possible you should find a measurable action on a page to help you tell these users apart. You may choose an analytics goal (as is usually the case with an advertising landing page) or simply use event tracking to measure actions that users can take without leaving the page, as covered in Chapter 12.

In light of all these possibilities, what do you do when you find a high bounce rate? There are really two familiar possibilities: plan a usability test that incorporates this page into a task, or bring your expert judgment to bear in evaluating the page to find things that may be wrong with it and how to potentially improve it.

High % Exit

The inconveniently named % exit metric shows you what portion of pageviews were the last time a user viewed a page on your website. A high % exit may not indicate a problem on a page, because while users may leave your website because they are frustrated with a page and give up, they may also leave because they have accomplished their goal.

If you find a % exit that is higher than average or at the extreme end of % exits, your first step should be to determine what that page is like. Does it make sense that users would leave the website after encountering it? Is it the end of a multipage registration process, a product page, or an article with information? Or is it in the middle of a multipage registration process or a navigational hub that should lead users to other pages?

When you examine the page, a problem may stand out immediately, otherwise, it may be worth trying to construct tasks in future usability tests that try to get users to encounter this page. Alternatively, as with the last section on high bounce rate, finding measurable actions that users can take on the page may give you more insight into whether users accomplished something they would want to do or not.

Page Value

Page value is an interesting and easy-to-misinterpret metric. When you set up goals, it is possible to give them a monetary value (either a fixed value or a value generated by event tracking code), discussed in Chapter 4. From a business analysis point of view, assigning value to each goal is a great idea, because knowing how valuable a conversion is lets you measure how much return you get on the money you spend to get that conversion and make informed decisions about the efficacy of your marketing efforts.

When you have values in place for goals, Google Analytics will start to show values for the page value metric. Page value is the total amount of all goal values divided by unique pageviews. It's only calculated based on goals that users completed after actually viewing a page. In other words, it's a way of measuring how much a page (or group of pages) contributed to users converting on the website. The higher the page value, the more times users went on to convert and/or the more expensive things they bought. The lower the page value, the less likely it is that users viewed a page some time before converting.

As with other metrics, a high or low value doesn't necessarily indicate a problem, but it is worth finding out so you can learn what pages users go to on their way to completing a goal. You may reveal that pages with low page value appear more interesting to a different segment of users than the ones who complete goals, or it may show that an important page is hard to find.

Not every company that uses Google Analytics puts values on goals; this issue may be politically fraught or stakeholders may simply find it to be a confusing metric, usually for anything other than e-commerce goals, where the relationship between a user's action and revenue is clear. UX professionals will typically be more interested in learning what pages users visited before converting as opposed to assigning monetary value to pages, which is something that can be done with segmentation (covered in Chapter 9). For these reasons, it is better to not assign values to goals and begin using this metric if it is not already in use.

Comparing Page Metrics to Similar Pages

Simply looking for bounce rates or whatever other metrics that are higher than the website average is easy to do, but it may be misleading because users interact differently with different pages. Perhaps you have an e-commerce website—you may have the following kinds of pages:

- The home page
- Boring but necessary pages such as privacy policy, return policy, customer support
- Pages for individual products
- Search results pages
- Some kind of category page that supports browsing your products

Users will probably interact with these types of pages in different ways, meaning that the bounce rate, time on page, and other page-level metrics may vary widely from one page type to another. There are a couple of ways to deal with this problem. The first is to use the filtering functionality in Google Analytics (or to export data to a spreadsheet and filter in Excel). Rather than entering in the URL of a specific page, you can filter according to part of a URL. Filtering is useful if there is a common component in the URL of pages that share the same template. Advanced filtering will also let you filter according to a series of AND or OR statements, or using regular expressions.

If you perform this analysis repeatedly, the most practical way to do so is covered in Chapter 14, where we discuss filters and profiles. You have to set up a separate profile where you rewrite the URLs of pages, such as:

- www.website.com/products/super-widget-3000/
- www.website/products/extra-large-widget-3500/
- www.website.com/products/electronic-thing/

Then merge them all into one fake URL like www.website.com/products/product-page. All of the data for those pages get merged together and, instead of seeing where users go after viewing an individual products page, you can see all of the pages users view when they view any product page. Unfortunately, this process takes some planning and can't be applied retroactively.

Google Analytics' "Content Drilldown" report, covered later in this chapter, may automate the clustering process. This report derives the hierarchy of pages on your website based on the URL; unfortunately, not every website has interpretable URLs.

More Reports

The next few reports are occasionally useful, but will probably not be used as often as the "All Pages" report.

"Landing Page" Report

A landing page is the first page of your website that a user views—the page that he or she "lands" on. Learning what pages users land on doesn't directly help you find any usability problems, but you can think of it as a prioritized list of pages that you want to make sure are friendly to people who have never seen your website before.

The "Landing Pages" report shows you the list of pages on your website organized by how many visits started with that page (in this report, "visits" will be the same as "entrances" on the "All Pages" report—it's how many visits started with an entrance on a given page). The "Landing Pages" report provides two more metrics that weren't available on the "All Pages" report:

- *Pages/visit.* Shows the average of how many pages users viewed after landing on a page.
- *Average visit duration.* Shows the average of how long users spent on the website after landing on a page.

You can also view the conversion rate for users who start their sessions on each landing page by switching from usage metrics to goals. Depending on how users get to the page and what goals they bring to the website, a low conversion rate may be an indicator of a problem (whereas on other pages like the homepage, it just means that a variety of users with different goals and interests land on the page).

For many websites, the homepage will be, by far, the most popular landing page. On the other hand, if you have a website that's well optimized for search engines or of which the business is to serve users who return frequently to some other page like a login page, then your homepage may appear further down the list of most popular landing pages.

The best use of this report, besides simply understanding the diversity of experiences users may have on your website, is if you have time and resources to improve the landing pages on your website and want to know what to prioritize. Finding out how many users land on a page can give you a sense of what to prioritize, whereas low pages per visit, average visit duration, or conversion rate or high bounce rate indicate that pages have potential problems.

PAID SEARCH LANDING PAGES

Your marketing team may engage in (or hire someone to do) paid search, or pay-per-click or cost-per-click, advertising. This kind of advertising puts ads in search engine results pages or on other websites with the goal of enticing people to click on the ad and come to your website. Landing pages are a critical topic for paid search advertising, since that's the page that makes or breaks the ad campaign. When you do paid search advertising, you spend money when people click on your ad; if users do not find the page they land on enticing and/or usable, you just wasted the money you spent getting them to your website. To wring more return on investment from paid search advertising, many companies design pages with the sole purpose of being landing pages for their campaigns. Other companies use existing pages on their website, such as product pages. Designing better landing pages is a big, interesting topic, but for now, suffice to say that bounce rate and conversion rate are critical metrics for you to look at for paid search landing pages.

LANDING PAGE (DIMENSION)

Every user who comes to your website has to start somewhere. The landing page is the URI of the first page that they visit. This dimension is very useful for measuring marketing efforts. Its main use for UX work is to learn more about a segment of users who interact with your website (the experience of using your website may be very different if you start on a deeply buried page versus the homepage) or to look for pages that you didn't realize so many users were landing on.

"Exit Pages" Report

The "Exit Pages" report provides you with "nice-to-know" information, for the most part. Whereas % exit is available as a metric in other reports, this report shows you the pages on your website organized around how many users exited from each page. It doesn't really provide you with anything more than % exit. What good does it do you to know how many exits there actually were during a given time period? Probably not very much. % exit is the more interesting metric. If you want to quickly find the pages where users exit most often and don't want to use the "All Pages" report, you can use "Exit Pages."

EXIT RATE (METRIC) AND EXIT PAGE (DIMENSION)

Exit rate is the portion of users who left the website (i.e., didn't do anything else on the website for more than 30 minutes). It can be measured for a single page or more than one page. Exit rate generally often appears next to bounce rate, which is the portion of users who exit the website without viewing a second page. The goodness or badness of a bounce rate depends on context, and with exit rate, this is even more true—a high exit rate may indicate that a page is turning off users, or it may indicate that users have gotten exactly what they wanted and are leaving the website happy.

The exit page is the last page a visitor opens before leaving the website. As with the landing page, you will mainly find exit page useful for segmenting users or to find pages that an unexpected large number of users leave the website after viewing.

"Content Drilldown" Report

This report is just like the "All Pages" report, except it organizes your pages according to the structure of your pages' URLs. It groups together pages and metrics for those pages according to the path (the "/widgets" in www.examples.com/widgets/page.html).

The "Content Drilldown" report can be very useful if you have a well-structured website where the hierarchy of pages from the users' perspective is clear from the path structure in URLs. You can easily roll up metrics for entire sections of your website. On the other hand, if the URL structure on your website bears no relation to how pages are laid out in your navigation, this report may be almost useless. It is worth exploring this report to find out how well it works for you.

PAGE TITLE (DIMENSION)

The page title dimension is like page, except instead of identifying pages by their URI, it uses whatever is in their HTML title tag. Page title can make it easier to tell pages apart if someone has put effort into giving all of your pages effective titles. Many websites have pages that have titles that make them impossible to tell apart.

For that reason you probably won't get a lot of use out of this dimension, even though it looks like it would be very useful and is common among web analytics tools. If, for some reason, you have a website that provides different content and page titles on pages that have the same URLs, then this dimension would be useful.

"Site Speed" Report

Responsiveness is important for user interfaces, so it follows that the speed at which pages of a website load is important to the quality of the user's experience. Google made data about how quickly pages are loading available through Google Analytics in 2012 as a section in the Content area. It takes a sample of 1% of visitors to measure how long it takes for pages to load for them. This sampling is why you may not have data for every page of your website.

High load times make a website harder to use and can annoy users. The main value of the "Site Speed" report is to find out if any pages have a high page load time, or if page load times are high across the website. Within the "Site Speed" report, page timings is the metric that shows you information for specific pages. This report also shows you with the page load sample metric how many pageviews it used to calculate load time, which is useful to know because one unusually high data point will pull the average load time up. The method for gathering page load time uses such a small amount of data that you would still want to confirm that a page loads slowly through other means.

In the end, the "Site Speed" report may be interesting to look at, but its scope is very narrow, so it may only warrant periodic viewing.

"In-Page Analytics" Report

The "In-Page Analytics" report, available as both as a standalone report in the navigation and as an option under the "All Pages" report, has historically been a seductive report. It displays actual pages of the website overlaid with markers denoting how many clicks each link received. In comparison to the "Navigation Summary" report, the "In-Page Analytics" report can be a far easier way to visualize the data.

Unfortunately, at the time of writing, the "In-Page Analytics" report can be misleading because, as discussed in Chapter 3, Google Analytics can't tell where on a page users clicked. That means if multiple links go to the same place, it can't tell which one users clicked on.

When you look at the "In-Page Analytics" report, it simply reports that the same number of users clicked on the same link. It also doesn't report on more interactive features like search buttons or playing a video.

The "In-Page Analytics" report is of limited value, not just because of the data it lacks, but because most of the methods described in this book involve comparing numbers. This visualization is less conducive to efficiently gathering metrics on where users click because it doesn't present metrics in a tabular format. It can be useful for quickly looking up how many users click on a particular link on a page or for easily creating an interesting visualization to share.

KEY TAKEAWAYS

- Content analysis will tell you where users go on your website and how long they stay there, what pages people enter your website on and from which pages they exit your website, and how they move from page to page.
- The main purpose of content analysis is to look for potential problem areas that you can probe through other means, such as heuristic evaluation and usability testing, as well as measuring the effectiveness of design changes.
- When looking at page usage metrics, look for these patterns:
  - The highest values for a metric.
  - The lowest values for a metric.
  - Pages that have metrics that deviate from the average value.
- A page may get many pageviews because many people are entering the website on that page, because links to it are easy to find and enticing (whether or not the page actually delivers on the promise of those links is a different matter), or it is really important to users.
- On the other hand, a page may get few pageviews because it is difficult to find, links to it are poorly labeled, or because users don't want to go there.
- When pageviews are much higher than unique pageviews, it indicates that users are frequently revisiting that page.
- Low time on page may indicate:
  - The content of the page doesn't match what users thought they were going to get.
  - The content isn't very interesting or is poorly written.
  - There isn't a lot of content on a page.
  - The page is very well organized and users can quickly satisfy their goals.
  - The purpose of the page is to direct users to other pages, like a search results page.
- High time on page only tells you that users are doing something on that page.
- High bounce rate indicates that there are potentially problems on a page for people who enter your website through that page.
- High % exit indicates a potential problem; there are some pages where a high % exit is appropriate.
- Page value can indicate how often users view a page before going on to convert.
- It is more meaningful to compare page metrics to other pages of the same type (or same template) rather than comparing two pages with completely different purposes.

Click-Path Analysis

INTRODUCTION

Getting insight into how users move from o
as click-path analysis, is a powerful capabilit
tant thing to remember: there is no way that
path" unless you have a very small and/or
people, this is disappointing to learn becau
how people move through their website. Consider Figure 8.1, a fictional
example website.

A user comes to the homepage in Figure 8.1, clicks on a link to page 1, goes
to page 4, goes back to page 1, goes to page 5, and then leaves. Another
user comes to the homepage, goes to page 3, goes back to the homepage,

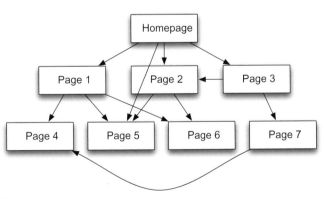

FIGURE 8.1

The difficulty of click-path analysis is that users have a tendency to traverse your website in diverse ways.
This diagram is meant to convey a sense of how many websites have not just top-down hierarchical
navigation, but also cross-linking between pages.

, and then to page 4. Yet another user enters the website on
s to page 5, then to page 1, and then to page 6. What's the most
path?

ously, this example is small and abstract, but the problem is the same
ven when the website is bigger and there are more users. Out of a thousand
users, only a small percentage will actually follow the same sequence of pages
through the entire website. To characterize how users move through a website, we must focus on navigation at a small scale—how users got to a page
and where they go after leaving a page.

FOCUS ON RELATIONSHIPS BETWEEN PAGES

You should focus on, page by page, where users went after leaving a page
and where they came from. Looking at what pages users viewed before getting to a page can help you confirm or adjust your expectations or learn of a
new way that users can move through your website. If you find that an unexpected page is sending a large portion of users to the page you're analyzing, you should go to the "Navigation Summary" report for that unexpected
page. It may be possible to create an interpretation that connects this page
to a sequence of pages, such as users moving from a search results page to
a product page, or from a high-level informational page to a more specific
subpage.

As with analyzing where they came from, when you look at where users
went to after leaving a page, you're looking for the unexpected—a number
that looks lower or higher than you expect, or a page that you wouldn't have
thought would be a destination. Keep in mind that when you throw enough
users at a page, they'll end up clicking on practically every link on that page.
However, the top 10 destinations will probably be enough to cover the majority of users.

You could use this information when planning user research activities like
usability testing to look for questions that you want to answer—that is, if you
see a "weird" next page, you can try to learn more about why users are going
there by constructing a task that incorporates the page that users leave when
they go to the "weird" next page. When doing an analysis of user research
findings, you can compare the participant behavior you witnessed to the
actual paths through the website to see how common the participants' behavior was. Even if you can't replicate the "weird" behavior, you may be able to
get insight into how users interpret what's on the page. If you can't conduct
further user research, simply knowing that users have gone from one page to
an unhelpful next page can help you find potential problems when you do
some kind of heuristic evaluation.

CLICK-PATH ANALYSIS TOOLS

There are other click-path, or click-stream, analysis tools (these two terms are used interchangeably). Besides Google Analytics, this capability is offered in SiteCatalyst, Webtrends, and in more tightly focused tools like Clicktale and Opentracker. In fact, depending on your research needs, Google Analytics may not be the best choice for looking at click paths.

In Google Analytics, much of your analysis time will be spent combining data from functionally similar pages (as described later in this chapter). In other tools like SiteCatalyst, this kind of "bucketing" is part of the initial setup. This means it will be easier to find out, for example, that users tend to move from the homepage to a search results page to a product page, because the data from all of the specific search results pages and product pages will already be combined.

ClickTale, mentioned in Chapter 3, is geared toward showing you where on the page users click. If your research is concerned with users' click paths and the nuances of where they click on individual pages, this is the type of tool you may find more useful. On the other hand, other analytics tools like Opentracker and KISSmetrics focus on showing you how individual users move through your website. If it is important to you to look at how a sample of individuals move through your website, this is the kind of tool that may suit your needs better.

NAVIGATION SUMMARY

In Google Analytics, there are two approaches to learning about click paths: the "Navigation Summary" report of the "All Pages" report (Figure 8.2) and the "Visitors Flow" report (Figure 8.3). This example of the "Navigation Summary" report is for a page on the Pure Visibility website, also pictured.

The Services page has a main navigation on the top and a subnavigation along the left side of the page. There are many places the user can go from this page and the data in the report reflect that diversity. It shows, for the 257 pageviews in this time period (which is unfortunately not actually listed on the report), what percentage of people entered the website on the Services page, how many people came to this page from other pages, what percentage of people exited the website after viewing this page, and how many people went to other pages.

The Services page is one of the items in the main navigation, and the greatest number of pageviews came after someone viewed the homepage. Nonetheless, only about 34% of the Services page's pageviews were logged after a user visited the homepage. The rest of the previous pages are scattered among a variety of pages and various depths in the website, each with a relatively small portion of previous pageviews. It's important to note that while some users entered the website on the homepage and then went

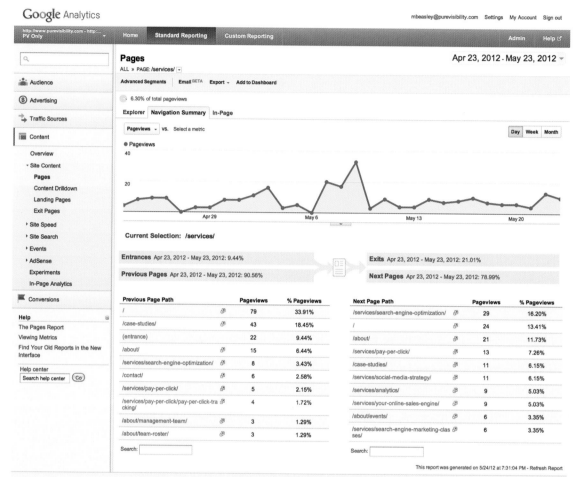

FIGURE 8.2

The "Navigation Summary" report of the "All Pages" report. You choose a specific page on your website (in this case, the Services page on purevisibility.com) and it shows what users viewed before the Services page and what they viewed after it.

directly to Services, some went off to view other pages first and then returned to the homepage. All we see in this report is one relationship between the Services page and the homepage (and the About page, and the Search Engine Optimization page, and so on).

On the other side of the report, the most popular destination after viewing this page was the Search Engine Optimization services page, but that was only 16%, compared to the 13% who went back to the homepage, 12% who went

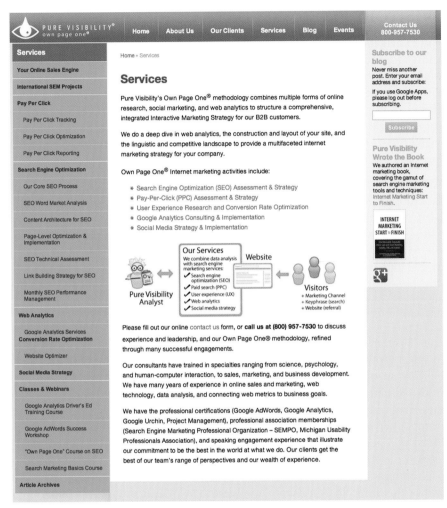

FIGURE 8.3

For context, here is the page shown in Figure 8.2. The page that a plurality of users viewed next is the Search Engine Optimization (SEO) Assessment & Strategy page, the top bullet point on this page. Other common destinations are the homepage, top-level navigation pages, and the Pay Per Click services page in the subnavigation to the left.

to the About Us page, and so on. We see that users are diffuse in their choice of where to go next.

By continuing to analyze further pages in the "Navigation Summary" report, we can begin to form a broader picture of the relationships between various pages.

"VISITORS FLOW" REPORT

The "Navigation Summary" report shows click-path data at a very small scale and is good for when you want to export numbers and transform them. Its weakness is that it doesn't tell you the actual sequence of pages users visit; for this reason, it's hard to tell if users are repeatedly moving around in a small cluster of pages. Whereas the "Navigation Summary" report focuses on the page, Google Analytics also contains a visualization for click paths that tries to tell the story of click paths from the perspective of users moving from their first page to their second page to their third page and so on.

You start on the left by choosing a dimension, such as medium, country, or mobile (the mobile "yes" or "no" dimension). Selecting a dimension divides users in the first column. From there, bars show how many visitors went to various pages in the second column, and from there how many left the website (pictured as a red bar fading out) or moved on to the next page. When users return to a page they've already been, it's shown in a new column further right rather than a loop back to a previous column. That's because the emphasis on this report is showing for how many users is a page the first page they view, for how many users is a page the second page they view, and so on.

The "Visitors Flow" report follows users on a continuous path from page to page. However, within a couple of clicks the paths that users take may become so diffuse that it is impossible to succinctly characterize them all. In this situation you can only look at the most common paths, even though they may only represent a minority of users. Let's look at that Services page from earlier in the chapter. Whereas the "Navigation Summary" report combined all data about pageviews for the Services page, as well as where those users came from and where they went, in Figure 8.4 we can see the Services page appears at least twice based on whether it was the second page users visited or the third. Sixteen users also visited it as their first page; it's folded into "+67 more pages," indicating that it is not a common page for users to land on. This feature that folds most of your pages into what is essentially an "et cetera" category is the reason why you will have to focus most of your attention on the handful of most common pages.

Now let's click on the Services page in the third column, called "1st Interaction" (the first page that the user clicked on after landing on the website). In Figure 8.5, we can see this page highlighted as well as the paths into and out of the page.

Whereas in Figure 8.2, we saw that 79 users went from the homepage to the Services page, we can now see that 67 users landed on the homepage and then navigated to the Services page. From there, 6 of those users went back to the homepage (shown in the third column, "2nd Interaction") and those same 6 users went from the homepage back to the Services page again.

FIGURE 8.4

The "Visitors Flow" report in Google Analytics. It first divides users according to a dimension such as medium or country, and then each column to the right is a page that users have visited.

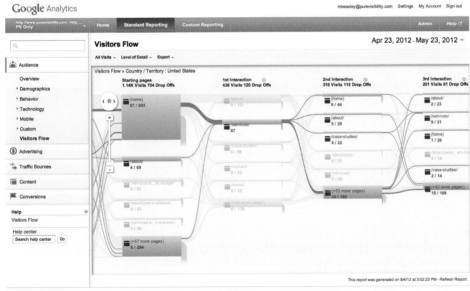

FIGURE 8.5

The "Visitors Flow" report again, but now the Services page when it is the first page users navigate to is highlighted.

With this report, you can answer specific questions about how users interact with particular pages, characterize the common paths on the website, or engage in an exploratory analysis of the data, looking for patterns that you can then attempt to understand from looking at the website itself or further user research. Some of the patterns you may see are:

■ *Pogo-sticking.* This is when users go back and forth between two pages (or flail between a small set of pages). We saw some users pogo-stick in the example from Figure 8.5, but there will always be some amount of users who engage in this behavior. The more users pogo-stick, the bigger the problem. The pogo-sticking pattern may indicate users who are confused about how to reach a page or find link/navigation labels difficult to interpret, or are trying to find something that doesn't exist.

■ *Many users go to an unexpected page.* To a certain extent, you will find that users go to all sorts of unexpected places. There may be times, though, when you find that a large portion of users are going to someplace that takes them away from accomplishing their task. Going to an unexpected page could mean that users go backward in a multistep process, such as registration or shopping cart checkout, access help or a FAQ, or go to a page with very dissimilar content.

■ *Many users exit from a page.* Of course, the "Visitors Flow" report is not the only way to find out if a page has a high % exit. You do, however, get a different perspective on the data from the "Visitors Flow" report than from looking at the average % exit because you will be able to see how many people viewed a page as their first, second, third, etc. interaction with the website and how many exited at each step.

In Chapter 9, we cover segmentation, a way of filtering data according to the metrics and dimensions available in your analytics tool. In Google Analytics, this functionality is also available in the "Visitors Flow" report and is an important way of interacting with this report. It lets you filter users according to aspects like how they got to the website (e.g., via a search engine) or how they interacted with the website (e.g., whether they landed on a particular page or viewed a specific page during their visit).

Segmentation gives you a way to reduce the diversity of user behavior to more manageable levels and to compare how different groups of users behave.

ANALYZING HOW USERS MOVE FROM ONE PAGE TYPE TO ANOTHER

So far we have talked about analyzing how users move from one specific page to another specific page. However, many websites have pages that contain different content but are otherwise functionally identical (e.g., a product page on an e-commerce website). How can we analyze how users interact with a class of pages? This analysis will be easier with some tools than others. For example, part of installing Omniture SiteCatalyst on a website is choosing how pages will be grouped into meaningful "buckets," how to name each type of page, and what data to capture about the individual pages within each category. It is a great deal of upfront work, but this work can remove the need for the following steps. On the other hand, Google Analytics is often set up without any grouping of similar pages. This means that to analyze users' click paths, you have some work ahead of you that is, at times, somewhat tedious:

1. Determine what kind of page you want to analyze (e.g., a product page, search results page, category page, or informational articles).
2. Find out the 10 most-visited pages of this type (or more pages, if you are feeling ambitious).
3. Starting with the most-viewed page, note:
   - The number of pageviews.
   - The top 10 pages (or, again, however many you can work with) users came from and how many viewed those pages.
   - How many entered the website on this page.
   - The top 10 pages users went to and how many went to those pages.
   - How many exited the website after visiting this page.
4. Repeat the process with the rest of the most-viewed pages, combining the data for the previous and next pages (you can certainly do this with more than just the top 10 most-viewed pages; the only real limitation is your time).

At the end of this tedious process you'll have a better look at where users go after viewing a class of page. Combining data from various pages should smooth out the idiosyncrasies of individual pages and may reveal patterns that are obscured if pageviews are distributed among many pages within a class.

From there, you can move on to other classes of page and form a more comprehensive picture of how users interact with the pages on your website.

An Example: AwesomePetToys.com

Probably the best way to describe this process is with an example. Let's go back to our online store for pet toys. There are several product pages, each with the following format: www.awesomepettoys.com/products/[manufacturer]/[productname]?product_id=[number]. For the laser pointer made by the (imaginary) company Toyco, you'd have the following: www.awesomepettoys.com/products/toyco/laser_pointer?product_id=2788897.

Table 8.1 Top 10 Highest Pageviews for Product Pages

Page	Pageviews
/products/toyco/laser_pointer?product_id = 2788897	2,540
/products/dogfun/squeezy_steak?product_id = 2784417	1,675
/products/toyco/cat_nip_bucket?product_id = 2840637	1,590
/products/dogsdogsdogs/tug_of_war_rope?product_id = 2784417	1,431
/products/woofy_fun/dog_catch_disc?product_id = 2757738	1,213
/products/trashforcats/stuff_on_a_stick?product_id = 2614716	1,156
/products/purrfectrealestate/kitty_apartments?product_id = 2843417	1,008
/products/trashforcats/crumpled_up_paper?product_id = 2860397	966
/products/toyco/squeezy_mailman?product_id = 2348536	946
/products/toyco/bowtie_novelty_collar?product_id = 2698176	936

Besides these product pages, AwesomePetToys.com has normal e-commerce website features: pages with information about manufacturers, a wish list, a way of showing related products on product pages, and a shopping cart.

Going to Content→Site Content→All Pages in Google Analytics, you can find a list of all the pages on the website that have been viewed, but you would want just the product pages, so the next step would be to filter the table to only show the pages with "products" in the URL. You're then left with a list where the top 10 highest pageviews belong to product pages (Table 8.1). You would now copy this list to a spreadsheet or, better yet, export the report and then work with that spreadsheet.

There are 19,235 pageviews of product pages, so this list obviously doesn't cover all of the product pages, but to make the workload manageable, we're working with a sample of the most-viewed product pages. This is a limitation that shouldn't make a practical difference, but is worth remembering.

The next step is to start at the top of the chart and look at the "Navigation Summary" report for each page in turn. Starting with the laser pointer product page, we see what is shown in Table 8.2.

Also, 65.35% of pageviews of this product page were followed by an exit from the website, which should work out to 1,660 exits. That's a jumble of pages with somewhat inscrutable names. Explore each of those pages on the website itself to find out what they are and rename them to generic categories, such as those shown in Table 8.3.

And then, in Table 8.4, combine the data for pages that fit into the same category.

Table 8.2 Previous and Next Page Data for the Laser Pointer Product Page

Previous Page Path	Pageviews	Next Page Path	Pageviews
(entrance)	1,560	/cgi-bin/basket?action= add&item_id=2788897	104
/products/cattoysinc/ super_laser_ pointer?product_id= 2346256	56	/browse-manufacturer/toyco	58
/cgi-bin/basket?action= add&item_id=2788897	42	/site_search/	48
/browse-manufacturer/ toyco/	33	/info/toyco.html	41
/cgi-bin/detail?product_id =2346256	32	/products/cattoysinc/super_ laser_pointer?product_id= 2346256	35
/site_search/	32	/cgi-bin/detail?product_id= 2346256	20
/products/toyco/pocket_ pointer?product_id= 234628	32	/cgi-bin/basket?action= add&item_id=234628	17
/products/yippeecats/ another_laser_ pointer?product_id= 2459267	28	/products/yippeecats/another_ laser_pointer?product_id= 2459267	10
/info/toyco.html	22	/info/yippeecats.html	9
/products/toyco/laser_ pointer_bundle?product_ id=2346274	12	/products/catfun/flying_ bird?product_id=5349564	9

Table 8.3 Forming Categories from Individual Page Types

Previous Page Path	Pageviews	Next Page Path	Pageviews
(entrance)	1,560	add to cart	104
related product	56	browse manufacturer	58
add to cart	42	/site_search/	48
browse manufacturer	33	manufacturer info	41
product detail page	32	related product	35
/site_search/	32	product detail page	20
related product	32	add to cart (related product)	17
related product	28	related product	10
manufacturer info	22	manufacturer info	9
related product	12	related product	9

Table 8.4 Combined Data for Pages in Same Category

Previous Page Path	Pageviews	Next Page Path	Pageviews
(entrance)	1,560	add to cart	104
related product	128	browse manufacturer	58
add to cart	42	/site_search/	48
browse manufacturer	33	manufacturer info	41
product detail page	32	related product	54
/site_search/	32	product detail page	20
manufacturer info	22	add to cart (related product)	17
		manufacturer info (other manufacturer)	9

Renaming necessarily involves some level of abstraction, and the correct level of abstraction is up to you and what you're trying to accomplish. In this example, we compressed multiple pages into "related product" but depending on the hypothetical design of this fictional website, we might have made different buckets depending on where the link was on the page, like if there were multiple places where related products were listed. You may also wish to keep some pages on your website, such as those in the top level of your navigation or other important pages, distinct rather than combining them with others.

And then the hard work continues! We move on to the next-most-viewed page, the Squeezy Steak product page, and repeat this operation of sorting the previous and next pages into buckets and adding them to the table, resulting in Table 8.5 here.

Clearly, there were some differences in how users interacted with the Squeezy Steak product page compared to the Laser Pointer page—the homepage, wish list, and help page all appeared on the list of next pages, and some pages moved up and some moved down the list. Since this example is fictional, it's impossible to go into a detailed analysis of what these nonexistent pages look like, but with these numbers, we would explore how the related products section works and possibly decompose that category in my analysis into smaller categories based on whether there's some hierarchy to the related product suggestions.

Users go on to read about the manufacturer, browse other products from the same manufacturer, and even read about other manufacturers, but relatively few read about the product details, which you would think would be an important thing to do (assuming for the moment that buying pet toys is a high-stakes game where product details matter). Perhaps

Table 8.5 Previous and Next Page Data for the Squeezy Steak Product Page

Previous Page Path	Pageviews	Next Page Path	Pageviews
(entrance)	8,045	related product	656
wish list	433	add to cart	486
related product	336	browse manufacturer	336
/site_search/	306	add to cart (related product)	325
add to cart	300	/site_search/	323
product detail page	264	manufacturer info	129
manufacturer info	236	manufacturer info (other manufacturer)	129
browse manufacturer	178	wish list	191
homepage	3	product detail page	32
		help	13
		homepage	3
		exit	10,952

examining the layout of the product page will reveal that the product details page is hard to find compared to the manufacturer information page. You may also wish to incorporate having users read about product details into other user research projects to learn about any difficulties participants have finding that link or why they may choose to click on one of the other links.

This activity will describe user behavior in a more generalized way than looking at specific pages' data. It will leave you with data that are easier to export and manipulate than the "Visitors Flow" report, and also allow you to intelligently cluster pages that are functionally identical (the "Visitors Flow" report does cluster pages in same cases based on URL structure, but it is practically impossible to override if you are unhappy with how it clusters pages). On the other hand, using the "Visitors Flow" report will let you get started more quickly on exploring the data and drawing insights. Manually combining click-path data is something that you may wish to do when your website's pages require a great deal of categorization to make sense or if you are in a situation where you need "hard numbers."

Whether you take this approach, use the "Visitors Flow" report visualization (or something similar in another tool) or simply look at navigation data for a single page, the value of click-path analysis lies in discovering potential problems and questions to follow up on, as well as simply understanding your users better. You can look at data about click paths at one point in time and then compare it another point in time to find out how changes to your website have affected how users move through your website.

CLICK PATHS ON HIGHLY INTERACTIVE WEBSITES

How does click-path analysis relate to web applications? Your website may not consist of a collection of distinct pages or may have richly interactive features that exist within a single page. Click-path analysis will probably still be possible, but you will have to do it by creating a series of virtual pageviews within your web application. You should go through your web application and identify the meaningful checkpoints or the distinct screens or areas of the interface users can interact with, and then work with a developer to add the necessary code to your website that will send data to your web analytics tool. You will then be able to analyze how users move from screen to screen or feature to feature using the same approach as you would analyze click paths on a website consisting of static pages.

KEY TAKEAWAYS

- You will probably find it impossible to pick out the most common path that users take on your website because user behavior can be so varied.
- Instead, focus on relationships between pages—from a given page, where do users come from and where do they go?
- Google Analytics offers two approaches to learning about click paths: the "Navigation Summary" and "Visitors Flow" reports.
  - The "Navigation Summary" report organizes data around page-to-page interactions and is more useful for summarizing all the behavior on a page.
  - The "Visitors Flow" report organizes the data around paths that users take and is better for showing the variety of ways users go from page to page.
- To analyze how users move from page type to page type (rather than individual pages):
  - Determine what kind of page you want to analyze (e.g., a product page, search results page, category page, or informational articles).
  - Find out the 10 most-visited pages of this type (or more pages, if you are feeling ambitious).
  - Starting with the most-viewed page, note:
    a. The number of pageviews.
    b. The top 10 pages (or, again, however many you can work with) they came from and how many viewed those pages.
    c. How many entered the website on this page.
    d. The top 10 pages they went to and how many went to those pages.
    e. How many exited the website after visiting this page.
  - Repeat this process with the rest of the most-viewed pages, combining the data for the previous and next pages (you can certainly do this with more than just the top 10 most-viewed pages; the only real limitation is your time).

CHAPTER 9

Segmentation

INTRODUCTION

Your users most likely come to your website with a variety of goals, different ways of expressing information through various means like organic search or clicking on a link on another website, and have different ways of exploring and navigating websites. Even if you have a website that has just one kind of user it targets, other people will still find their way to your website. Some of the most exciting analyses you can do involve segmenting your web analytics data.

Segmentation is the filtering of data according to metrics and dimensions so you can just analyze specific users, the ones you care about. By now, you have already seen basic segmentation according to dimension in action. For example, the "Mobile Overview" report in Google Analytics divides users according to whether or not they accessed your website with a mobile device, and shows website usage metrics for the segment of users who use mobile devices and those who use laptops and desktops. The "All Traffic" report divides users according to what source and/or medium brought them to the website.

So far, we have dealt with basic segmentation where we have used one or two dimensions to segment metrics data. This chapter covers the creation of your own, more complex segments. Complex segments involve setting up one or more filters on practically any dimension or metric available in web analytics, and then your web analytics tool goes through each visit to the website that it measured and filters out all of the data from every visit that don't fit the criteria that you specify. You can match the value of dimensions, or filter, according to whether a metric is greater than, less than, or equal to a value you specify for any given visitor. You can then explore any of the analytics reports, seeing only this segment of data.

WHY SEGMENT DATA?

Let's go back to AwesomePetToys.com. Their website gets visited by their target users, pet owners with an unusually strong attachment to their pets, as

CONTENTS

Table 9.1 Bounce Rate Data for AwesomePetToys.com

	Number of People Who Bounced	Total Number of People	Bounce Rate
People who arrived on the website accidentally	4,000	5,000	80%
A secondary kind of user	1,800	2,500	72%
Target users	500	2,500	20%
Total	6,300	10,000	63%

well as less-wealthy pet owners and people who accidentally reached their website or who explored it and decided that buying pet toys online wasn't for them. On top of that, AwesomePetToys.com also has a secondary target, pet boarding services that buy bulk orders of toys and other accessories. When one looks at their web analytics data, all these people are grouped together.

That means, for example, if AwesomePetToys.com had an overall bounce rate of 63% in August 2012, that bounce rate could include the data shown in Table 9.1.

As you can see, the 63% bounce rate masks a huge difference between the bounce rate for AwesomePetToys.com's target users and the large number of people who weren't their target users. This level of segmentation is not something you would get through any default reporting; rather, it requires understanding the web analytics data you have available and making choices about the metrics and dimensions to sufficiently differentiate your groups of users.

You segment data so you can see and analyze data for just that segment of visits instead of all visits within a given time period. For example, Figure 9.1 shows data from the "All Pages" report in Google Analytics, showing data for all users. Figure 9.2 shows the same report, but after a segment has been applied to show only users who used a mobile device. Note that the metrics have changed considerably.

You explore other reports and the data in them will also reflect the segmentation. It is also possible to show data from different segments side by side— Figure 9.3 combines both the data from all users with the mobile devices segment, from Figures 9.1 and 9.2, respectively.

After a short how-to guide to segmentation in Google Analytics, this chapter will cover a few of the most useful ways to segment data to answer UX questions.

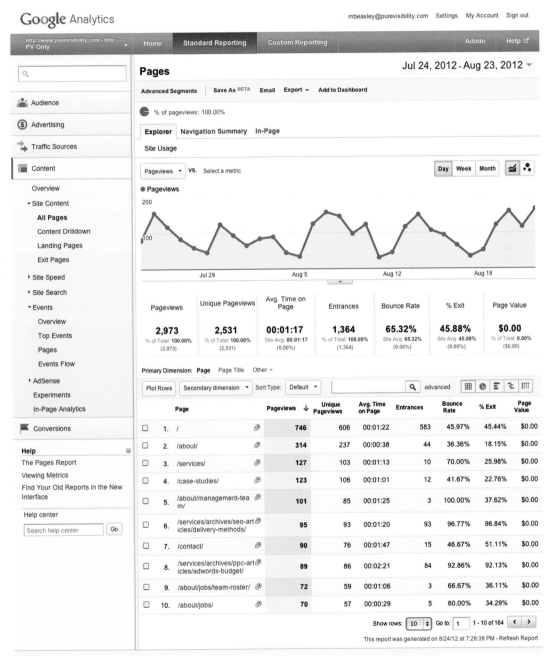

FIGURE 9.1

The "All Pages" report from Google Analytics, with no segmentation applied.

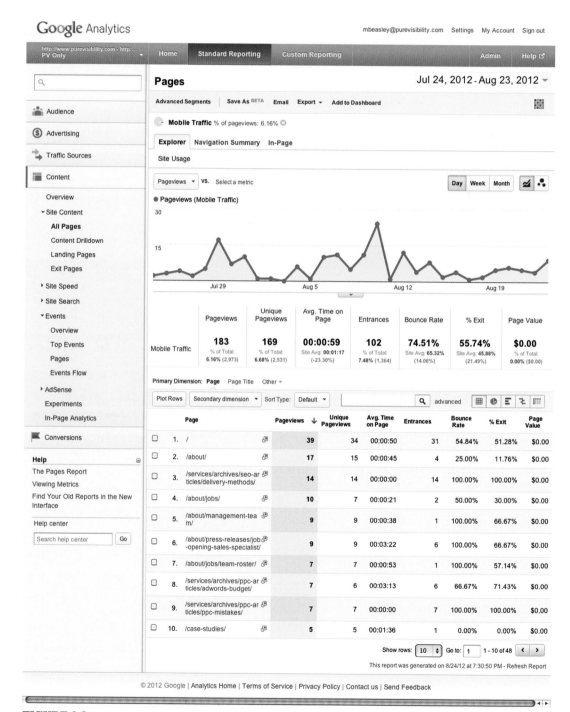

FIGURE 9.2

The same report in Figure 9.1, but showing only data for users who used mobile devices.

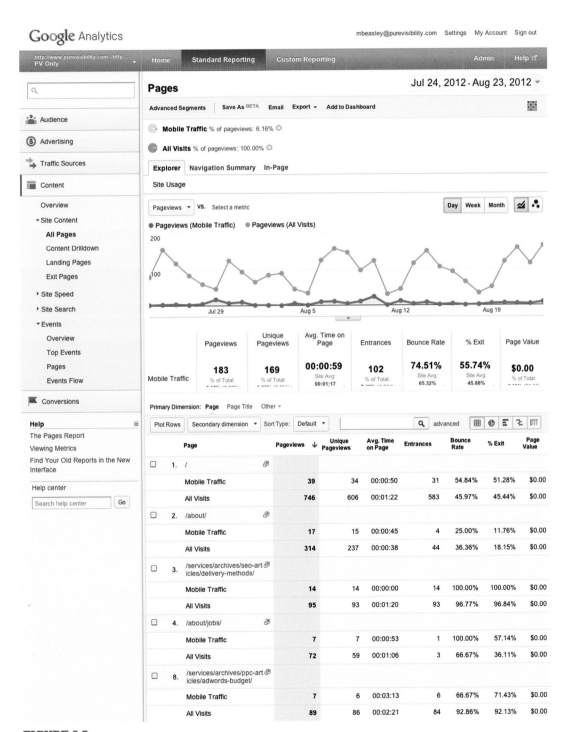

FIGURE 9.3
Both data from all users and the mobile devices segment, side by side in the same report.

☐	9.	/services/archives/ppc-art icles/ppc-mistakes/							
		Mobile Traffic	7	7	00:00:00	7	100.00%	100.00%	$0.00
		All Visits	29	29	00:04:51	28	92.86%	89.66%	$0.00
☐	10.	/case-studies/							
		Mobile Traffic	5	5	00:01:36	1	0.00%	0.00%	$0.00
		All Visits	123	106	00:01:01	12	41.67%	22.76%	$0.00

Show rows: 10 ⇕ Go to: 1 1 - 10 of 164 ‹ ›

This report was generated on 8/24/12 at 7:35:19 PM - Refresh Report

© 2012 Google | Analytics Home | Terms of Service | Privacy Policy | Contact us | Send Feedback

FIGURE 9.3 (Continued)

HOW TO SEGMENT DATA

Recall the general analysis process:

1. Pose the question.
2. Gather data.
3. Transform data.
4. Analyze.
5. Answer the question.

Segmentation is a way of transforming data within your analytics tool to make them better suited to answering the question you have posed.

When you have a question you wish to answer with web analytics data, consider:

1. What are the ways I can tell the relevant users from the irrelevant users?
2. How do these factors translate to metrics and dimensions that web analytics tools measure?

This is the intellectual work in segmentation. After these steps, all that's left is manipulating your web analytics tool.

Let's look at the AwesomePetToys.com example. After considerable research, they develop personas to describe their primary user, secondary user, and their anti-user (the pet owner who just doesn't have the disposable income to spend on expensive pet toys). Their primary user, Emily, is described in this way:

It's early Saturday afternoon, and Emily is settling down on the porch swing on her east-facing porch to relax for a while with a cup of herbal tea. It's easy to let the house go during the week, when she works at the main branch of the library, and Saturday mornings usually bring with them a flurry of chores that Emily shares with her partner, Christina. Emily looks through the window into her living room and sees one of their cats, Toonces, and remembers that she has meant to buy a new ToyCo laser pointer, their last one having been lost in the recent move to this house after years of excellent service.

Emily is never far from the Internet, though, and she opens the cover on her new iPad, opens Chrome, and searches for "ToyCo laser pointer." On the Google search results page, she sees, among other results, both an ad for AwesomePetToys.com as well as an organic listing. Emily clicks on the organic listing and arrives at the ToyCo laser pointer product page.

There are elements of this story that can be used for segmentation:

- Time of day (the hour dimension in Google Analytics)
- Browser (the browser dimension)
- Device (the mobile device model dimension)
- Keyword (the keyword dimension) and which search engine Emily used (the source dimension)
- Landing page (the landing page dimension)

This persona was packed with a rich level of detail, meant to help the entire design team at AwesomePetToys.com imagine their target user, Emily. The downside of segmenting at this specificity level is that the number of users who actually meet all of these criteria *may* only constitute a tiny portion of AwesomePetToys.com's users—maybe 10 out of the 6,300 visits.

While the specificity of a persona can be useful for helping people empathize with what is realistic, it can cause you to leave out data from users who are also the right kind of user, but who didn't follow the narrative in your persona. Is it possible to generalize some aspects of the persona, leave out elements that are too specific, or to go back to the research on various real users who went into the persona to find traits you can filter for?

In the case of AwesomePetToys.com, time of day, keyword, and landing page may simply be too specific for the purposes of segmentation. The time of day was intended to add detail to Emily's story, but early afternoon is not the only time that the people fitting the primary persona use the website. On the other hand, Emily shopped on the weekend, which could be a useful way to differentiate users. AwesomePetToys.com sells a wide variety of products and when users search for these products by brand name, it indicates that they are probably specifically seeking these high-end products. Building out a segment for AwesomePetToys.com's primary persona should involve coming up with a longer list of search keywords for specific products (as well as, perhaps, people searching for "expensive pet toys" in general). Segmenting according to the landing page as well as according to keyword is often redundant. As our hypothetical AwesomePetToys.com researcher widens the scope of keyword segmentation, it is safe to stop segmenting according to the landing page.

Although the browser may be too specific and not highly relevant to understanding Emily's behavior, the fact that she uses an iPad is probably a marker of having disposable income. However, iPad use among AwesomePetToys.com's target users may still be uncommon. If the research on AwesomePetToys.com's users showed that they were primarily Apple users, then it may make sense to filter according to the operating system (OS, where the dimension is either Macintosh or iOS). Looking at the user research may also show that the user's device wasn't enough of a defining trait to be useful and should therefore not be used for segmentation.

Finally, research may have uncovered other ways to identify users like Emily who didn't make it into her persona, like clicking on a link on a website that caters to the interests of pet owners with disposable income to spend on their pets.

So far, we have discussed segmentation as a way of identifying users according to their traits or how they got to the website. It is also possible to segment according to users' behavior on your website, something we will cover in this chapter.

After you have identified ways to distinguish the users you are interested in from the rest of your analytics data, it is time to actually build the segment.

Google Analytics' Advanced Segments

If you're using Google Analytics, you can very easily make up your segment as you go and iterate quickly. Let's make a segment that includes AwesomePetToys.com's primary persona, Emily, as well as other relevant users who don't fit that exact story.

1. In Google Analytics, you can access advanced segments by clicking the Advanced Segments button near the top of almost every report (Figure 9.4). Clicking this button shows a list of prebuilt segments as well as the list of all of the segments you've segmented.
2. There is a button in the lower-left corner of the list of the segments you've built, + New Custom Segment. This button brings up the form where you actually build the segment (Figure 9.5).
3. First, you should give your segment a name. You will probably create a great deal of segments over time and never have time to curate your collection, so try to be descriptive and succinct. We can use "Primary Persona—Emily."
4. Next, it's time to start adding filters. You will start with "Include *Ad Content* Containing" and then a blank text field.
   - You can change "include" to "exclude."

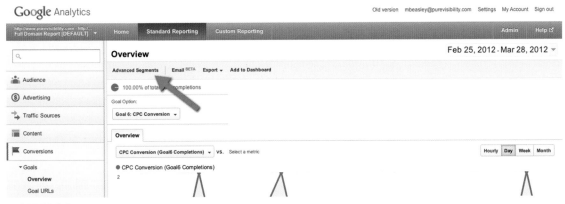

FIGURE 9.4
The Advanced Segments button in Google Analytics—where to get started with segmentation.

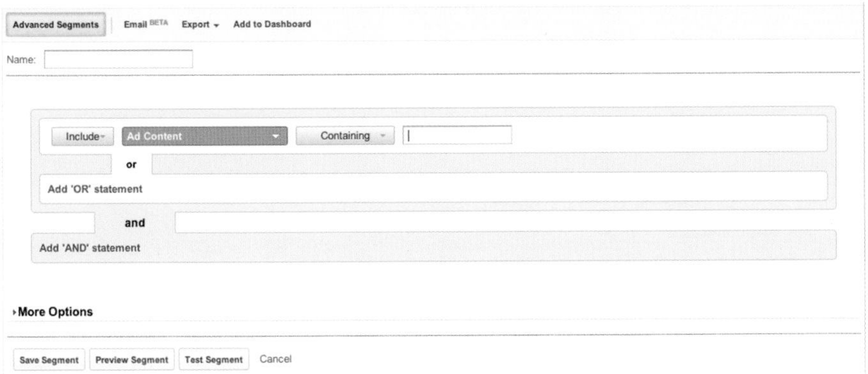

FIGURE 9.5
The form in Google Analytics where you can create segments.

- Click on "Ad Content" to change this field to another metric or dimension.
- Change the method of matching.
- Enter what you'd like to match.

5. At this point, you can click on "Add 'OR' statement" or "Add 'AND' statement" to continue building your segment, and repeat step 4 as many times as you need. Figure 9.6 shows the "Primary Persona—Emily" segment with several filters entered.

6. You have three options after you're done adding filters:
- The Save Segment button saves the segment, takes you away from this form, and applies the segment to your data.

FIGURE 9.6

One possible approach to the Emily persona segment. The OS for the device she uses to access AwesomePetToys.com is specified as created by Apple, indicating her high amount of disposable income, and then a set of keywords and a referring website that show her goal to be the purchase of expensive pet toys. In the real world, this segment would contain a more expansive set of keywords and referring websites.

- The Preview Segment button keeps the form open, but applies it to your data. This can be incredibly useful for experimentation or addressing one-off questions.
- The Test Segment button runs all of the filters and tells you how many users each filter captures. Doing so can be useful for troubleshooting.

7. After you have either saved or previewed the segment, you can begin to explore the reports in Google Analytics with data segmented.

Under "More Options" you also have the choice of applying your segment to all profiles that you have access to, or choosing specific profiles. This feature can be useful if you work with multiple clients or have multiple profiles since it will make it easier to sort through your list of segments if you only see ones that are relevant to the profile you're looking at.

WHAT ARE THE WAYS YOU CAN SEGMENT DATA?

You can segment data according to almost any metric or dimension that appears in your web analytics tool, in a combination of AND and OR statements. This section explores some of these ways.

AND, OR, and Sequence of Filters

Segmentation often involves combining two or more filters. You join these segments in two ways:

1. With an AND statement, meaning *both* conditions *must* be true.
2. With an OR statement, meaning *only one* of the conditions *must* be true.

In Figure 9.2, a screenshot from Google Analytics, there are four filters to segment the people who got to the Pure Visibility website through a search engine, by searching for something other than the name of the company, and who visited more than three pages during their visit—users who probably were not previously aware of Pure Visibility and are now possibly interested in its services (at least interested enough to not leave after looking at a couple of pages). This segment provides a nonexhaustive look at people who reached Pure Visibility while researching online marketing, although it's worth noting that it casts a wide net; not only does it capture people searching for "online marketing," but also five people who searched for "amazing birthday cakes."

In Google Analytics, each step of the filtering process either includes or excludes visitors according to whatever metrics or dimensions you choose (Figure 9.7). *Include* means that visitor data are shown when you use the segment. *Exclude* means that all of the data from visitors are left out when you use the segment.

This advanced segment's filters are grouped into three clumps: one that handles page depth AND another that handles keywords AND another that that specifies that the users came in through either organic search OR paid search. These filters are not sequential; changing the order won't change your results.

Metrics

You segment metrics according to a numeric threshold. In Google Analytics, you have the option to filter according to whether a metric has a value greater

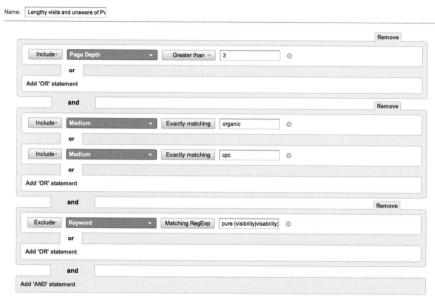

FIGURE 9.7
An example of an advanced segment in Google Analytics, using filters joined by AND and OR.

Table 9.2 Sample Metric Filters in Google Analytics	
Exclude *Visit Duration* Less than 60	Shows no data for any visits that lasted fewer than 60 seconds.
Include *Product Revenue* Greater than 20	Shows only data for visits where users bought more than $20 of products (not including tax and shipping).
Include *New Visits* Equals 0	Shows only data for users who have visited the website before. New visits have the value 1 and returning visits are 0.
Exclude *Goal 1 Completions* Equals 1	Filters out any data for users who completed goal 1.

than, less than, or equal to whatever number you specify. Table 9.2 shows some examples.

Dimensions

Dimensions have text values and therefore you have different options for filtering them. In Google Analytics, you get the filters shown in Table 9.3. Some examples are shown in Table 9.4.

Table 9.3 Filter Options for Dimensions	
Exactly matching	Only values that are completely identical to what you enter, with no additional characters.
Matching RegExp	If you know how to use regular expressions (and if you want to analyze search queries, regular expressions will be essential) you can use this option.
Begins with	Looks for values that start with what you enter.
Ends with	Looks for values that end with what you enter.
Containing	Looks for values that have the exact string you enter somewhere in the this field.

Table 9.4 Sample Dimension Filters in Google Analytics	
Include *Country/Territory* Exactly matching "USA"	If you want to, for example, see only visitors who are in the United States, this would be the way to do it.
Include *Medium* Exactly matching "organic"	To filter users according to whether they followed a link from another website, used a search engine, clicked on an ad in a search engine, or directly typed the name of your website.
Include *Mobile* Exactly matching "yes"	Shows only data for users who came to your website using a mobile device.
Exclude *Keyword* MatchingRegExp "pure (visibility|visability)"	This simple regular expression would filter out most of the people who went to the search engine of their choice and typed in the name "Pure Visibility" as well as a common misspelling. This filter could be useful if you don't want to see data for people who already know about Pure Visibility (admittedly, such a filter is of limited value if you don't actually work for Pure Visibility).

USEFUL WAYS TO SEGMENT FOR UX QUESTIONS

Segmenting According to a Page

Segmenting users according to whether or not they visited a particular page during their visit is a useful technique for studying how a page may have affected user behavior. You can't use analytics to directly answer a question like "Did this page make it more likely that people bought something?" because the answer relies on learning about people's motivations. What you can do, however, is find out how people who visited (or didn't visit) a particular page behaved. That means you can answer questions like:

- Were the people who visited the About Us page more likely to convert than the people who didn't visit this page?
- Did the people who visited the amenities page have a higher conversion rate than the people who visited the floor plan page?
- How many people visited both the SEO section of my website AND the UX section of my website?

- What else were the people interested in super laser pointers also interested in looking at?

The mechanism here is simple—you choose a page, and the segment either includes users who went to that page sometime during their visit to the website, or you exclude users who went to that page sometime during their visit to the website. Of course, you could specify multiple pages with AND or OR relationships. You can even specify whether the page was the landing or exit page, but you otherwise can't explicitly filter according to when they visited a page during their visit.

In Google Analytics, you specify either the dimension page, landing page, or exit page. You can also select the matching option that best fits your needs— "Exactly matching" is best suited to situations where you have a specific page in mind, but you may want to match a class of pages with similar URLs.

Example 1

Let's go back to AwesomePetToys.com. It is an e-commerce website and part of the process of purchasing standards is entering payment information. This page of the shopping cart has the following URL: /cgi-bin/billing.tmpl.

If AwesomePetToys.com made design changes to this part of the shopping cart, they'd want to see if it increased sales. To assess the effectiveness of the changes, the only people who AwesomePetToys.com cares about are the ones who actually saw this page and not all of the people who clicked around the website but didn't proceed to the checkout. They would build the segment in Figure 9.8.

They would then compare the time period to the time period before the change to see if more users make it from this page to the next page in the checkout process.

Example 2

In 2012, one of Pure Visibility's clients, Learning Care Group (LCG), replaced several of the pages on their five websites. LCG is a provider of childcare in the United States, with almost 1,000 centers across the country. Each center has its own page on LCG's website, each using the same design template. This template was the one that was redesigned in 2012.

LCG wanted to know, quite reasonably, if the new pages were better at enticing users to contact them and schedule a tour of their local childcare center than the old pages. Every center's page used the following format:

- /our-schools/austin-tx-7529
- /our-schools/riverside-ca-7191

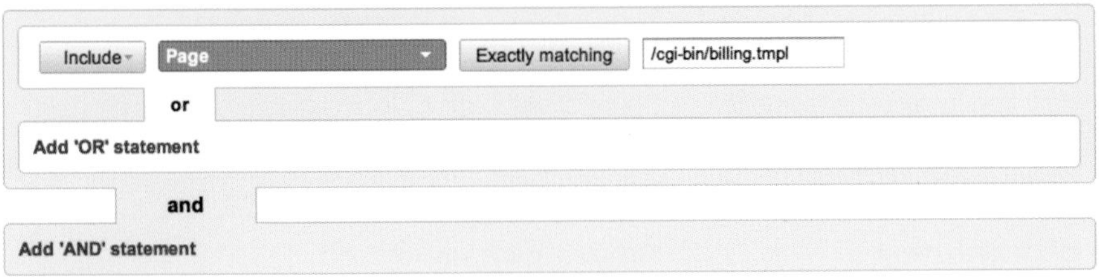

FIGURE 9.8

Segmenting according to whether users viewed a page during their visit.

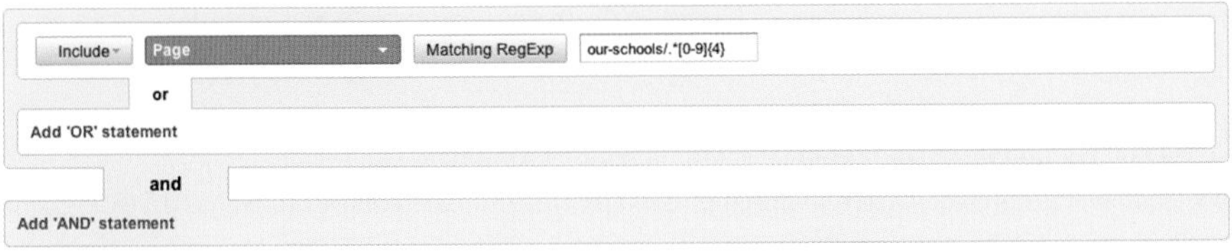

FIGURE 9.9

The advanced segment that filters out any visits where the user didn't reach the childcare center pages at some point.

and so on. The only visits we wanted to analyze were the people who actually visited these center pages, so we used a segment like the one shown in Figure 9.9.

It uses the page dimension—that means Google Analytics will go through all visits for the selected time period and show only the ones where the user viewed this page at some point. This filter looks for pages that match the regular expression—that is, pages in the "/our-schools/" directory and having a four-digit number in the URL.

It was then just a matter of looking at the conversion rate (i.e., what portion of users contacted LCG to schedule a tour) before and after the pages changed. The good news was that the new pages worked very well! Obviously, tying the improvement in conversion rate to the new pages was an inference, but a reasonable one.

PAGE AND TIME ON PAGE

You can use the ability to segment according to whether or not a user visited a page as a rough proxy for whether the user was interested in the content on that page. The obvious problem with that assumption is that it will not be true that every user who reaches a page was actually interested in it. Unfortunately, Google Analytics can't segment according to whether users spent more than a certain amount of time on a page. Use this approach with care.

Table 9.5 User Traits Translated into Metrics and Dimensions	
How frequently users come to your website	Count of visits, days since last visit, hour, visitor type
Where users come from, geographically speaking	City, continent, country/territory, language, region, subcontinent region
Information need	Keyword, page, search term
Where users come from on the Internet	Source, medium, referral path
Technological aspects of the user	Browser, browser version, connection speed, domain, flash version, Java support, mobile, operating system, OS version

Segmenting According to User Traits

As discussed earlier in this chapter, if you have found aspects of your personas that map well to analytics dimensions and metrics, you can create a segment that captures these users so you can eliminate the noise from users who don't match your profile. There isn't really a specific task that follows from creating this kind of segment; rather, it sets you up to explore the data and help answer a variety of questions more accurately.

Some dimensions and metrics that you may find useful are shown in Table 9.5.

Segmenting According to Information Need

By now, we've discussed how you can learn about users through the search keywords that bring them to your website or the search terms they use in your website search. You were able to look at user behavior at a high level (average time on website, bounce rate, etc.) in these reports, but with segmentation, you can do a deeper analysis of what users do on your website based on what they searched for.

To segment according to information need, you simply create a segment with filters for the keywords in one of the categories you discovered. Let's go back to the example from Chapter 6, the Pure Visibility website. One of the categories was "Branded," or people who searched for Pure Visibility by name. Creating a segment that included only users who searched for Pure Visibility by name would simply be a matter of listing some common variations on the name, as shown in Figure 9.10.

Another category was "PPC services" (pay-per-click [advertising] services). This category has a more diverse set of keywords, but many of the keywords are variations on:

- Pay-per-click company
- Pay-per-click business
- Adwords company

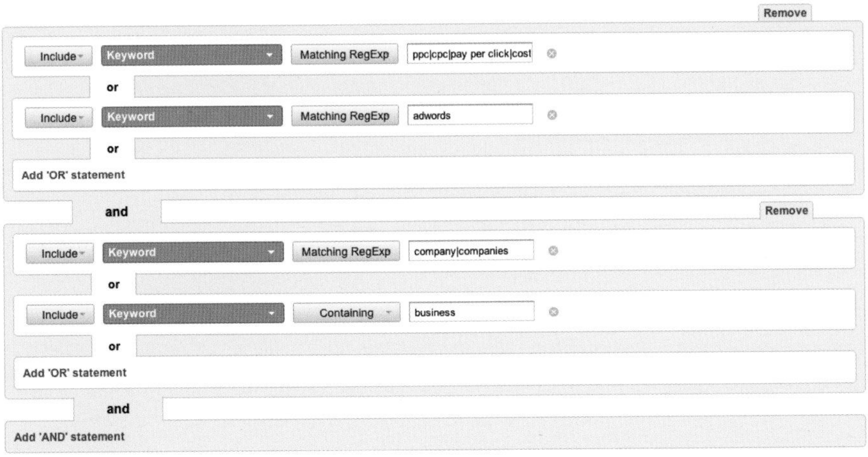

FIGURE 9.10

The segment of users who searched for pay-per-click services. Due to how small the text fields are, these filters are built less efficiently than they could be.

The important elements are a variation on the name of the service, combined with "company," "business," or some other word for business. A segment that isolates these users could take the form of Figure 9.10. In the figure, we have a cluster of keywords describing the service, and a cluster of keywords describing the business.

With trial and error, iteration, and creativity, you can make your segment more precise. Create filters, apply them, and then explore how many and what keywords you have captured. Are you missing keywords from your segment that you know are relevant? Alternatively, you could build a segment that *excludes* the keywords you want to capture, and then see what remains— are there any keywords that you can add to your segment?

You have to strike a balance on how comprehensive you want to be. Looking at the "PPC services" category, do we also want to capture people who searched for "online marketing pay per click," "adwords management Indianapolis," "p.p.c. management marketing," and so on? The more variations you want to include in your segment, the more effort it will take to create your segment, particularly if it's a keyword with a lot of ways to misspell it.

Put simply, you can trade effort to get accuracy—the question is just how much extra accuracy will you get for your trouble. This book does not have a specific method for determining that point; unscientifically, roughly 80–90% coverage of visits that could fit within a keyword category will probably be a point with diminishing returns on accuracy.

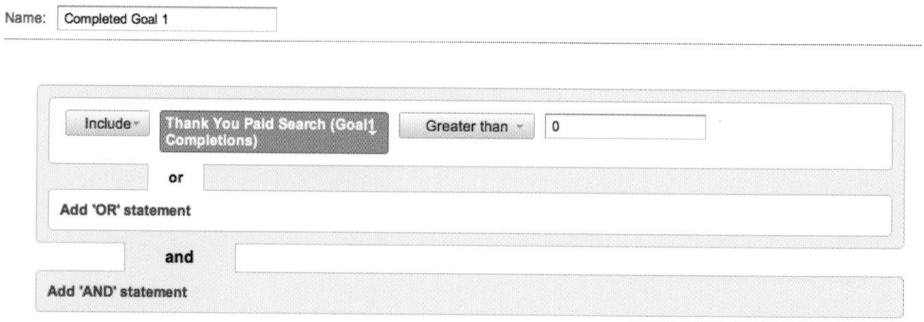

Name: [Completed Goal 1]

[Include ▾] [**Thank You Paid Search (Goal1 Completions)**] [Greater than ▾] [0]

or [ ]

Add 'OR' statement

and [ ]

Add 'AND' statement

FIGURE 9.11

An advanced segment that will show only users who completed goal 1; that is, who filled out a form on the Pure Visibility website.

You also don't have to do an exhaustive search query analysis before building this kind of segment. The main disadvantage of skipping the effort is that you will not have a good idea of exactly how many visits fall within a category of searches. You can still gain valuable insights, though, from just creating a segment that captures the few, most common keywords, particularly if you are looking at trends over time.

Whether or Not Users Completed a Goal

If you've gone to the trouble of setting up goals on your website (and it would be a good idea to do so), you may want to analyze the behavior of the people who actually completed one of those goals (perhaps in comparison to users who did not complete a goal). There is even a default "Advanced Segment" report in Google Analytics that will let you just see data for users who completed any kind of goal (the "Visits with Conversions" advanced segment). You can also go down to the level of the individual goal, which is relevant if you have more than one goal set up for your website.

In Google Analytics, you simply specify a goal and whether the user didn't complete it (0) or completed it (1), as shown in Figure 9.11. Selecting 0 or 1 is a very engineerish way to express this concept. You can put in numbers greater than 1, but it simply won't match anything.

You might create this segment to explore the behavior of people who converted—what pages did they visit and spend the most time on, where did they enter the website, what keywords did they search for in search engines or on your website's search functionality, and so on.

What Pages Users Landed On

You could segment users according to what page of your website they landed on (i.e., the first page of your website that they saw) to explore the behavior of the users who came to your website with a specific interest.

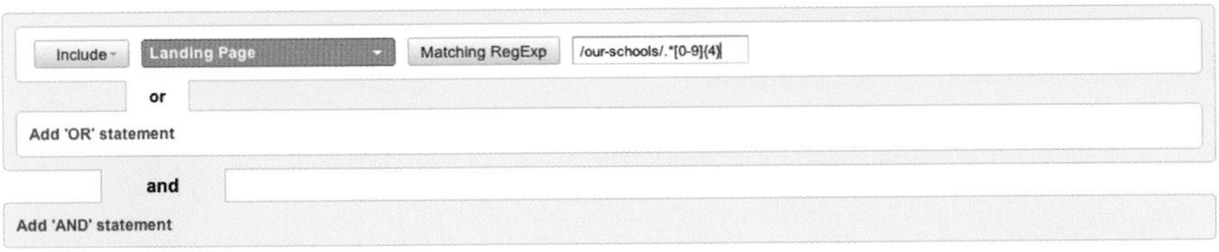

FIGURE 9.12
The segment capturing only users who landed on one of the childcare center pages, as opposed to simply encountering it any time during their visit.

The ability to segment according to the landing page is useful for answering very narrow questions. Typically, you would only do a segment by landing page if you wanted to find out how well a landing page serves users: Does it do a good job of providing immediate benefit to users and entice them to take some sort of action (e.g., buying something or exploring the website further)? Otherwise, you would be better off segmenting in a different way that captures more users. Recall the example from earlier in this chapter, one of Pure Visibility's clients, LCG.

Besides simply wanting to know how the pages for these childcare centers affected whether or not users contacted LCG to schedule a tour, these pages were also important for SEO and paid-search advertising, as a place where we tried to get users to land. What did these users do on the website after they landed on these pages?

Instead of creating a segment that looked for any visit where the user viewed a page matching "/our-schools/.*[0–9]{4}" at some point, we instead used the landing page dimension, as in Figure 9.12.

What Pages Users Viewed/Didn't View
Whether or not a user viewed a page, while not perfect, is still a way of differentiating users based on what they want to do on your website. Emily is interested in shopping for cat toys. We can create a segment that includes users who, at some point during their visit, viewed a product page in the cat toys section of the website. AwesomePetToys.com has toys for other kinds of pets, a section of the website for selling toys in bulk to other businesses, a careers section on the website, and so on. It is possible to create a segment that includes only users who viewed a cat toy product page and did not view any pages in these irrelevant sections of the website. This segmentation will obviously exclude some users who just accidentally find their way onto the irrelevant pages, but if there are enough data to work with, then it's worth it.

This kind of segment is much like the landing page segment described in the last section, except instead of the landing page dimension, you would use the page or page title dimension.

CUSTOM VARIABLES

So far in this book, we have discussed what are for the most part universal metrics and dimensions that you will find, one way or another, in any web analytics tool. Now picture these scenarios:

- AwesomePetToys.com has users who browse the website anonymously, and users who log in to their account. How can they segment these two kinds of users?
- In a similar vein, it would be useful to be able to tell users who bought something in the past from those who didn't—this won't necessarily be the same division as logged-in versus not-logged-in.
- Better yet, AwesomePetToys.com's CRM system may store demographic data that analytics would not normally know about, like gender, purchasing habits, or specifics of their pet ownership. Segmenting according to persona would get even more powerful with access to these data.
- Searching for products can be as simple as typing a word into a search box, but it can be a complicated affair with filters on price, manufacturer, and more. None of these advanced features show up in the URL. What if the people at AwesomePetToys.com want to get a better understanding of how people use search?

Google Analytics and Omniture allow you to define additional dimensions that you can fill with practically any kind of data you want, such as the users' interaction with a page, their visit to the website, or about the users themselves (across multiple visits). The only limit is your programming ability, which is why this topic will have to remain largely outside the scope of this book. To expand the amount of data you can access in web analytics, you should talk to your IT department or a developer about what is possible with your organization's infrastructure and website.

THE TIP OF THE ICEBERG

This chapter has presented a small list of versatile tools. We have only scratched the surface of what is possible with segmentation. As with much of web analytics (and life), the best way to expand your knowledge is in reaction to real-world problems that you must solve.

KEY TAKEAWAYS

- Segmentation is the filtering of data according to metrics and dimensions so you can just analyze other users, the ones who you care about.
- You segment data so you can see and analyze data for just that segment of visits instead of all visits within a given time period.

- Some of the useful ways you can segment data are:
  - Whether or not users viewed a page during their visit.
  - According to user traits, such as mobile device use, geographic location, or data you feed into analytics through custom variables.
  - According to what users searched for to get to your website, or in website search.
  - Whether or not users completed a goal (e.g., buying something or filling out a form).
  - Where and/or how users entered your website, such as what page they landed on.

CHAPTER 10

Pairing Analytics Data with UX Methods

INTRODUCTION

Web analytics belongs in a portfolio of UX methods, supporting and supported by those other methods. This chapter discusses how you can use web analytics in combination with personas, usability testing, usability inspection, and design deliverables.

PERSONAS

A *persona* is a description of an archetypical user of your website—a specific, fictional user of your website meant to focus design decisions around whether or not they serve the needs of a concrete user rather than every stakeholder's individual idea of what constitutes the website's user. Personas are made up of details gathered from research on a sample of actual or potential users, synthesized to reduce the variability found in real-world users into the story of a single user. Personas take advantage of our capacity for empathy with other people and the power of storytelling as a way of communicating information.

We already touched on personas in Chapter 9, discussing how to draw upon them for a way to segment analytics data. This chapter expands on the use of data in web analytics to further refine personas and use the research that went into personas to improve analyses and open new lines of inquiry.

Segmenting Based on Personas

In Chapter 9 we looked at how the specificity of personas can make it challenging to build segments directly based on them. We used the example of Emily, the pet owner who AwesomePetToys.com wishes to target with their website. Let's take a better look at Emily and the scenario of her using the website:

Emily: "Our pets are our family." Spoils her pets Income: $50,000 Education level: postgraduate Job: access services librarian Motivation: pamper her pets Goal: replace her ToyCo laser pointer, a particularly high-end cat toy Pets: Joy, American shorthair calico cat, age 6 Toonces, American shorthair tortoiseshell cat, age 6 Pepper, golden cocker spaniel, age 4	It's early Saturday afternoon, and Emily is settling down on the porch swing on her east-facing porch to relax for a while with a cup of tea. It's easy to let the house go during the week, when she works at the main branch of the library, and Saturday mornings usually bring with them a flurry of chores that Emily shares with her partner, Christina. Emily looks through the window into her living room and sees one of their cats, Toonces, and remembers that she has meant to buy a new ToyCo laser pointer, their last one having been lost in the recent move to this house after years of excellent service. Emily is never far from the Internet, though, and she opens the cover on her new iPad, opens Chrome, and searches for "ToyCo laser pointer." On the Google search results page, she sees, among other results, both an ad for AwesomePetToys.com as well as an organic listing. Emily clicks on the organic listing and arrives at the ToyCo laser pointer product page.

Many details in Emily's story are so specific that only a tiny number of AwesomePetToys.com's users would actually fulfill those criteria, as would be the case in any website that does not receive an enormous volume of visitors (and even then, the portion of corresponding users would still be small).

The best thing you could do to build segments that allow you to explore the behavior of your different kinds of users is to go back to whatever original user research you used to develop your personas. Reviewing your research should provide you with a broader set of values to use for the dimensions and metrics that may help you identify your desired users.

The following subsections describe some of the ways you could segment analytics data based on your user research data.

Segmenting According to Technology

We saw that Emily uses the Chrome browser on her iPad to find and use AwesomePetToys.com, but what other software and devices did AwesomePetToys.com's users use to get to the website?

You may find that the browser is irrelevant, and that AwesomePetToys.com's pet owners with disposable income to spend on their pets predominantly use iPads, or that they use a mix of tablets, laptops, and desktops, but mainly Apple devices. Then again, this detail in Emily's scenario may have been an arbitrary decision and there is too much diversity among browsers and devices to differentiate pet-spoiling owners according to that dimension.

While AwesomePetToys.com sells toys to people who may use a wide variety of devices, there may be situations where you expect your users to have a much more constrained set of choices for technology. If you expect your users to work in a corporate environment where an IT department controls what computers and software is available, you may be able to use the operating system, OS version, browser, and possibly even browser version to identify the right users.

BUILDING PERSONA SEGMENTS WHEN YOU DON'T HAVE MUCH DATA

Unfortunately, personas do not always come from extensive user research, and your judgment comes into play even more than deciding what aspects of research to use for segmentation. When segmenting analytics data without user research, it is important that you can justify your decisions.

One thing that you can do to help verify the usefulness of your persona-based segments, whether you are building them from research data or from judgment, is to look at whether the segment you have built has a higher conversion rate than the rest of your users (or otherwise is more likely to take whatever action you use to judge success—in the case of AwesomePetToys.com, they want to make sure that their Emily segment buys more pet toys than the general population).

Segmenting According to Demographic Aspects

Web analytics can't tell you much about who your users are without being linked to another data source (see the "Custom Variables" sidebar in Chapter 9, which touches on integrating other data sources with Google Analytics). You may be able to segment according to two demographic dimensions with the data you get with the standard setup that most people will encounter:

- Where your persona lives (city, metro area, state, or country)
- What language the user's browser is set to

Many readers will not find these to be useful ways to differentiate users, but your situation may be different. AwesomePetToys.com is an e-commerce website and, as such, will sell awesome pet toys to pet owners no matter where they live. Geography and language simply isn't a useful way of differentiating users since they found that cultural differences aren't as important as other factors like pet ownership and disposable income. On the other hand, a company like Thomson Reuters Techstreet, a Pure Visibility client that sells technical standards documents in various languages, might be interested in understanding any differences between users with different native languages—particularly with regard to what documents they search for and purchase.

Segmenting According to Behavior

Segmenting according to user behavior is what web analytics does best and, being familiar with your options, you may wish to adjust your user research agenda to collect more data that you can use for segmentation.

Some of the behaviors that you can use for segmentation and possibly learn about directly from users are:

- When users visit (day of week or time of day)
- How often they visit (have they visited before, and how often they visit)
- How they get to your website
- What they search for, either in search engines or on your website
- What page they land on
- Whether or not they visit a page or type of group of pages
- Whether or not they complete a goal

Or, to put it another way, when they access your website, how they access your website, and what they do on your website. What users search for on or off your website and whether or not they view pages (or take other actions on your website) are the areas where you infer their motivations based on their behavior.

What Can You Do with Segmentation?

There are two primary things you can do with segments that you have based on the research you used to create personas: explore analytics data to find patterns and answer specific questions in a more accurate way.

Exploration involves looking at data in various reports to see how your segment compares to the general population of users or to another segment to see what patterns may emerge. This activity may drive further research or uncover data that you can incorporate into your personas to give them greater verisimilitude.

Answering questions more accurately simply means that for any kind of analysis, you could use your persona-inspired segment rather than unsegmented data. You could examine common paths to and from a page or analyze keywords and search terms for your segment, or verify whether changes to your website have affected the right user in the desired manner. The important thing to remember is that any segment you create based on other kinds of user research is just going to narrow down the amount of data you look at—it can't give you a perfect view of just your target users and no one else.

You may attempt to segment to answer a question more accurately when a trend is too slight to notice when you look at data for all of your users.

Otherwise, because your focus is on trends over time, it is often not necessary to go to the effort for this additional accuracy.

For example, AwesomePetToys.com not only serves pet owners with money to spend on their pets, it also sells to businesses that these pet owners use. If AwesomePetToys.com changes its main navigation to make it easier to identify the wholesale section of the website, they could use their business purchaser segment to filter out the noise of pet owners who accidentally go to the wholesale part of the website, and therefore get more accurate measurements of user behavior before and after they change the design.

Because pet owners probably wouldn't actually purchase large quantities of awesome pet toys wholesale, segmenting data according to whether they visited the wholesale section wouldn't really make any trends in sales more clear. On the other hand, changes to the wholesale section of the website may actually drive away pet owners who accidentally stray into that part of the website, lowering pageviews for all of those pages when you look at data for *all* users. In this situation, segmenting to show only business users would paint a better picture of performance, perhaps showing that business owners are more engaged with the wholesale section of the website, even while pet owners are fleeing.

Building Better Personas

You can use web analytics data to build more realistic personas by looking at how common your persona's actions are and adding realistic data. The challenge is to examine the right data—the data that describe the people your persona represent.

The way you build better personas from analytics data is through iteration—start building a segment based on what you know about your users and then explore the data to look for other patterns that fit with what you know, such as common search keywords, pages users visit, or when they use the website. Optimally, you go on to verify this information through further user research, otherwise this is, of course, informed guesswork.

Instead of building the Emily persona segment we described earlier, AwesomePetToys.com could build a segment showing data only for people who purchased pet toys in the consumer portion of their website. Using this segment, the analysts at AwesomePetToys.com could then study the keywords that users searched for that lead them to the website and find ways that their keywords differ from the rest of the website's users. In the case of AwesomePetToys.com, they found that people who bought pet toys reached the website by searching for some variation on "AwesomePetToys" or by the brand of toy (e.g., "ToyCo laser pointer"). They could build up a collection of keywords that Emily may search for that would capture pet owners who spoil their pets—both the ones who purchase expensive pet toys and the ones who don't. In this way, they could back into what would hopefully be a similar segment.

> ## DEFENDING ANALYSES
>
> As with other research activities, you interpret the data to derive meaning. Other people could look at the same data and draw different conclusions. There is no bulletproof way to approach this situation—in fact, debate is usually healthy. The best thing that you can do is keep track of where your data came from or how you got them, and the intellectual steps you took from raw data to conclusions. In many cases, being able to describe a thought process is enough to assuage the concerns of others.

USABILITY TESTING

You can incorporate web analytics into usability test planning and when you analyze your findings. With usability test planning, you can use analytics data to help discover potential problem areas or raise questions that you can answer with usability testing. When analyzing data, analytics data can provide evidence for patterns that you observe during testing.

Test Planning

Naturally, web analytics data should not be your only source for research questions. They are merely one input into your research plan and strategy. You will find that in some cases (e.g., why users spend a long time on a page) you may be able to come up with test tasks that focus on the potential problem you have identified. In other cases (e.g., understanding why users express a search in a certain way) it may be more fruitful to explore the matter with interview questions before or after the test. There is no one-size-fits-all way to turn a specific kind of question from web analytics data into a test task. The benefit of these data is in giving you the questions that you can translate into usability testing, just as you would any other research question.

Using Goals

If you have elicited and created goals, then you already have one or more excellent candidates for tasks. Our running example, AwesomePetToys.com, is a fairly typical e-commerce website, and for their Emily user, they have a few goals: purchasing something, adding an item to a wishlist, and signing up for the weekly specials newsletter. Any of these actions would be a good focus for a usability testing task. In fact, an e-commerce checkout can be a long-enough action for multiple tasks, focusing on different aspects of the checkout process.

Prioritizing Tasks

Usability testing is an expensive undertaking and you will probably not have enough time to cover every part of your website. What tasks will you create? In addition to learning about what aspects of your website are the most important based on talking to stakeholders and learning about your organization's goals, web analytics data can provide additional context for selecting tasks.

You can look at how frequently users encounter a page to gauge how vital it is to your testing. If a page has a high number of pageviews relative to other pages or is among the most popular landing pages, then it is a good candidate for inclusion in testing, by building a task that attempts to have test participants interact with the page.

When you look at web analytics data, you may find that users are visiting a page you would not have thought to be important based on business goals. You may find yourself able to incorporate such pages into tasks or prepare test moderators and notetakers to pay attention for pages like the one that you are curious about.

For example, Learning Care Group, one of Pure Visibility's clients that we discussed earlier, had a page on their website, available in the main navigation, labeled Enrollment. At the time, it was difficult to discern the purpose of the page just based on reading what was there, yet it was a highly viewed page, beating out other, more important pages. While in this case it was difficult to construct a task that tried to get participants to view this page, it was something we wished to learn more about during a round of usability testing, so we prepared to note when participants went to that page and to ask about that behavior. We more carefully noted behavior related to that page and spent more time probing participants' interactions with that page during the test and the post-test interview.

Identifying Potential Problem Areas

Throughout this book, we have run into a barrier when analyzing data: not being able to explain why users do what they do. When you have the opportunity to conduct a usability test, you have the chance to begin solving items on your list of mysteries.

You may have been perplexed by the places users go after visiting a particular page on your website; having users perform a task that includes this page may provide you with qualitative data to help you answer the "why" question. You may have found pages with outlier metrics, such as an unusually high time on page or % exits, or you may be curious about what users mean when they search for certain keywords.

Test Analysis

When you analyze data from a usability test, for every finding, consider how you can translate it into something web analytics can measure so you can compare your usability test finding to the web analytics. At times, doing so may prove infeasible, but when it works, you can gain additional context to help you better analyze your findings and additional proof for your findings.

By now, we have covered analysis of how users move from page to page and usage metrics. You can compare your findings on how users move through your website and interact with pages to these metrics. Say that the AwesomePetToys.com UX team observed three out of five test participants moved from the shipping address page back to the billing address page instead of moving on to review their order. Web analytics data could tell the AwesomePetToys.com UX team how many other users exhibit this behavior—it is unlikely that they would find out that precisely 60% of users acted the same way, but they may find that the actual number is of a similar scale, or that the problem is less common than their test indicated.

Another example: Every product page on AwesomePetToys.com has a link to a page with instructional videos on how to play with your pet with various pet toys. They conduct a usability test and none of their participants go to that page, and the participants who mention the link express no interest in click-ing on it. The AwesomePetToys.com UX team concludes that this link simply doesn't seem interesting to their test participants, but is this behavior wide-spread? When they go to their web analytics data, they find that in the last six months, only 1.3% of their users actually went to that page, and even then, the average time on page was only 11 seconds—not enough time to watch any of the videos! They have evidence that this page, as currently designed, may simply not correspond to users' interests.

What if You Find Out Something isn't a Common Problem?

What does it mean when analytics data indicate that a problem is not com-mon, or not as common as usability testing led you to believe? Analytics data do not indicate whether or not a problem you observed during testing is actually a problem—rather, they simply indicate the scale of the problem by helping you understand how common it is. If you observed a participant encountering a problem with a website and later find out that the participant behaved in a very uncommon way, you have still found a problem with the website you're testing. You just may not prioritize it as highly as other, more common problems.

BEYOND PAGE USAGE METRICS

In Chapter 12, we discuss measuring more complex interactions than movement between pages—things like interacting with anything that doesn't make you leave the page, such as picture editing, a commenting and rating system, a tool for finding directions, and so on. What is relevant here is that, with the help of your IT team, if it is possible for users to do something on your website, it is probably feasible to track it, and you then have access to more evidence to incorporate into your analysis of test findings.

After testing, you may find gaps in your tracking of user behavior on your website, actions you want to track but currently do not. You will not be able to measure this behavior retro-actively, but you can find a way to start, and then analyze the data in a few days or weeks.

Usability Test Reports

Don't create special sections for analytics data in your usability test report (whatever form that may take). The proper place for analytics data is right in line with your explanations of the problems you have discovered.

Let's look at an AwesomePetToys.com example. Imagine that their website's homepage has a prominent area where they highlight new or discounted products—a rotating "carousel" where one ad shows for a couple of seconds the next ad for a couple of seconds, and so on (Figure 10.1). After a round of usability testing, their UX team produces the following finding:

There is No Clear Call to Action on the Carousel Ads

Severity: Low

Page: Homepage

These ads display a picture name, and price of the item, but do not state that the items are on sale or provide a call to action. Four of our six participants commented that they did not understand the purpose of the carousel ads. Participant 2 stated "Why's this here? I didn't come here for a squeezy steak. I thought I was supposed to be looking for cat toys. I don't care about a squeezy steak right now." None of the participants clicked on a carousel item and none identified the carousel ads as showing toys that were on sale. We examined the last four full weeks of ads (7/16/2012–8/12/2012) and noted that out of 5,632 homepage pageviews, only 2.3% of the next pageview was for a product featured in an ad. There were no significant differences between individual ads.

FIGURE 10.1

An example of a carousel ad on AwesomePetToys .com. Note the lack of any copy identifying this item as a sales item or call to action (e.g., "Add to Cart" or "Learn More"). The lack of context leads to few users clicking on carousel ads.

When you recommend design changes to address the problems you have found, are there any relevant metrics that you hope to move? For example, you may want to make it easier for users to find a page or fill out a form on your website. When you describe your design recommendations, you can also tell stakeholders that you wish to increase the portion of users who view a page or increase the conversion rate. It is impossible to predict how much you will affect these metrics, but you can point out what metrics you will monitor after your changes have rolled out to determine their effectiveness.

Recommendation: We recommend adding two elements to the carousel ads: an indication that the item is on sale or new, and a call to action. The indication that the item is on sale or new should consist of copy stating either that the item is new, or displaying the regular and the sale prices. The call to action should be the words "Order Now" (although different calls to action could feasibly be tested). We expect this change to the carousel to increase the portion of visitors who reach the featured product pages higher than the 2.3% average we have observed.

In summary, there were three components to this example report:

1. An explanation of the observed behavior, usually with an image to help readers understand. This component should be familiar to people experienced writing usability testing reports.
2. Citation of any relevant analytics data to support the observation. The citation and the explanation of observed behavior can appear in either order, depending on what makes sense for the issue you wish to describe.
3. A recommendation on how to address the problem, generally with some kind of design change, including a description of any metrics that you expect to be affected by this design change.

USABILITY INSPECTION

Integrating web analytics with usability inspection methods like heuristic evaluation is, for the most part, similar to integrating it with usability testing. You can look to analytics to provide you with clues as to potential problem areas, and for evidence of potential problems you have identified or to describe the scale of a problem.

Identifying Potential Problems

As with usability testing, web analytics data can point to potential problem areas. When you have observed outlier metrics (e.g., an unexpectedly high or low average time on page) or simply metrics that are higher or lower than expected, then you have a page or portion of your website that you should ensure you touch upon during your inspection.

Evidence for Problems

A drawback of usability inspection methods is that they are not based on evidence from actual users. Web analytics data are a kind of evidence that can show that users are behaving in a way that you believe they would, based on your professional judgment. It's important, however, to remember the limits of this kind of evidence. As we have discussed, analytics is for "what" questions, not "why" questions. It follows, then, that you are still using your judgment to guess what may motivate users or what they may think when they misinterpret part of a website.

Nonetheless, data on how users interact with your website can make your description of potential problems more compelling. As with your usability test report, analytics data should simply be baked into the descriptions of potential usability problems, rather than relegated to a separate section.

DESIGN AND DESIGN OBJECTIVES

As discussed earlier in this chapter, you should point toward analytics metrics that you wish to affect when designing. Again, you cannot predict specifically what results you will get before real users begin to interact with your design, although it is possible to test a design and measure how users interact with it before pushing it out to all of your users through A/B testing. What you can do is outline what metrics you will use to measure the performance of your website after design changes and what behaviors you expect to find. This means stating objectives such as:

■ The effectiveness of a website redesign of AwesomePetToys.com will, at the highest level, be measured by how much the conversion rate increases for subscriptions to the weekly specials newsletter, addition of items to users' wishlists, and purchase of items (goals 1, 2, and 3 in web analytics).
■ For any given week, the product pages for items that are the weekly specials on AwesomePetToys.com will be the most-viewed product pages among users who entered the website on the homepage.
■ The portion of users who go to the manufacturer description pages after looking at a product page will increase after the AwesomePetToys.com redesign.

The metric-related objectives that you choose should flow from your design goals, which should, ultimately, flow from business goals. You shouldn't simply take it for granted that increasing an average time on page is a good thing—why does it matter to you whether or not users spend more time on a page (or whether more users view a page, or more users watch a video, and so on)? Explicitly describe how an objective you will measure with analytics relates to a business goal.

While the design work you do for your website should ultimately be geared toward steering the appropriate users to one of your website's analytics goals (such as in the case of AwesomePetToys.com, people buying pet toys), not every change you make to your website will have an easily measurable effect at this high level. A change may only affect a small portion of users or have an effect that is indirectly related to the end goal. Sometimes, stakeholders simply have their own agenda for the website, things they want added or changed that you must support but that don't have any practical value.

We can also articulate intermediate objectives, such as increased pageviews, that let us indirectly measure the effectiveness of our work. While we cannot say with certainty that increasing the portion of users who view a page will increase the conversion rate on that website, we can provide a rationale for using this metric as an objective, and using it as a standard for judging success leaves us better off than if we measured nothing at all. Think back to the example of the AwesomePetToys.com ad carousel. Each week, a new set of products is featured with an ad that sends users to that product's page. Not only must users be enticed to click on the ad, they must also interact with the product page itself and determine how much they actually want it. These factors (and possibly more) affect how many users ultimately buy the featured products. Improving the design of the carousel ads can really only affect one link in this chain: increasing how many users reach the featured product pages.

These objectives that we set for design changes should be thought of as something to strive for, something to shape the overall design direction, knowing that sometimes, it will turn out that a new design won't influence user behavior in the intended way and more work will be needed. We should embrace this opportunity to gain greater certainty about our work, even though it opens the possibility of alarming outcomes.

Coming up with thoughtful and specific design objectives that minimize ambiguity will take practice and is an activity that will definitely benefit from collaboration with other stakeholders, particularly the web analytics team. Expect to go through at least an iteration before coming to the objectives that everyone can agree on.

How Much Will You Improve a Number?

There is no way to predict how much you will improve the conversion rate or how many more visitors will reach a page. You can only state the goal of increasing or reducing a metric.

We simply don't know enough about cognition to make any such calculations. Because there are so many variables that go into design (size, shape, color, placement, font, artwork, browser, computer, where the user is located, the users' motivations and cognitive capabilities, etc.), it is doubtful that it ever will be possible to calculate something like "making this button 10% bigger will increase the conversion rate 5%."

This lack of concrete numbers may be a tough thing for some stakeholders to accept if they are used to more explicit estimates or projections. Such a situation calls for education about the obstacles to estimating specific changes to metrics and stressing the accountability that comes from measuring the effectiveness of design changes. Even if you can look to how similar design changes affected metrics, there's still no way the data from one situation are applicable to another.

Although sometimes it is impractical to take steps to mitigate risk, there may be times when you can implement changes on a smaller scale and measure the effects of those changes (as we will discuss in Chapter 11). Starting with smaller-scale changes could mean changing a single page rather than several pages on a website all at once, and not just measuring whether this design change affected the relevant metrics, but the degree to which they changed.

KEY TAKEAWAYS

- You can create segments based on your personas to get a more accurate analysis of what your target users do on your website.
- Step back from the specificity built into personas, otherwise your segment will probably be too limited; you can go back to your original research to learn about more ways to segment data.
- You can also use analytics data to build more detailed personas through first segmenting data based on what you do know, and then exploring the remaining data to find patterns.
- Exploration of web analytics data and unanswered questions from earlier analyses can feed your usability test planning by giving you ideas for test tasks. You can also use web analytics data to help prioritize tasks according to how many users encounter a part of a website.

- You can use web analytics data when analyzing usability test results to add more context and evidence for usability problems.
- Similarly, you can use analytics data during usability inspections to help you find and provide evidence for potential usability problems.
- Incorporate analytics data into the reports of your usability testing and inspection findings. When creating design recommendations, indicate metrics that you hope to impact with through your design changes.

CHAPTER 11

Measuring the Effects of Changes

INTRODUCTION

A vital use of web analytics is to measure the effectiveness of design changes by comparing the effectiveness of one design to another (e.g., comparing a new design to the way things used to be on your website). It is a way of being accountable—accountable to ourselves and to the stakeholders of the website.

When we see our designs get implemented, it is in our best interest to learn, as best we can, whether they are working. If they do, fantastic! But even failed experiments teach us what design choices do not work as intended. It may be scary or challenging to report to stakeholders that a design did not work as intended, but it is important for our professional credibility that we are willing to measure the effectiveness of our designs and to change direction when needed.

What does it mean for a design to be successful or unsuccessful? Every design change should have a reason, and when this reason is to change user behavior, there should be a way of measuring that influence. Even in cases where you are exploring past changes, you should still be able to express the purpose of the design change as some kind of measurable objective.

This chapter does not focus on A/B or multivariate testing, which are good approaches for specific circumstances. Instead, the focus of this chapter is on "working on the airplane while it's in flight"—that is, making changes to your website and then seeing what happens.

As such, this chapter is not specifically about designing and running experiments (although, as per Chapter 10, if you are making design changes to a website, it is a good idea to find a measurable aspect of user behavior that you hope to affect with your change). This chapter is about looking at the analytics data for your website before and after a design change to determine the effectiveness of that change according to something that web analytics can measure. You can measure the effectiveness of changes to your own

CONTENTS

website that you have just rolled out, or you can analyze changes that happened over three years ago, for example, so long as you know what happened to the website and when.

REFRAME AS A RATE

The key to measuring the effectiveness of design changes is thinking about a broader set of user actions as though they were conversion rates. In Chapter 4, we discussed the conversion rate, which is a way of measuring website performance by taking specific actions users can take on a website and looking at what portion of all users perform that action. You can look at the conversion rate in one time period and compare it to another time period to assess how the website's performance has changed over time. Although conversion rates are based on goals that you define in advance, nothing stops you from applying the same approach to other metrics; if something is a binary action (the users either do it or they don't), it can be treated like a conversion rate.

CHOOSE WHAT TO MEASURE

Before you can measure whether a design change was successful, you must decide what to measure. At this point, you should have a good idea of the kinds of things that web analytics can measure. While not every design change is reducible to a web analytics metric, some of the ways you can measure how a design change changed user behavior are:

- Bounce rate: Can you hold the attention of users who enter the website?
- % exit: Can you keep users from leaving the website?
- Whether or not users reach a certain page.
- % search exits: Can you keep users from abandoning your website after performing a search?

Aside from these binary metrics, you also have continuous metrics, where rather than measuring "yes" or "no," you measure something on a scale. What that means, practically speaking, is:

- Average time on page
- Average time on website
- Average pages per visit

The latter two metrics can be used as goals in Google Analytics, making it possible to treat them as binary metrics. However, other than these exceptions, it is more challenging to measure the effectiveness of any designs intended to influence these metrics, as we will see later in this chapter.

How do you choose a metric to measure the effectiveness of a design change? As discussed in Chapter 10, choosing is ultimately a matter of judgment about what you are trying to accomplish. Are you trying to get more users to see a piece of content (i.e., visit a certain page)? Do you want to increase their engagement with your website? You can measure engagement as pages per visit or time on page, or in terms of some action on your website users can take that more directly implies engagement. The important thing is to find an aspect of user behavior that can be measured even when it only gives you indirect insight into the users' experience with your website.

Choose When to Measure

You also must choose two time periods for your analysis: before and after the design change. The first should be the longest time period possible where the website did not undergo any significant changes and there was no mean- ingful seasonal variation in user behavior. That means the two time periods you analyze should have no unusual events such as website outages, national holidays, breaking news that drove lots of visitors to your website, other changes to the website, and so on. Choosing the longest time period pos- sible will give you the most accurate measurement of the conversion rate (or whatever other change in a metric you wish to measure, as per the previous section). It would be best if both time periods, or at least the first, was able to capture all seasonal variation, but your website may not be stable enough for this to be possible.

Finding the right amount of time after the design change is going to be more challenging, because it will depend on how many users you get and how large the change in conversion rate is. The smaller the change in user behavior, the more data (and time) it will take to conclude with confidence that there is a meaningful difference in performance. The number of visitors matters for the same reason—if you need data from many users, it will take longer to get those data if you have hundreds of visitors per week rather than thousands.

If you are simply investigating a change to the website that happened a long time ago, choose the longest time period possible where the website was sta- ble. If you are trying to measure the effects of a change that just took place on your website, a good heuristic is to gather two weeks of data (or about 5,000 visitors) and then analyze them. You may then find that you have enough data to conclude which design is better, or decide that you should wait longer.

SAMPLE SIZE ESTIMATION

It is possible to take a more rigorous approach to sample size estimation where, based on your desired confidence level and power level, you can estimate how many users must reach the page you have changed before you can detect a difference in performance. Sauro and Lewis' *Quantifying the User Experience* (2012) is a good resource, and there are also calculators available online for binomial sample size estimation. The main value of doing calculation is to get an idea of how long it will take to get results. In practice, you may find yourself lacking the necessary information to perform these calculations, and either waiting as long as possible before measuring results, or measuring results frequently and repeatedly until you find a significant difference or conclude there is none. Unlike usability testing where you must determine how many participants to recruit, there is no direct cost to gathering more analytics data.

TYPES OF CHANGES

Your approach will remain the same no matter what metrics you are attempting to change with your design. The following sections describe some of the nuances in measuring changes with different metrics.

You will go through the same high-level steps no matter what you are measuring:

1. Choose the time period before a design change.
2. Wait and gather data from after a design change (or, for changes that happened in the past, choose a time period following the design change).
3. Determine the conversion rate and sample size before and after the design change.
4. Compare the designs; use an A/B test calculator (or do the math by hand) or wait for very large samples of users and eyeball the results.

Conversion Rate

Measuring changes in the conversion rate is something web analytics tools are well suited to doing in terms of how easy it is to access the data. As discussed in Chapter 4, there is a report in Google Analytics specifically for showing you the conversion rate and conversions over time.

To test whether a design has improved the conversion rate, you simply have to choose the time periods you wish to analyze and the goal you wanted to have an impact on. You should then have the data you need. At this point, you can stop—if you saw a dramatic change in the conversion rate or showed in a chart that it was consistently higher over a long time period, then you can tell a compelling story.

However, to get more certainty about whether the change you observed is due to your design change or chance, you should use a statistical significance or A/B test calculator, or employ the chi-square test if you are comfortable with the math.

CONFIDENCE INTERVAL AND CONSERVATIVE ESTIMATION

For the sake of completeness, you should calculate the confidence interval around the improvement so you can report a more complete picture of how certain you are that you've really improved the design. You could be very conservative when you talk to stakeholders and use the low end of the confidence interval.

However, unless you have run a usability test with a huge number of participants, you probably have a wide confidence interval that includes the possibility that you've made the website worse. For this reason, you should use the completion rate you observed. However, if you have observed such a dramatic improvement that even the low end of the confidence interval is an improvement over the old benchmark, try using that instead to give stakeholders a more conservative estimate that provides you with more leeway.

Let's imagine an example from AwesomePetToys.com. For September and October, a stable time period on their website, they had 14,276 visits and a conversion rate of 1.43% for people purchasing awesome pet toys on the consumer-facing portion of the website. At the end of October, they made a change to the shopping cart to make it easier to buy without setting up an account and then waited two weeks. During that time period, 3,922 users visited and converted at a rate of 1.47%.

Plugging in these numbers to the A/B test calculator, we find that the two-tailed p-value is 0.8164, meaning that there is only an 18.36% chance that the conversion rates of these two designs are different.

After waiting another two weeks, AwesomePetToys.com has 8,041 visits and a 1.46% conversion rate. After using the calculator to compare this result to 14,276 visits/1.43% conversion rate, we find that now there is only a 12.48% chance the designs are different. In addition, at a 95% confidence level, the actual conversion rate for the new design could be as low as 1.2%.

This finding is obviously disappointing. In practical terms, if this design change has already gone live on the website, as long as it does not perform worse than the previous design, then it is probably here to stay. In addition to avoiding the embarrassment to the website's stakeholders of rolling back a design, if a new design appears, at worst, to be performing the same as the old design, then it is probably not worth the cost of reverting to the old design.

Fortunately, in other situations, it will quickly become clear that there is a meaningful difference in designs. If, instead of 8,041 visits and a 1.46% conversion rate, AwesomePetToys.com had measured a 1.68% conversion rate, then they would have obtained a p-value of 0.1428, meaning there was a 85.72% chance that the designs are different—still not good enough for situations where lives are at stake, but quite arguably good enough for an e-commerce website.

For more on the subject of the chi-square test, you can look to Sauro and Lewis' *Quantifying the User Experience* or use the A/B test calculator on the Measuring Usability website (http://www.measuringusability.com/ab-calc.php).

Other Rates

You may wish to affect other rates like bounce rate or % search exits. You test changes in these rates just like you would a change in the conversion rate. The only real difference is where you look in your web analytics tool to pull the data. In Google Analytics, for example, instead of goals reports, you would look to the content reports to find out the bounce rate for a specific page or group of pages that your design has affected. Otherwise, the procedure of determining appropriate time periods for data remains the same.

In Chapter 12 we will delve into tracking behavior that does not result in new pages loading. In Google Analytics this functionality is called event tracking, and practically anything that a user does on your page can be tracked, provided someone can write appropriate code to add to the page. These events can be used as goals, but even if they are not tracked as goals, they can also be used to measure the effectiveness of a design change, since they can also be thought of in terms of the conversion rate.

Redirect Traffic

Another major category of change that you can measure is redirecting the flow of traffic through your website. Imagine you have a particular page on your website that you want more people to see and you make some changes to try to persuade more users to click on the link to that page or make it easier to find that link. You want to look at the portion of all users who view that page before and after you make the changes. In other words, you treat whether or not users go to that page as a conversion rate. Unfortunately, you will have to piece together the data from a couple of different reports.

There are a couple of approaches you can take: Did you drive more users to a particular page regardless of what path they took, or did you get more users to click on a specific link on a specific page on your website?

Did Users Reach a Single Page from Any Other Page?

To find out if more users reached a page, regardless of how they approached it, take the following approach:

1. How many users visited the website before and after the change? Use unique visitors.
2. How many unique pageviews did the destination page receive before and after the change?
3. You now have two conversion rates:

$$\frac{\text{Unique pageviews before change}}{\text{Unique visitors to the website before change}}$$

and

$$\frac{\text{Unique pageviews after change}}{\text{Unique visitors to the website after change}}$$

You can now compare these two rates and determine if there is a statistically significant difference. For these calculations, we use unique visitors and unique pageviews because visits and pageviews may inflate the numbers since users may view a page multiple times during their visit.

Did Users Reach a Single Page from a Specific Page?

What if you have changed a specific page to try to get more people to go from that page to another page? The formula is conceptually similar, except that instead of looking at whether or not users viewed a specific page sometime during their visit, now you look at whether users who viewed a specific page clicked through to another page or not.

$$\frac{\text{Clicks through to destination page}}{\text{Pageviews of page that changed}}$$

Recall Chapter 10's example of the carousel ads on the AwesomePetToys.com, where the AwesomePetToys.com UX team tried to entice users to click on ads for products that were on special in a given week. They made changes to their ads to make them more enticing to users (actually mentioning how much money users could save on the product, emphasizing the newness or special-ness), with the goal of getting more people to click on the ads. They need to gather the following information:

- For the time period preceding the design change:
  - Pageviews for the homepage.
  - How many times users clicked through to the destination pages—that is, for the time period, counting up every time a user went to the product page for a product that was on special.
- For the time period after the design change:
  - Pageviews of the homepage.
  - How many times users clicked through to featured product pages.

With all of this information, you will have two proportions you can compare with an A/B test or statistical significance calculator.

Did Users Reach Any of a Group of Pages from Any Other Page?

You won't always be focused on getting more users to a single page. Sometimes, you may want to make a whole section of your website or a whole class of pages more visible to users. You may also have a page that is functionally the same as far as users are concerned, but has a different URL every time users look at it.

You can measure the portion of people who view any of a group of pages. First, for a given time period, find out how many unique visitors the website had without any segmentation. Then, either filter the "Pages" report or apply a segment that includes only users who viewed one of the destination pages (in Google Analytics, "include page exactly matching [page A] OR include page exactly matching [page B] OR include page exactly matching [page C]").

$$\frac{\text{Unique visitors who viewed one of the destination pages}}{\text{All unique visitors to the website}}$$

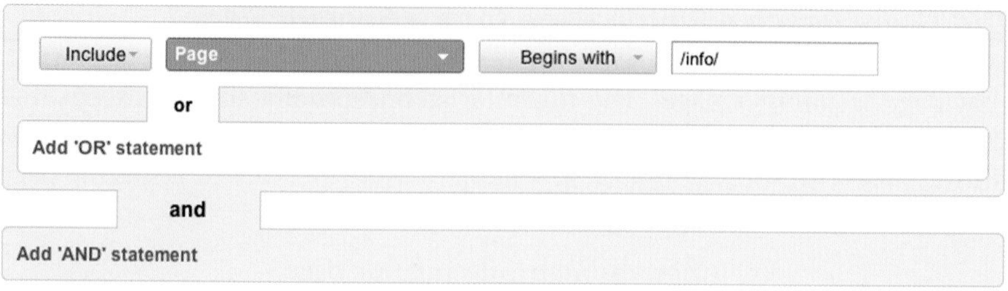

FIGURE 11.1

An advanced segment in Google Analytics that shows users who viewed a manufacturer page sometime during their visit to AwesomePetToys.com. This segment will filter out any visits where the user didn't, at some point, view a page with "/info/" in the URL.

Imagine AwesomePetToys.com made changes to their search results page, the way customers search for products, to promote manufacturer description pages and try to get more users to view them. They roll out this change to the website on July 1, after a time period where the design has been stable for three months, and then they try to measure the effects of this change on August 1.

First, they note that there were 10,000 unique visitors to the website from April 1 to June 30, and 3,000 unique visitors from July 1 to August 1. Next, they find the URL of the manufacturer page: http://www.AwesomePetToys .com/info/[manufacturer].html. Examples would be pages like /info/toyco .html or /info/yippeecats.html. Using Google Analytics, they then build a segment that shows users who viewed one of these manufacturer pages at some point during their visit or simply use the filtering function in the "Pages" report (Figure 11.1).

Applying this segment reveals that 2,000 unique visitors viewed a manufacturer page between April 1 and June 30, and 500 unique visitors viewed a manufacturer page after the change to the website:

$$\frac{\text{Unique visitors who viewed one of the destination pages}}{\text{All unique visitors to the website}} = \frac{2,000}{10,000} = 20\%$$

and

$$\frac{\text{Unique visitors who viewed one of the destination pages}}{\text{All unique visitors to the website}} = \frac{500}{2,000} = 25\%$$

So far, so good—it looks like the portion of people who view the manufacturer pages increased after AwesomePetToys.com changed their search results page. When we compare the two designs using the A/B test calculator, the good news continues—this difference is almost certainly statistically significant. The large sample sizes and dramatic difference in the portion of users who viewed a manufacturer page leads the AwesomePetToys.com UX team to conclude that the difference they measured was probably not due to chance.

More Variations

There are potentially a great many different permutations using the same basic idea. Instead of measuring how effective a design is at sending users to *any one* of a set of pages, you could measure how well it sends users to *all* of a set of pages. You would do so through a segment with a series of AND filters, specifying each page you expect users to visit.

It is possible to measure how many users go from a specific page to *any* of a set of pages. This is similar to finding whether they reached a single, specific page from another specific page; you simply add all of the click-throughs for the various destination pages.

Unfortunately, it is practically challenging to measure how well a group of pages sends users to another group of pages. To answer this kind of question, you should answer on a page-by-page basis, and in the case of there being too many pages to comprehensively analyze (e.g., a frequently used template like a product page), you should simply analyze a sample of pages.

Time on Page and Other Continuous Metrics

The proper way to compare two average times on page (and other continuous metrics where there isn't an either-or outcome) would be to use the two-sample *t*-test, which you can find online and in statistics books. Unfortunately, one vital ingredient of this equation is missing: the standard deviation, a way of showing how far all the individual times on page spread out from the average. This information is simply unavailable in Google Analytics and, without it, we can't use the two-sample *t*-test to calculate whether a difference in average times on page is due to random chance or a meaningful difference.

That leaves us without a rigorous way to measure how much a design changes users' average time on page. Nonetheless, you can still measure any change in time on page and infer whether your design change was effective. Besides looking at the average time on page for two time periods, you can also look at a chart of the day-by-day, week-by-week, or even month-by-month average times on page to see if the new average is consistently higher (or lower) than the old one (see Figure 11.2), or if the new average time on page after the design change is the result of an outlier on a specific date.

In Chapter 4, we discussed Google Analytics' ability to use time on website or pages per visit as goals, as a way to approximately measure engagement. For either of these two metrics, you can set any threshold and every user who

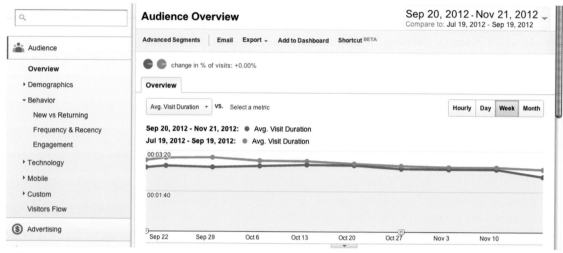

FIGURE 11.2
A chart in Google Analytics showing the average visit duration for two time periods. There were significant changes on this website on September 20 geared toward making the website easier to navigate, which appear to have decreased the average visit duration for the time period following the change compared to the same time period in the previous year.

exceeds it is counted as a conversion. While this capability isn't nimble (you can't adjust the threshold retroactively or temporarily change it without permanently recording conversions), it nonetheless represents a way to turn these two continuous metrics into rates, which you can compare.

CHANGING MANY THINGS AT ONCE

It is not always practical to make a single change to your website, intended to affect only one metric. You will often want to bundle multiple website changes into a single release for the sake of efficiency, like changing both the call to action and the content on the same page, changing the labels on links to that page, and adding a couple of other pages to the website that may entice users into viewing them instead.

The challenge of making multiple changes is that they may affect the same aspect of the user's experience of your website and may provoke unintended consequences from making multiple changes. You may then have some detective work ahead of you to try to understand how specific changes may have affected users when multiple elements on the same page have changed.

One of Pure Visibility's long-term clients, Learning Care Group, made big changes to their websites in 2011 within the space of a few weeks. Two of these changes were to add a link to their "Find a School" feature to the main

FIGURE 11.3

The Child Care Comparison Checklist page on lapetite.com, where there is both a link to "Find a School" in the main navigation and a way to perform a search on the page with the "Search by ZIP" badge.

navigation, and adding a search form to most pages of their websites that allowed users to search for a nearby childcare center by ZIP code (the "Search by ZIP" badge). These features are shown in Figure 11.3.

The main navigation link sends users to a search form, where they can enter their address or click on a map, and then end up on a page with search results. The brief search form on most of the pages takes users directly to the search results page. Although it is relatively easy to find out if a greater portion of users are reaching the search form because of the change to the main navigation, both changes were intended to drive more users to the search results page. We were fortunate that more users actually did reach the search results page after these changes rolled out, but were both changes beneficial, or only one?

In this case, we were able to look at how many users reached the search form to judge the efficacy of the change to the navigation, and to add code to the "Search by ZIP" badge that allowed us to count how many users used it (through event tracking, one of the topics in Chapter 12). We could indirectly count how many users reached the search results page through the new "Search by ZIP" badge.

We were lucky to be able to disentangle the data in this way, but when you change multiple parts of your website at the same time, it will not always be possible to do so. When it is impossible to isolate the effects of changes, it may be time to turn to other user research methods to learn about how users interact with the new iteration of your website, or to simply analyze the bundle of changes as a single change to the website.

COMPLETE REDESIGNS

Your design recommendations may also be incorporated into a complete redesign of your website. In situations where everything (or practically everything) changes at the same time or where you can't really map an action on the old website to an action on the new website, it may be difficult or impossible to isolate the effects of any single change in analytics data.

In the case of website redesigns, the best course of action is to focus on the high-level goals of the website (e.g., buying things, getting people to register, newsletter subscriptions, or having users read several pages). If the new design improves the website's performance on your goals, then you have the luxury of time to explore the performance of individual design elements. It is when a new design does not perform as well as the old design that stakeholders become concerned and want immediate answers on how they can improve the website—a situation where there are no easy solutions but where the immediacy of web analytics data is handy.

REPORTING

The stakeholders in your website want to know how the website is doing, and when they change the website based on your work, they want to know how those changes worked out. Obviously, web analytics gives you another way to address their needs, as well as a discount method of following up on design changes.

Whatever format your reporting takes, storytelling is essential to helping others make sense of the data. Rather than simply showing stakeholders a set of numbers, tell them what those numbers mean.

Of course, numbers are important for the credibility of your findings. In addition to actual numbers (e.g., "this design change resulted in a 5% increase in the conversion rate, from 1.25% to 1.31%"), it is often very effective to include a visual. Use a chart that shows the conversion rate (either the actual conversion rate or something that you are treating as a conversion rate) before and after the design change, to illustrate the point where it changes. Providing a visual can be as simple as taking a screenshot of your web analytics tool, or you could export day-by-day or week-by-week data and construct a chart in Excel. In fact, you may have to export data and create a chart elsewhere if you built a compound metric to measure whether you have managed to bring more users to a page or set of pages. A side benefit to creating your own chart is that it emphasizes to stakeholders the effort that went into your analysis in a way that a screenshot of your analytics interface does not.

New Designs Don't Always Work

If you do not get the desired result—that is, if you have found that the new design does not perform better than the old design—at least you have learned something about what doesn't work, and there is no shame in trying and failing. No one likes the thought of rolling back a new design, so it is important to find out if the new one is actually worse than the old one or simply no better. Additionally, you may have generated data from the way people used the new design that will help you understand what didn't work through further analysis of web analytics data, as well as through other user research methods.

It is also worth double-checking the data you used for your analysis. Did you pull the time period that you thought you had? Are you sure that there were no other changes to the website or to your users before or after the design change that may have affected users? If so, you may need to alter the time periods that you look at. You may have also targeted such a small portion of your website's users that any actual improvement in the conversion rate is getting lost among all the visits to the website that you do not care about. Improvement rates can be obscured when your website has multiple audiences with distinct needs, and you may need to use segmentation to take out irrelevant users.

KEY TAKEAWAYS

- Every design change should have at least one metric you can measure to find out how you have influenced user behavior.
- To measure the effectiveness of a design change, find a way to reframe the relevant metrics as a rate.
- Reframing will work for binary metrics like bounce rate, pageviews, and, of course, conversion rate, but it will be difficult to measure changes in continuous metrics like time on page in a statistically rigorous way.
- To test whether users reached a single page from any other page, compare unique pageviews divided by all unique visitors to the website from before and after the design change.

- To test whether users reached a single page from a specific page, compare clicks through to a destination page divided by pageviews of the page that changed from before and after the design change.
- To test whether users reached any of a group of pages from any other page, compare unique visitors who viewed one of the destination pages divided by all unique visitors to the website from before and after the design change.
- Sometimes, many things will change on the website at once; this will require you to do careful sleuthing or to focus on high-level objectives like the conversion rate for analytics goals.

PART

3

Advanced Topics

CHAPTER 12

Measuring Behavior within Pages

INTRODUCTION

So far in this book, we have mainly dealt with measuring how users move from page to page on a website. We now turn to measuring what users do *on* a page. Historically, measuring on-page activity has been a challenge, but tools for doing so are now easily available.

This chapter first looks at the out-of-the-box functionality in Google Analytics, continuing our tour of this commonly available tool. We then briefly look at tools that can record anywhere that users click on a given page, before finishing the chapter with a section on configuring page tagging tools to measure practically any interaction users have with your website. The last approach, though the most technically complex, may offer you the most rewarding possibilities for analysis.

GOOGLE ANALYTICS IN-PAGE ANALYTICS

At the time of writing, Google Analytics' "In-Page Analytics" report looks powerful but has significant limitations with regard to what kinds of interactions it can actually capture and display.

The "In-Page Analytics" report, shown in Figure 12.1, displays a page of your website, page-level website usage metrics (including the average load time metric, which is available in few reports), and annotates the page you are looking at with the portion of clicks each link has received in the selected time period.

At the time of writing, the "In-Page Analytics" report only displays clicks on links to other pages and can't differentiate between multiple links to the same destination page. Any interactive elements that keep users on the same page or JavaScript or HTML code that forms elements that take users to a new page don't have any data associated with them in this report. We will address this limitation later in the chapter, although advances

FIGURE 12.1
Google Analytics' "In-Page Analytics" report. Fortunately, it is possible to expand the report to see more of the page without scrolling.

in Google Analytics may make it possible to associate data with these elements.

A useful feature is that you can change from all clicks to a segment showing users who completed one of the goals you have configured. Doing so gives you a way to visualize pages that "contributed" to the user completing a goal, because rather than showing how all users moved through the website, it just shows what pages the people who converted looked at.

This report is basically the Navigation Summary tab of the "All Pages" report. However, it does not show how users got to a page, and instead of displaying what pages users went to next as a list, it does the overlay. Depending on your personal preferences, the "In-Page Analytics" report may be easier to comprehend. However, it is difficult to use the data from this report for more complex analyses that involve combining and/or manipulating the data because there is no way to export them; instead, you must click around with your mouse and write down the data.

MAKING THE "IN-PAGE ANALYTICS" REPORT BETTER

Google Analytics has recently made available code that can be added to the tracking code on every page to separate clicks on multiple links to the same destination and display clicks on form and JavaScript elements—in other words, code that will make the "In-Page Analytics" report show everything that users may interact with. Unfortunately, this feature is new enough that, at the time of writing, I have not seen it successfully implemented or read another's account of using it.

CLICK ANALYTICS TOOLS

There are web analytics tools that you can use to measure where people click on the page. These tools record the coordinates of every place that users click on a page, whether it is a link or not, as well as users' keystrokes. They then allow you to either view, on a page-by-page basis, the total number of clicks at each coordinate for a given time period, or to play back an individual user's session on your website as they move from page to page, recreating their clicks and keyboard input.

These tools can be useful for answering specific questions about website usage. Learning where users click on a certain page can show you what elements stand out or appeal to users and, importantly, show you places where they click that is not actually an interactive part of the website.

The main drawback of a tool for measuring where users click on a single page is that it is not integrated with other web analytics data from other tools. You can *only* answer questions about where users click on a page—you can't learn more about what else they did on your website and how they got to it. You will only be able to answer questions about a single page at a time; even if you measure clicks on multiple pages of your website, you still won't have a picture of users' whole interaction with it, but rather just snapshots of any time any user encountered a given page. Unfortunately, this kind of tool does not necessarily handle dynamic pages very well (i.e., pages where the layout or content can change), and may only show the page as it appears when first loaded.

Tools for recording entire sessions on your website obviously solve the problem of not being able to see users' entire sessions. You can, with such a tool, play back a user's session on your website as though you were looking over their shoulder.

The main issues that you encounter with this kind of tool are:

- Foremost, you have a huge amount of data to sift through. Although you may be able to filter through the recordings based on which pages users encountered or actions they took, the data defy aggregation. You must watch the recordings to learn what is in them.
- You don't know anything about the users—who they are, what they came to the website to do, what they think about the website as they interact with it, and how they interpret what they see. Obviously, web analytics data in general do not give you insight into what the user thinks, but it is easy to get the impression that session recording offers more data than it actually does.
- It is less of a challenge of the tool and more of an ethical issue, but there are those who are wary of the privacy issues involved in recording individual users' complete sessions and potentially capturing personally identifiable information.

Watching recordings of sessions may give you ideas for places where users have difficulty on your website, although because you lack context about users, you will probably want to follow up on any discoveries you make by looking to more quantitative web analytics data or other user research methods.

Both session recording and single page–click analytics tools may encounter difficulties with highly dynamic and/or interactive websites. Because they are not actual video recordings of pages and do not actually "understand" how a page can change in response to user actions, they may not properly display all of the parts of a page that users may interact with.

MAKING CLICKS MEASUREABLE IN PAGE TAGGING ANALYTICS TOOLS

Anything that users do on a website can feasibly be tracked by web analytics. The only problem is that for any action that does not result in a new page of your website loading, this requires the insertion of additional code on your website to communicate with analytics (Figure 12.2).

Before we go any further, we need to define an important piece of terminology: an *event* is any action that a user can take on a website. So far, we have skirted around this term, but we have already measured a certain kind of event—users clicking on a link to another page of the same website. We now turn our attention to making other kinds of events measurable.

Some of these on-page events could be the user clicking a button to post a comment on an article, subscribe to a newsletter, or download a document. It could be clicking a link leading to someone else's website, or starting, stopping, or completely watching a video. You could track someone playing a

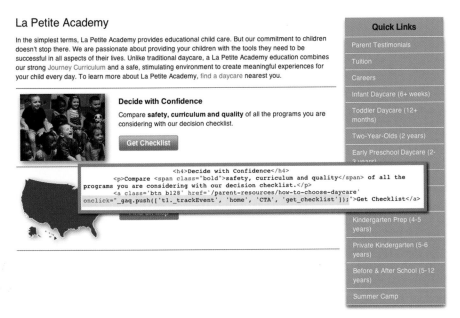

FIGURE 12.2
The Google Analytics' event tracking code on a button on the homepage of one of Pure Visibility's clients, highlighted in yellow.

Flash game for a certain amount of time, reaching specific objectives in the game, or adding items to a shopping cart. If you can articulate what you want to measure about *what* the user does, with the right support or programming skills, you can measure it in web analytics.

Anything is possible, but you will either need to be comfortable specifying code to add to the website or have someone to help you write and add code. On top of that, some user actions will be more complex to measure than others—whereas tracking when users click on a simple HTML button will require a standard, repeatable chunk of code, tracking actions in Flash or AJAX widgets will require greater facility with interpreting and writing code.

Defining Events

When you want to start capturing events beyond pageviews, you should ask what you want to measure and why. The first question will probably be easy, but the "why" issue will have ramifications for what data you capture and how. The best way to explain events and event tracking is through examples.

Example 1: What Videos Did Users Watch?

Let's start with our example from last chapter, AwesomePetArticles.com (a spinoff of AwesomePetToys.com providing information on taking care of pets). They have a library of videos on their website and they want to know if anyone is actually viewing them. They're played in a Flash video player embedded in pages, and if the tool records how many times the videos are played, no one knows from which pages. Fortunately, this information can be captured by web analytics.

We now know what AwesomePetArticles.com wants to measure—what videos are played—to determine what content is the most enticing and engaging to users. To this end, it follows that they would need to record two pieces of data: the name of the video and that it was played.

These data tell us whether a video was enticing enough to be played, but what about how engaging or useful users found the videos? The typical approach is to record how much of the video users watched before stopping it, and also capturing when users watched a video to completion. AwesomePetArticles.com ends up with three events instead of just one:

- The name of the video and that it was played.
- When a video is stopped, at what time it was stopped, and the name of the video.
- When a video is watched to completion and the name of the video.

These three events allow the AwesomePetArticles.com team to tell what users wanted to watch, and what they actually watched.

Example 2: Where Did Users Click on a Page?

Popular page tagging analytics tools do not, by default, pay attention to where on a page users click, only on the pages they view. What do you do when you have multiple links on the same page leading to the same destination and you want to know which one users clicked on?

This was the problem facing one of Pure Visibility's clients, Learning Care Group, a major provider of childcare in the Unites States. On their websites, a typical page has a main navigation where users can go directly to many of the pages on the website. The most important of these pages also appear in a set of "quick links" that appear on almost every page of the website. In addition, every link in the main navigation reappears in the footer on every page, and depending on the content, further links may appear in the body of the page.

The most important thing for users to do on the websites is to find a childcare center near them and then schedule a tour. There may be four different links on a given page leading to the search form, so which one did users click on? Here, "what do you want to measure" was how many users clicked on the links available, and the "why" was to find out which were most visible or appealing.

The trick here was to make the act of clicking on any of those links into an event that gets recorded in analytics in addition to the pageviews from the destination pages, with a labeling scheme that lets us tell them apart. This event tracking scheme was rolled out across the entire website, so we could determine, for example, how many users clicked "Find a School" in the header and on what pages they did so.

The main drawback of this kind of tracking is that, deployed widely on a website, it can produce a large amount of data. That makes labeling important, and we will cover labeling schemes later in this chapter. For one-time questions about where users click on a page, you may be better off using a click tracking tool—it all comes down to the specifics of your situation.

Example 3: Did Users Get Any Search Results?

Another Pure Visibility client, vRide, wants users to search for vanpools that they can join to save money on their daily commute to work. What we wanted to find out was whether users' searches turned up any search results or not, so we could break users into two segments and analyze their behavior. It turned out it was easiest to record this information in analytics, in addition to enabling some interesting analyses.

We used event tracking in Google Analytics to record every time there was a search, what that search was for, and the number of search results returned. Instead of "firing" when a user clicked on the Search button, this event was triggered when the search results page loaded in the user's browser.

Configuring event tracking like this gave us a richer data set to work with than the website search reports in Google Analytics could provide. vRide's search tool asked the user to enter a start and destination point and used these data to generate the search results, and Google Analytics' website search tracking functionality would only let us track one search term or the other. In addition, the interactivity of the search results page was more complex than Google Analytics could deal with, most notably with regard to telling us whether or not a search had any results.

Putting It Together

In these examples, we have gathered or defined the following pieces of information:

- What to name the event according to what action the user performed.
- A way to describe the event (e.g., with what the user searched for, in the case of vRide).
- A numeric property of the event (e.g., the number of search results or how much of a video was played).

Every analytics tool handles events in its own way, with regard to what sort of data you can record about events. You ask the "what" and "why" questions so you can figure out what data you want to record within the rules of your tool.

Google Analytics' events can record the following data:

- Category
- Action
- Label (optional)
- Value (optional)

The first three fields can contain any string of characters. Value can only contain numbers. You can put anything you like in these fields—you can choose practically any action that users can take on your website and record it using any labeling scheme you want.

The idea behind category, action, and label is that you will come up with a classification scheme that makes sense for your website and what you want to learn, and is robust enough to accommodate all of the events you would ever want to track.

The trickiest part is category. Do you want to categorize by type of user action, section of the website, or something else entirely? Even action can be tricky because you must choose how fine-grained to get. Will every event get a unique identifier, or will you give similar events the same event identifier and tell them apart by using the label field? Or, ignore the label field altogether and simply look at what page these events happened on?

There isn't a single right approach. Rather, you use the scheme that makes sense for your situation. If possible, take the opportunity to audit your entire website for actions users can take that are not getting tracked so you can come up with a flexible naming system. However, if you end up later violating your naming conventions with newly tracked events, the only problem it will cause is poor organization of data that may make it more difficult for newcomers to understand the data.

ANALYZING EVENT DATA

Now that you've added code to your website to track the desired events, what can you do with the data besides just counting how many people take these actions? Broadly speaking, you can look at what pages events take place on, use event tracking data to make rates you can compare to other rates, and use event tracking data as another way of segmenting analytics data.

Pages and Events—What Happened Where?

If you have the same event on multiple pages of your website, you may want to find out where users are taking that action. On the other hand, if you have multiple events that users can trigger on a single page, you may wish to get a sense of the variety of things that users are doing on this page. Both situations were the case with tracking links to the "Find a School" page for Learning Care Group, where besides multiple links per page, many pages had links to "Find a School."

In Google Analytics, there are two main approaches depending on what you want to know: For a given event, on what pages did it happen, or on a given page, what are the events that happened?

On What Pages Did an Event Happen?

This information is available in Google Analytics, but only with some clicking around. Go to the "Top Events" report, which shows you the most frequently triggered events that you can view by category, action, or label. Now click on the Secondary Dimension button and add the page dimension, as shown in Figure 12.3. You now have a table that shows all of the pages on which every event is triggered.

Looking at a list of events further segmented by where they happened is most useful for simply characterizing the different places where users perform an action, or for looking for places where they take that action the most or the least.

TOTAL EVENTS AND UNIQUE EVENTS (METRICS)

In the screenshots from Google Analytics, you will see two metrics: total events and unique events. The latter is how many individual people triggered an event one or more times, whereas total events counts how many times an event was triggered, regardless of whether the same person did it multiple times.

What Events Happened on the Page?

Getting this information is essentially the opposite of what you did to find out on what pages an event happened. The "Event Pages" report (Figure 12.4) shows you a list of pages on the website and how many events happened on each of those pages. Alone, it will probably not be useful to simply have a list of pages where users performed some unknown actions. You must add a secondary dimension, such as event category or event action, to break out each individual action. You can then sort the table to see how many times each action was performed on a page.

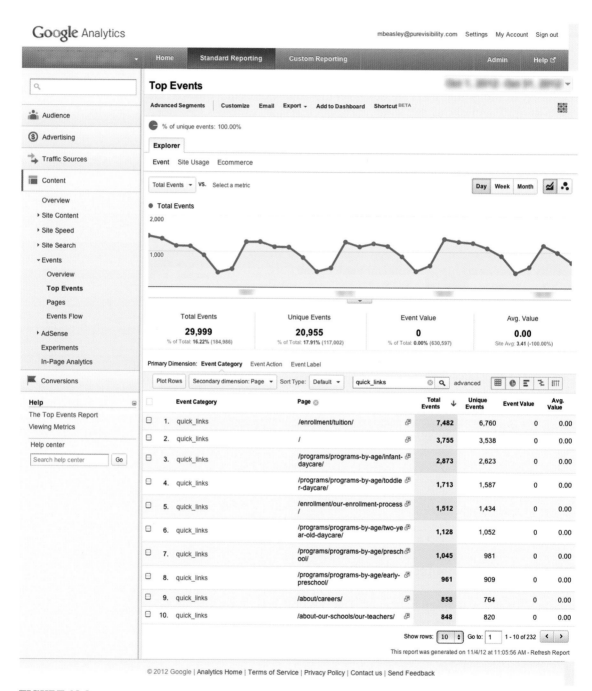

FIGURE 12.3

The "Top Events" report, with a secondary dimension added to show what page each event happened on.

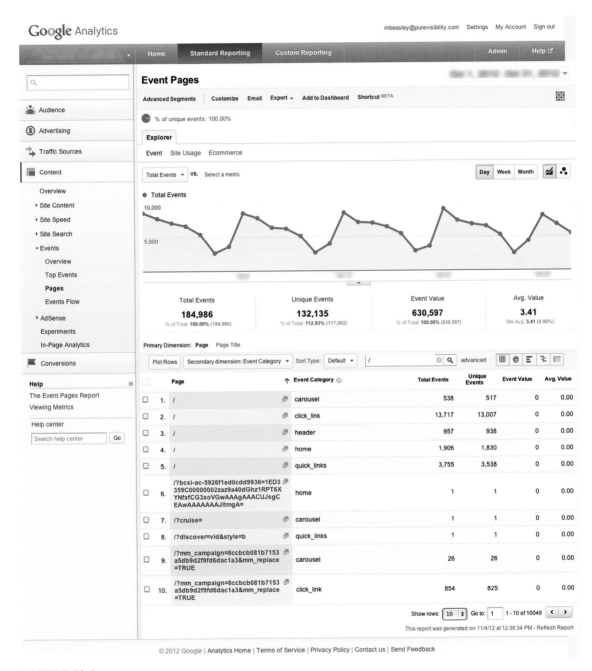

FIGURE 12.4
The "Event Pages" report with a secondary dimension added to show what event happened on each page. It currently shows event category, but we could use action or label instead.

Making Rates

By now, we have discussed many ways to make a rate out of two kinds of numbers, and data from event tracking are another kind you can use. It is typically useful to do so to compare how many people want to do something and/or are successful at doing it, either in two different timeframes or between two tasks or designs.

Here are some of the rates you may wish to calculate:

- How many users took an action out of all visitors?
- How many users took an action out of a subset of visitors, such as just those who viewed a certain page or who took another action recorded as an event?
- Out of the users who took an action recorded as an event, how many of those events had a value greater than x?

A common use is to make a design change intended to get more users to take an action, and then compare how many users take that action before and after the change.

In Google Analytics, one of the goals you can create besides matching a specific page on the website, or counting how many users exceed a threshold of time on the website or pages/visit, is how many users trigger an event. You can match against the category, action, label, or events that exceed a specific value, or some combination of the four.

Segmentation

The events that you create in web analytics can also be used as dimensions for segmentation (and in the case of event value, a metric). If you read Chapter 9, then you should have the background you need for creating segments. Events give you more ways to differentiate users according to their behavior on your website.

EVENTS FLOW

There is one more notable report in Google Analytics covering events, and that is "Events Flow." It is similar to the "Visitors Flow" report, which showed how many users moved from one page to another, and organized the pages by whether it was the first one that a user looked, or the second one, or the third one, and so on.

The "Events Flow" report is similar, except instead of pages, it shows the sequences of events that users trigger. How useful the "Events Flow" report is depends on how much your website uses event tracking and in what way. If you use event tracking to measure a handful of isolated actions on your website, then it will probably not be meaningful to look at the sequence of events. On the other hand, if you use event tracking extensively on a highly interactive website, this report may be the most effective way to look at these data sequentially.

VIRTUAL PAGEVIEWS

You can also add code to your website that fakes a pageview. You specify the name of the page—either a unique URL that doesn't exist anywhere else or an existing URL—and then decide when you want that code to be triggered. You would use a virtual pageview when the user reaches a piece of content on your website that is a discrete location but where there is no actual HTML page corresponding to that content.

Imagine that the AwesomePetToys.com checkout process, instead of consisting of a discrete set of pages like /review_cart/, /payment_information/, and shipping_information, actually took place on a single highly dynamic page. Without additional code, the user's movement through these steps of the checkout process would be invisible to web analytics. You can analyze the data you get from these virtual pageviews in the same way you do actual pageviews.

As with event tracking, the code itself for sending data to your analytics tool is relatively simple and repeatable. The tricky part is placement, which will depend on the circumstances in which you want the virtual pageview to occur.

WEBSITE DEVELOPMENT SHORTCUTS

On many websites, interactions that *look* like they take users to a new page actually change the content of the page and the user stays on the same URL. This interaction is then invisible to web analytics without additional code to track the event. An example is when a user fills out a registration form, clicks the Submit button, and then sees the form replaced with a thank-you message or is simply taken to whatever page he or she was on previously, rather than going to a unique page that users would only reach if they had filled out the form. You can overcome this problem either through virtual pageviews or through event tracking. Neither solution is appropriate for every situation, but unless it would be useful for you to be able to analyze data about user behavior as though they had viewed a page on your website, it will probably be better to use event tracking.

KEY TAKEAWAYS

- Measuring the actions users take on your website that do not result in new pageviews can be challenging, and there are situations where you would resort to specialized tools to do so.
- With additional code, anything that users do on a website can be feasibly tracked by website-wide page tagging web analytics tools like Google Analytics.
- It is up to you to determine the naming scheme for event tracking; it is important to understand ways your web analytics tool allows you to describe events and to come up with a system that is flexible.

CHAPTER 13

A/B Testing

INTRODUCTION

A/B testing is when you take two competing designs for a page, select a single metric for determining success (typically, the conversion rate), and send users to both pages until there is a statistically significant difference in the conversion rate. One could compare a brand new design against an existing design, or compare two new pages.

This technique allows you to confidently make decisions about competing designs on a page-by-page basis, rather than as a network of multiple pages. Just remember that A/B testing does not give you insight into why one page or the other "won," only that users took a specific action on one design versus another.

This chapter discusses designing an A/B test and interpreting results. It also touches on tools and the help you may need to deploy a test.

DESIGNING AN EXPERIMENT

At a high level, the steps of designing an A/B test are:

1. Select a page that you wish to improve.
2. Determine a metric for judging improvement.
3. Design one or more alternatives.
4. Add code to the page(s) and execute the test.

Select a Page That You Wish to Improve

There is no real magic to selecting a page that you wish to improve, but generally speaking A/B testing is most effective on pages that give users an opportunity to complete one of your website's goals, and often with a high number of users exiting from those pages. A common use for A/B testing is to improve landing pages for advertising campaigns—that is, the page that users land on when they click on an online ad. A landing page has to capture a user's

CONTENTS

attention, explain the company's product, and persuade the user to take some kind of action, such as buy that product, typically without sending him or her to any other pages. It is self-contained, and self-contained pages that focus on getting the user to take some kind of action make good candidates for A/B testing.

More broadly, you should choose pages that are important to your website where the user can take some kind of measurable action that he or she would have to do intentionally that is important to you. Instead of a self-contained landing page, you may instead choose a page at a critical point in a longer process, like a page in a multipage registration or shopping cart checkout process. The important thing is that there is an action users can take on the page that signals that they were successful and a significant number of users are not doing it.

Determine a Metric for Judging Improvement

That brings us to the second part—determining a metric for judging improvement. A/B testing, as it is typically used, compares the conversion rate of one page against the conversion rate of one or more alternatives. As we have discussed in this book, many actions can be reframed as a conversion rate.

Design One or More Alternatives

You must then design one or more alternatives to what exists, or, if there is no existing page, two or more designs to pit against each other. Although the term *A/B testing* implies testing just two designs, the only reasons you would not test additional pages would be the cost of designing and developing additional pages, and because it will take longer to get results if you test more pages.

Designing new pages for your website is outside the scope of this book, but it is important to remember that, generally speaking, small changes to a page will produce small effects on user behavior.

If you are using a tool that requires you to do much of the development work in-house, or if you are using highly dynamic pages on your website that are difficult to change, you will probably get more value out of testing dramatic changes, even though your experiment will not have the kind of rigor that lets you isolate the effectiveness of individual design changes to a page.

On the other hand, of course, if you can easily and rapidly produce variations on a page and/or do not experience time pressure on getting results, then a series of experiments testing changes to one design element at a time will help you better understand *why* one design is better than another. Specialized A/B testing tools will generally allow you to alter the appearance of the page that is already live on your website, which means there are design elements like labels, copy, images, and arrangement of page elements that you can test without a great deal of support from your organization.

This chapter focuses on comparing one design for a page against another design. Later in the chapter, there is a sidebar on multivariate testing, of which a set of individual design elements within a page are tested to arrive at a combination that has the highest conversion rate.

ORGANIZATIONAL CHALLENGES

The hardest part about A/B testing may be getting all of the participants in your organization to work together. Depending on your situation, you may have separate individuals responsible for:

- Wireframing/high-level design
- Visual design
- Coding the page
- Producing the A/B testing tool's tracking code
- Quality assurance on newly developed pages
- Deploying a page on the website

These people may be in-house or outside vendors, and they all have their own things to do besides helping you, and their time has a cost (either directly or just an opportunity cost).

The point is that it may be costly and time consuming to build and deploy new, experimental pages that may end up getting discarded at the end of the test. While A/B testing is an effective approach to optimizing a website around getting users to take some specific action, it's important to remember that the scope of the operation is not trivial. However, depending on what you wish to test (e.g., changes in copy versus changes in visual elements) or your organization's willingness to pay for additional tools, you may not face as many hurdles.

Tracking Code

After you have chosen the page you wish to test and the metric you will use and designed one or more alternatives, you then need to add additional JavaScript code to the page(s). The code you have added will allow your tool to randomly choose which design alternative to display to users throughout their visit to your website. Typically, your A/B testing tool will generate this code.

Tools

Not surprisingly, Google Analytics has an integrated A/B testing tool. If you are already using Google Analytics, then you have access to the Content Experiments feature. The downside is that this tool requires a great deal of help from your organizational support for installation and to construct the pages to be tested (as described previously in the "Organizational

Challenges" sidebar). There are other tools available with a broader range of features, such as multivariate testing or that reduce your need to rely on your own organization's IT people for help, such as Optimizely or SiteSpect, which allow you to test page elements without building entirely new pages.

If you want to test things like changing copy, changing the color of text, swapping images, or even rearranging elements on a page, then it will probably be worth using a specialized A/B testing tool so you have more control and can affect changes yourself.

Google Content Experiments

The Content Experiments feature is currently in the Content menu. Setting up an experiment entails the following steps:

1. Enter the URL of the page you wish to test.
2. Enter the URL of one or more pages that you wish to compare to the original page.
3. Select one of your existing goals (or, at least, a goal that you have just set up in Google Analytics).
4. Set other, optional options, such as how many visitors to include in the experiment and the confidence threshold.
5. Google Analytics will generate the code you must add to the pages you wish to test.
6. Finally, you can start the experiment.

The idea behind the Content Experiments feature is that it will run your experiment until it has gathered enough data to declare one design has a higher conversion rate with a high degree of statistical certainty. As previously mentioned, it requires you to fully develop one or more pages to use as alternatives rather than swapping out design elements on-the-fly, which most likely entails cooperation across multiple parts of your organization.

Specialized Tools

There are tools that specialize in A/B and multivariate testing. They will cost money, but their greater flexibility may be worth it to you.

While a tool like Optimizely will do all the things that Google Analytics' Content Experiments feature will do, you will have the aforementioned additional flexibility to also test some changes to your page without the involvement of developers to create new pages. This can greatly reduce the amount of time it takes to go from designing new pages to starting a test, meaning you can reasonably choose to perform many tests with the intention of isolating one variable at a time.

As with Google's tool, these tools also work by way of implanting a small amount of JavaScript code on the pages you wish to test.

MULTIVARIATE TESTING

Multivariate testing is an exciting and weird concept. Rather than testing one entire page against another entire page, multivariate testing involves dividing a page into sections, producing alternative designs for each section of the page, and then the multivariate testing tool presents users with a random combination of components until it arrives at the best performing combination.

The math involved in this kind of test will not just show you the winning combination, it will also show you how much of an effect each part of the design had on the page's performance. The downside of multivariate testing, besides the additional overhead of design and setup, is that it will take a huge number of users when compared to a simple A/B test. A good rule of thumb is that for a one-month test, for every additional combination, you will need 2,000 visits per day. So a four-way test would require about 8,000 daily visits to complete in one month.

Estimating the Length of a Test

It is impossible to accurately predict how long a test will take because you will not know how big the difference in performance between the two designs will be—it may take weeks or months to detect a 1% difference in the conversion rate. In my experience, most A/B tests will take a month or more than 5,000 visitors, but a huge difference in performance can become evident within days. An A/B test may take longer if your website receives few visitors, and it may be shorter for very high-traffic websites or when it turns out that there is a great difference between designs.

We touched on sample size estimation in Chapter 11, pointing out that you could refer to Sauro and Lewis' *Quantifying the User Experience* for guidance on how to estimate how many users you will need to produce results in your test. Estimating sample size may be useful if you are under pressure to produce a timeline because other resources must be scheduled (e.g., a developer to roll out a new page). After you calculate how many users you need, you can measure the current average amount of unique visitors who view the page you wish to test on a daily basis and come up with a number of how many days the A/B test may take before you have statistically significant results. The risk, however, is that if you're waiting to reach 95% (or more) statistical significance and the difference between the two pages' performance is small, the test could drag on and on. That brings us to the next section.

MONITORING AND "WINNING"

A full description of the math involved in A/B testing is beyond the scope of this book and different tools may use different statistical techniques. Overall, A/B testing tools judge the outcome of a test by calculating the conversion rate for each variation (i.e., the number of conversions—that is, people taking whatever desired action, divided by the number of users who viewed the page) and then calculating the confidence interval around that rate. That's because the test is just looking at a sample of all possible users, and so even though you have observed a conversion rate of 1.64%, for example, the actual value may be higher or lower. The confidence interval gives you the range of values where the actual conversion rate *probably* lies. As the A/B test gathers data from more users, the confidence intervals get smaller until the two confidence intervals do not overlap, meaning that there is only a very small chance that there's no difference in performance. At this point, the tool declares that one design has a higher conversion rate.

Alternatively, after a few weeks of testing, the performance of the two pages may be so close that there is still a great deal of overlap between the two confidence intervals, often with both pages alternating which one performs better from one day to the next. This is a situation where you would conclude that the new design(s) is no better than the page that currently exists. Or, in the case of choosing among two or more brand-new pages, you will have to choose one on criteria other than performance.

DON'T WATCH IT CONSTANTLY

Do yourself a favor, and don't obsess over the results. There is no harm in checking the data once a day, twice a day, or as many times per day as you want, but doing so will drive you crazy. Check during the first 24 hours to make sure the test is working properly and collecting data, and then leave it alone for at least a week before you check it again. You can set up your A/B testing tool to notify you when the test is complete.

Ending a Test Early

If you are fortunate, one design will clearly have a higher conversion rate, either the original page or a challenger. You may also find that all of the variations you are testing have about the same performance. There is another possibility: you have a page that *looks* like it may be better, with a higher conversion rate but a confidence interval that overlaps another page, indicating that there is still a reasonable (but small) chance that it is not better.

Your tool will show you the probability that one design is better than another design. When the probability reaches 95% (or some other threshold that you set), the tool declares the test complete. In this situation, you may have had a page that performs consistently better than the other over several days, but the probably that this page is superior is still less than your threshold.

Whether or not to end or keep running the test comes down to your tolerance for risk and how much of an improvement the new page gives you. Would you accept 90% certainty? 80%? Attaining 95% or even 99% certainty is a convention for publishing research or for when the stakes in a decision are high. The stakes in choosing a page design in other contexts may be considerably lower, particularly when the risk of being wrong simply means you end up with a new page that is just as good as the one it replaced. In these cases, 80% or even 50% may be more appropriate.

PEAK OPTIMIZATION

A/B testing will improve your website a page at a time, probably in small increments, but occasionally in leaps. It's important to remember that it is a way of improving your website within its existing design and architectural framework. It is not a way to reimagine entire sections of your website or interactions at a high level.

The upshot is that you may reach a point where you stop finding ways to improve the website. That doesn't mean that you have the perfect website, just that your page may be as good as it can be at this time, with your current users, and in the overall context of the current website. The only way to improve the website may be to go back to the drawing board and redesign it (or entire sections of it). Or to put it another way, a more creative approach may break through a peak you have reached through A/B testing.

KEY TAKEAWAYS

- A/B testing is when you compare two competing designs for a page according to a metric of success by randomly sending users to one or the other.
- At a high level, the steps of designing an A/B test are:
  1. Select a page that you wish to improve.
  2. Determine a metric for judging improvement.
  3. Design one or more alternatives.
  4. Add code to the page(s).
- Choose pages that are important to your website where the user can take some kind of measurable action that they would have to do intentionally that is important to you (i.e., a web analytics goal).
- It is possible to use sample-size estimation calculations to estimate how long a test will take, but it is ultimately unpredictable how long it will take to conclude that there is a statistically significant difference between two pages (and it may never happen in any practical timeline).
- A good starting point for an A/B test is one month or about 5,000 visitors.
- A/B testing tools often default to declaring a "winning" page at 95% signficance; calling a test early depends on your appetite for risk, but in many contexts, a higher degree of uncertainty is appropriate.

CHAPTER 14

Analytics Profiles

INTRODUCTION

This book has, for the most part, skirted around the topic of installation and configuration. Such information tends to have a short shelf life and works better as online documentation rather than as a book. In addition, the skill sets of many UX professionals just isn't a good match for tool configuration and writing code and it is more effective to seek help from specialists.

Profiles, a way of organizing web analytics data, and the filters that determine how those data are organized are another area where the help of a specialist will probably be necessary. Nonetheless, it is good to know what is technically possible, and this chapter is about setting up alternative ways of displaying web analytics data to make analysis easier. *Profile* is a term specific to Google Analytics, but you will find a similar concept in comparable tools, such as Omniture's Reporting Suite.

CONTENTS

PROFILES

An analytics profile is a subset of all of the data available in an account (Figure 14.1). It may contain some or all of the data about a website, or data from multiple websites combined, and in all of the examples so far in this book, we have been interacting with data in profiles in Google Analytics. You can think of a profile as a way to set boundaries on what data you see.

Why wouldn't you want to see all of the analytics data about a website? It is unlikely that you would want less than full access to all data, but it may be the case in large organizations that people in a specific department may only be given access to the analytics profile containing data for their department's part of the website. They would see how users interact with just their department's pages and nothing about any user behavior on any other page. This configuration can make for some strange data because users may not respect your organization's departmental structure as they explore your website—that

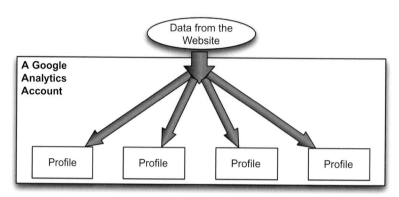

FIGURE 14.1

In this figure from Chapter 3, we see data about website usage flow into a web analytics tool and then into one or more profiles. In Google Analytics, an account receives the data and contains one or more profiles.

means that click paths and website usage data, such as time on website, may become unreliable.

It is also worth noting that in Google Analytics, profiles are essentially permanent records of data starting from the day they are created. One cannot create a profile to contain historical data, and any changes to the configuration of the profile are not retroactive. They are not a tool for casually exploring data and rather require planning.

The best way to understand why it would actually be useful to have more than just one profile displaying all of the data about your website is to talk about some of the different ways you can filter the data in profiles.

WHAT ARE PROFILE FILTERS?

The mechanism for determining what data are displayed in a profile is the *filter*. We have encountered this term before, as a way to describe what happens when you segment data and as a way to manipulate what data are displayed in a table. There are also filters that one can set up to determine what data are recorded in a profile.

Filters can do relatively simple (but common and important) things like prevent spurious or misleading data from getting displayed when looking at data from actual users. For example, you may want to filter out any data from your own company's employees by filtering out IP addresses of your office or the name of your Internet service providers.

On the more complex and dramatic end, profile filters let you choose which pages of your website to include or exclude, and to even change how the URLs of pages are displayed.

Filters are powerful, complex functionality for cleaning data and combining data sources. A full description is outside the scope of this book on practical UX work—it is an area where cooperation with experts is important. Our interest in filters lies in building alternate profiles that allow us to view data in different ways and as a supplement to the unfiltered data.

WHERE TO FIND FILTER PROFILES IN GOOGLE ANALYTICS

In Google Analytics, you configure profiles or simply inspect how they are configured in the administration area (the same place you would go to configure analytics goals), accessible via the Admin button in the upper-right corner of the interface. If you do not have administrator access to an account, though, you will not even be able to see what filters are in place, let alone alter them or set up new ones. In this case, finding out how profiles are set up is going to require the help of an administrator—probably someone in your organization's IT department or web analytics team.

Making URLs Easier to Read

Some websites have difficult-to-read URLs—their URLs may contain strings of meaningless-to-humans characters or there may be meaningful words buried in a long chain of meaningless words. This may be a problem because a website has a significant amount of dynamically generated content (for the former situation) or because a website uses a content management system that generates unfortunate URLs (in the latter situation).

You would use filters that match the contents of the uniform resource identifier (URI, also known as the stuff in the URL after "example.com"). You can match the entire URI, URIs that contain a string you specify, or use regular expressions. You then specify whatever text you want the URI to be instead. You can rewrite entire URIs or just part.

While rewriting can make it easier for you to identify pages and display them in reports, you must either be able to identify a pattern that lets you alter many pages with few filters, or you must create a separate filter for every page on your website that you wish to rewrite.

Rewriting URIs will unfortunately be a brittle solution, because if new pages are created, you may not have any existing filters to rewrite those URIs. Also, if the URIs on your website change for some reason, it may make your filters obsolete. Although you can always go back and add or fix filters, you will still end up with a period of time where you recorded the hard-to-read URIs in your profile.

Ultimately, this kind of filtering may not be worthwhile unless you have pages that are egregiously difficult to identify by URI. It does, though, bring us to another kind of profile.

Easier Click-path Analysis by Combining Pages

We touched on this subject back in Chapter 8: a challenge to analyzing how users move through your website is the diversity of paths they may take. One of the approaches we took to addressing this challenge was grouping pages into logical "buckets," such as grouping all of the product pages on AwesomePetToys.com together and combining the click-path data for these pages, and then looking for patterns in how users move between the "buckets."

If you intend to perform click-path analysis frequently, you may wish to add a profile to your account that rewrites the URIs of pages to merge them into your categories. The data for individual pages will be combined—what pages users come from and went to as well as usage metrics like % exit, average time on page, and so on. You can easily summarize how users interact with pages, at the cost of being able to drill into categories to learn more about specific pages.

Let's reexamine the AwesomePetToys.com example from Chapter 8. There, we looked at some examples of different kinds of product pages:

- /products/toyco/laser_pointer?product_id=2788897
- /products/dogfun/squeezy_steak?product_id=2784417
- /products/toyco/cat_nip_bucket?product_id=2840637

The AwesomePetToys.com team could write a profile with a filter that takes these URIs and rewrites them as "products/product-page" or whatever other naming system makes sense to them. Then, when looking at reports in Google Analytics, instead of seeing data for these individual product pages, there would only be one page, with all of the page usage data combined.

TESTING CHANGES TO PROFILES

Google Analytics unfortunately has no "sandbox" for testing profile configurations to find out immediately whether they are working. Any time you change a profile, from setting up filters to configuring goals, there is no way to learn if you did it right until at least 6–24 hours have passed and the profile has accumulated data from after the change. If you must fix a problem, you then wait up to another day to find out if you have solved the problem. In the meantime, all of these bad data are permanently recorded in the profile.

This permanence underscores the importance of maintaining a "raw" profile with data in which you are confident, and of being deliberate and thoughtful when making changes to profile configurations in Google Analytics.

A Profile for UX Data

Another reason you may set up a profile is to maintain a separate set of goals that are meaningful from a UX perspective. You may do so because there is no space in an existing profile to set up new goals or because there are political objections to you modifying an existing profile.

A positive side to this kind of setup is that you will have a clean, well-organized profile to use where goals are oriented toward measuring user behaviors that show your designs are working rather than more purely marketing-oriented goals. You may also take advantage of this opportunity to make further customizations to your profile since you will not interfere with any other stakeholders.

For one thing, you can do any URI rewriting we have discussed in this chapter. You could also make use of custom variables (a way of integrating additional data sources with web analytics data and creating your own dimensions) and event tracking (a way of adding data about users' actions that do not result in loading a new page). Although we have glossed over this detail previously, custom variables and event tracking are actually set up at the level of the profile. As a result, you could create event tracking code to measure something on your website and only send the data to your own UX-oriented analytics profile.

CROSS-DOMAIN TRACKING

It is likely that you, like most people, will look at web analytics data for a single domain. There are situations, though, where you are interested in users' behavior as they move across multiple domains—that is, connecting the data a single user generates while moving from one website to another instead of treating the data as though they were generated by separate users. It is possible to combine data from multiple websites in a single web analytics profile, requiring changes to the analytics tracking code placed on the website and some way of rewriting URLs in the profile's filters to tell the pages from one website apart from pages from another website. Setting up cross-domain tracking will require help from an analytics expert but, depending on your situation, can be useful.

KEY TAKEAWAYS

- Data in web analytics tools like Google Analytics are organized into one or more profiles.
- Filters determine what data are presented in a profile and how those data are presented.

- Some kinds of profiles you may create are:
  - Make URLs easier to read when they are not human-readable.
  - Rewriting URLs can make click-path analysis easier when multiple pages' URLs are rewritten to present them as the same page.
  - Giving the UX team a place to create their own analytics goals and collect event tracking data that are relevant to them.

CHAPTER 15

Regular Reporting and Talking to Stakeholders

INTRODUCTION

Any UX team should include web analytics in its repertoire of user research methods. It is important that we use all of the data sources at our disposal to learn about users rather than treating web analytics as a separate activity. Throughout this book, we have discussed using web analytics to learn about your users. This chapter focuses on using web analytics to talk to the stakeholders in your organization. One aspect is determining metrics and setting a rhythm for reporting on web analytics data to stakeholders. Another part is using analytics data to justify the implantation of new designs based on your team's work or to help negotiating budget for user research activities.

It is common for another team or department other than user experience to "own" web analytics. These tools and talent may be part of an IT department or in their own silo. Other teams may be the gatekeepers to web analytics and can be an important ally, but when you explore how to use web analytics to communicate with stakeholders, it is vital that you do not step on their toes.

REPORTING CULTURE

This book proposes that a vital element of any UX team is to continually monitor the state of the user experience on the website and report on this status to business stakeholders. Reporting means choosing what metrics are most important to share and describing what they actually mean and what actions they may warrant.

That previous sentence cannot be stressed enough. In a perfect world, we only look at data when there is a reason to do so. While in practice, people may just want the reassurance of knowing what is going on, even when data do not lead to action, you should point out when the data indicate that all is well or going according to plan or is a mystery that you will continue to monitor.

Web analytics data help the UX team report to business stakeholders on a regular basis. Doubtlessly, you already are responsible for informing

CONTENTS

stakeholders about your team's activities (and justifying its continued existence and funding). You may be called on to describe the overall state of usability on your organization's website.

One of the things you can do with analytics tools is get data on a regular basis that describe users' behavior. In light of the previous chapters, how you approach regular reporting should not come as a surprise. You must select a handful of metrics that serve as KPIs, metrics that provide the best summary of the most important aspects of the experience you try to provide for your users, monitor them continually, and report and interpret them for business stakeholders.

Choosing metrics and deciding what to include in a report is an act of storytelling, an editorial process where you choose the pieces that will create meaning. You have an important responsibility to balance transparency and not create needless panic. Crafting a report also means that it is important to put data in context, to tell stakeholders why they are seeing data, whether it is the continuation of a trend, a new development, something you can explain, or something you will investigate further, and how it relates to the rest of your findings, currently and historically.

You are also choosing metrics that will tell you and others important things about how your website is working for users. This purpose is distinct from other people who may use web analytics for their reporting, notably online marketing. The focus with online marketing is on describing the effectiveness of efforts to bring users to the website and then ultimately generate revenue from those users, which necessarily includes measurements of how effectively the website "converts" those people into revenue-generating visitors. Your own reporting should ultimately tie into how users generate money for your business (or otherwise fulfill the mission of the organization), but your work will undoubtedly go into greater detail on users' interactions, including ones that are further removed from revenue than, for example, a shopping cart checkout, but that still capture how well the website is meeting the goals that your organization has agreed on. Figure 15.1 shows an example of how you could approach the report.

Why You Report Analytics Data

You probably already have some kind of rhythm for reporting on UX initiatives to one or more stakeholders, such as a manager, director, or even one or more executives. You should fold data from analytics into whatever regular communication you have.

Reporting metrics you identified as critical on a regular basis to stakeholders gives you a framework for showing progress on initiatives over time, and quite simply gives you another reason to remind stakeholders that you exist.

AwesomePetToys.com User Experience Status Report

Shopping Cart Success	60.32%		Customer Satisfaction	4.50
Wholesale Order Success	95.40%		Phone Support Calls	30
Purchases from Wish List	10.20%		% Search Exits	36.98%
Account Signup Success	54.33%			

FIGURE 15.1

An example of a slide or section of a document for a spinoff of AwesomePetToys.com, AwesomePetArticles.com. The goal of the website is to provide information to users through articles and videos, breaking the articles into categories and rolling up the much smaller library of videos into a single number. The focus of this report is much more on the quality of the content than on task completion, with pageviews per visit providing a way of showing that users are interested in the content. Depending on stakeholder concerns, time on page would also have been a useful approach.

On top of all that, you are creating better-informed stakeholders who know even more about their customers—a vital edge for your organization.

Also, it will always be the case that some people respond better to what they see as "hard" numbers, to data involving large numbers collected in an objective manner. Web analytics data gives you a way to speak their language and improve your credibility with these stakeholders as well as whomever they in turn report to; the reports you create may, after all, get reused by others. In fact, you will help the stakeholders who value hard numbers make better decisions because you will be able to supply them with the type of data they want, rounded out by the other insights that UX methods can offer.

Exposure to web analytics over time also teaches you what kinds of questions you can answer. This means that over time, stakeholders will start to want to know more, want to stretch beyond the constraints of the story that you can tell with the data you have. Regular reporting and discussion of what you can measure is a good way to build more interest in your team's work.

Why You Monitor Analytics Data

Setting aside the matter of reporting on the data, the three big reasons to monitor web analytics data for your website are:

- Building your web analytics skills
- Detecting changes to your website
- Detecting changes in your users

The first reason should be obvious—repeated exposure is the best way to learn tools and methods. When the data change in an unexpected way from one week or month to the next, the next step is to try to learn as much as you can from web analytics before turning to other (possibly more expensive) approaches. The constant stream of novel challenges will expand your skills.

The second reason, in a perfect world, would not be necessary, because there would not be any changes to the website that take the UX team by surprise. However, when many stakeholders are involved in an organization's website, there will always be rogue agents, last-minute changes, or executive decisions that alter the website. A change in the data may be your first clue that something about the website has changed, such as a sudden drop in the conversion rate or the appearance of a new page in the list of top pages. Not only can web analytics help you identify when changes happened, it can also give you some of the earliest evidence of the effects of those changes upon users.

Lastly, the composition of what different kinds of people comprise your website's users can change. Your organization's marketing efforts affect which users show up to your website, and as those efforts change they may drive more or fewer users, or influence what goals people have that bring them to the website. You may also find signs that forces beyond your control are at play, such as other companies' marketing efforts or broad changes in the market, economy, or popular culture. Obviously, you won't be able to actually detect any of these changes in the data themselves; rather you will find evidence that *something* has changed about your users, and once you rule out changes to the website, you are left with the possibility that it's your users who are different.

Choosing Metrics to Report

Among the metrics you can report, first and foremost will probably be whatever goals you or your organization have set up in your web analytics tool. These metrics provide a high-level summary of how the quality of the website affects the bottom line or otherwise helps your organization fulfill its mission. It is possible, when you are not the sole user of your web analytics tool, that there are analytics goals that you do not find meaningful. What to use will involve your judgment.

Beyond analytics goals, you should report on any other metrics that you have identified as capturing how well the website delivers on business goals, as discussed in Chapter 4. Are you trying to engage users? In what way are you engaging them? Are you trying to help them find specific content or just stick around for a long time? Speaking to business goals could mean describing how many users reach a page or group of pages, or simply showing average time on website or pages per visit, for example. What other actions that are not configured as goals are you trying to get users to perform? For example, if website search is an important aspect of your website, then perhaps you will report on how many users abandon the website after a search or how many go on to buy something.

GOALS ARE JUST METRICS WEARING A CROWN

A goal is just a way of highlighting specific metrics that you could measure through other means. There may be things that you want to measure for your reporting that could, in fact, be designated as a goal. It just isn't always possible from a political perspective to go around adding new goals in analytics. That doesn't mean that you can't compile a report that highlights the metrics that you believe best describe users' experience of your website. In fact, you should.

You should probably avoid simply displaying counts, like the number of pageviews or forms filled out. Rather, put numbers like these in the context of "out of how many people had the chance to take this action"—that is, state them as rates. While rates aren't immune to external factors like seasonal trends in your users' behavior, they are the best way to tell a consistent story about users.

That said, sometimes stakeholders want to know the visitor count, the list of top search terms, or month-over-month comparisons of how many users bought something. Reporting can involve balancing your expertise and what information your stakeholders need to feel informed and in control. When stakeholders want to expand the scope of your reporting, it is an opportunity to collaborate with whoever owns web analytics in your organization to ensure you are not encroaching on their territory and to hopefully let them handle the information needs that do not fit squarely in the realm of user experience.

GETTING IN AT THE BEGINNING

You may be involved in the implementation of web analytics on your website, which is a great opportunity to capture important data right from the beginning and to marshal resources while your organization is focused on installing a web analytics tool, rather than negotiating for developer time to make changes to an existing implementation. Installing a web analytics tool varies in complexity based on how many aspects of usage you want to measure and how many features the tool has. UX teams can have the most impact on how more complex tools like Google Analytics and Omniture get set up because of the degree to which they can be customized.

Perhaps the most important contributions that user experience can make to an analytics implementation project is inventorying and prioritizing all of the things users can do on a website to ensure they are tracked. User experience can contribute useful taxonomies for labeling on-page events and naming pages so they are grouped properly for useful click-path analysis. Also, by being involved in the setup of a web analytics tool, the UX team will have a better understanding of how the tool works, reducing the learn curve and making the tool useful more quickly.

Reporting Frequency

You should report to management or stakeholders on a schedule that balances their desires against your ability to deliver high-quality work in a timely way. That said, the best frequency for reporting analytics data is probably going to be monthly. More frequently than that, and you risk spending more time analyzing data than actually acting on them. Less frequently, and you may miss new developments and possibly lose visibility for your team.

If you are pressed for a weekly rhythm for reporting analytics data, advocate reporting easy-to-obtain measurements on a frequent basis and performing any more complex analyses, if any, on a monthly schedule. It's common for management stakeholders to want as much data as frequently as possible, but the best defense you can use is that it is better for you to spend more time actually making the website better rather than reporting all of the time.

Keep It Concise

The idea of KPIs is that you focus on a few metrics that indicate how well something is performing. When choosing what to report regularly, use the fewest metrics possible to convey what is most important for stakeholders to know. The more numbers you put in front of stakeholders, the harder it will be digest your message.

Optimally, a single slide could give stakeholders a summary of how the website is performing, or a single sheet of paper, such as in Figure 15.2, which is another example of how a report could look. Include enough context to make current numbers meaningful, like last month's performance or last year's performance, but not so much to waste people's time (like all data stretching back two years).

If you have more to tell stakeholders in a given month, you can always expand your reporting temporarily—just beware of the reporting creep, where one-off analyses become permanent fixtures of a regular report.

AwesomePetArticles.com User Experience Report
July 2013

Category	Pageviews/ Visit	% Change MoM	% Change YoY
Dogs	3.63	1.11%	−0.06%
Cats	3.48	1.75%	1.15%
Birds	4.79	0.42%	−0.30%
Ferrets	2.12	−14.17%	−2.35%
Lizards	5.22	−1.69%	−1.39%
All Articles	3.75	0.27%	0.43%

Complete Video Views	41.36%	3.12%	0.98%
Successful Newsletter Signups	64.10%	5.55%	4.30%

Overall, users' interest in pet articles remained steady month over month. The exception is ferret articles, which dropped significantly month over month and modestly year over year, even though there has been no change to the contents of that section. We will continue to monitor and analyze the situation for trends and recommend an article-by-article analysis to determine if particular articles drove the decrease.

The portion of users who completed the newsletter signup process after starting it increased 5.55% compared to the previous month and 4.30% compared to the previous year, indicating that the recent changes to the form had a positive effect.

FIGURE 15.2
Another example, this one of a slide or section of a document the AwesomePetToys.com UX team could use for their report. It captures data on a small set of valuable user actions and provides recent historical context through spark lines, the thumbnail-size line graphs. Notably, this report includes two metrics that would only be available outside of web analytics: customer satisfaction and the volume of calls to the support center. Collaboration with other teams is essential.

MAKING THE CASE FOR USABILITY ACTIVITIES

Web analytics data can help you make the case for doing usability activities by showing stakeholders how many users will be affected by your work and perhaps even allowing you to estimate how many additional users will benefit from this work.

Making the Case for Design Changes

Making the case for design changes using web analytics data means giving stakeholders a sense of scale, of how many users may be affected by a design change combined with an estimate of how much they will be affected. As previously discussed, it is impossible to predict how much a design change will affect users' behavior until real users have actually interacted with it. You can draw upon usability testing for this information or, if that is not possible, you can still calculate how many more users will take the desired action if you make only a minimal improvement to the website.

It is vital that UX professionals become fluent in this language. While everyone can agree that it would be nice if the website was easier to use, when it's time to actually spend money improving the website, user experience must compete with other stakeholders who can better articulate their return on investment (e.g., marketing or IT infrastructure) or have a flashier pitch (e.g., a fantastic-looking new feature for the website).

Giving stakeholders a sense of scale simply means describing how many users may be affected by a design change. If you want to change a page, show stakeholders how many people view the page now. Want to improve a checkout process? Show them how many people start this process. In other words, show stakeholders how many users currently have the opportunity to take whatever action you want them to take.

The other part is describing to stakeholders what kind of gain you may get from implementing a design. In a perfect world, you've conducted usability testing on a new design and measured how much you will improve the completion rate based on your previous benchmark.

Start with calculating how much you improved performance over the benchmark:

$$\% \, Improvement = \frac{New \, design \, completion \, rate - Old \, design \, completion \, rate}{Old \, design \, completion \, rate}$$

This formula should not be surprising at all in light of Chapter 11.

Next, find the current conversion rate in Google Analytics for the task you wish to improve and calculate your estimate for the new conversion rate. The time range should be a recent time period when the website was stable and nothing unusual was happening:

$$New \, conversion \, rate = Old \, conversion \, rate \times (1 + \% \, Improvement)$$

Take the number of visitors to the website during that time period, or the number of users who had the opportunity to take the action you wish to improve:

$$Additional \, conversions = (New \, conversion \, rate \times Visitors) - (Old \, conversion \, rate \times Visitors)$$

You now can talk about how many users in a given time period will be affected by your design change, and how many more may take action as a result of those changes. Providing numbers like these should strengthen your argument for development time.

Let's go back to AwesomePetToys.com. Pet owners purchase pet toys on the website, using the checkout process. According to earlier usability testing, 80% of users who start the checkout process complete it without encountering any major usability problems. The AwesomePetToys.com UX team redesigns the checkout process on the website and then runs a usability test to find out if the new design is an improvement. They find that the new completion rate is 90.9%, and they are confident the actual completion rate is between 60.1% and 100%, and there's about an 80% chance the new completion rate is higher than the old benchmark. The new design could be a 13.6% improvement over the original design, although there is a chance that it could be worse than the current design.

Now the AwesomePetToys.com UX team can go to web analytics and look at how many users start and complete the shopping cart checkout. It's 63% rather than 80%, because there are more factors influencing users than in the usability test (e.g., some people may decide the price is too high and abandon their shopping cart). Going by the 13.6% improvement observed during the usability test would take the completion rate from 63% to 71.57%. If AwesomePetToys.com has 1,000 users starting the checkout process per month, that's an additional 86 purchases per month.

Of course, this is just an estimate, one that has the benefit of being based on data but with flaws that must be acknowledged. Foremost, the actual increase will almost certainly not be 13.6%, and there is a greater possibility of it being smaller than larger (and the new design may actually be worse than the old design). How exactly you discuss this matter with stakeholders will depend on their temperament, and one approach is to lowball the estimated improvement to something that is still within the realm of possibility but still great enough to justify the development work.

With the number of users who will be affected by the design change and the estimated improvement in the conversion rate, you can show stakeholders an estimate of how many additional users will purchase awesome pet toys or take whatever kind of action you care about over the next month, six months, year, or whatever time period stakeholders care about. An estimate can help you make the case for investing in a design change, particularly if you can link your design change to revenue—in the case of AwesomePetToys.com, that would be done by taking the average revenue per order and multiplying it by the estimated amount of additional people completing the checkout process.

What happens if you can't do any usability testing with a new design to find out how much of an improvement it is over an existing design? You have to guess conservatively. Pick a low number, like a 5% improvement in the conversion rate or whatever rate you want to improve. For example, improving the conversion rate from 3.22% to 3.38% on a website with only 5,000 visitors per month would mean conversions would go from 61 to 64 per month. Would this small of an improvement be worth the cost of development time? That would depend on how much the business values each conversion. If each conversion is worth $100 to the business, in a year that's an extra $3,600. What if, instead of 5,000 users per month, there were 20,000? Would the additional users generate enough extra sales?

Making the Case for User Research

You may be in a position of having to negotiate a budget for UX research activities. The basic idea behind using web analytics to make the case for user research is the same as for design changes, except that you have no way to estimate how much you will improve the current design. You determine how many people are in the group that you want to study, such as how many people use a feature that you want to study through usability testing or how many people fit into a segment of your users who you want to study through field research.

Let's go back to the AwesomePetToys.com shopping cart checkout example. In the previous section, the AwesomePetToys.com UX team had come up with a new design and conducted usability testing on it. Let's say that earlier they had to justify conducting usability testing on the old shopping cart checkout design to find out where users were having problems with it. With 1,000 users attempting to use the shopping cart checkout per month and about 630 completing the process successfully, even a 1% improvement in conversion rate would yield an additional 12 or 13 purchases per month.

Obviously, the example here is somewhat facile—in real life, it should be a no-brainer to argue for conducting usability testing on the shopping cart checkout process on an e-commerce website. Nonetheless, this is the approach that you can take to describe the scope of any kind of work that you may wish to do to learn about users. Even when you can't directly link the actions of these users to revenue, the idea is that whatever part of the website you wish to study is still relevant to business goals, and therefore it is possible to convince stakeholders it is worth understanding its users.

KEY TAKEAWAYS

- Web analytics data and tools don't just help you do your work better— they help you communicate with business stakeholders as well.
- Include web analytics data in your regular communications with stakeholders to quantify the success of the website and keep stakeholders informed.
- Choose the fewest metrics possible that are meaningful and conceivably actionable.
- Keep your reporting concise.
- The best rhythm for communicating web analytics data will probably be monthly, but your situation may vary.
- To make the case for design changes, you can use web analytics data to show how many users will be affected by the change, and how many additional users will take the desired action based on either the observed improvement in usability testing or a minimal, conservative guess when no data are available.
- Similarly, analytics data can help you advocate for user research by helping you put a number on how big a portion of your website's users you want to study.

CHAPTER 16

Web Analytics in the Near Future

INTRODUCTION

Web analytics should be a core competency for any UX professional working with websites or mobile applications, one of many skills in a profession where generalism is important. It behooves us to seek out data on users wherever we can and form alliances with the experts in those domains where we benefit from their skills and we help them better understand their users. Web analytics is, of course, one such domain.

Throughout this book, we have looked at the ways that the current generation of web analytics tools can help you learn about users by providing valuable quantitative data and help you speak the same language as business stakeholders. In return, UX research can give web analytics data context, making them an even more powerful tool. These tools have changed a great deal in just a few years and web analytics tools are certain to continue changing and growing in power and usefulness in the years to come. This chapter briefly surveys technology and features that may become important trends in the years following the publication of this book.

MOBILE APPLICATION ANALYTICS

The same technology for measuring usage of websites can be used for measuring usage of mobile applications. This practice is still young compared to web analytics, but it is happening now and the tools will become more mature as the market for mobile applications grows in the years ahead.

The fundamentals of mobile application analytics are the same as web analytics. You can measure things like how users came to find and install your application (an important thing to do if your interest is in marketing). You can study demographic and technological aspects of users. You can also analyze how people interact with your application—how often they use it, what screens they look at, how they move from screen to screen, what actions they perform, and so on. Like web analytics, it is imperative that you figure out

CONTENTS

what actions you want users to take that signal your application is successful and use these actions as analytics goals.

Mobile application analytics has its own application-specific metrics and dimensions, but taking on analysis of mobile applications will be less about learning a whole new domain and more a matter of applying the same basic skills to a new data set.

CROSS-DEVICE MEASUREMENT

Web analytics tools determine whether you are a new or returning user by putting a cookie on your computer. If you change to a different device or even a different browser, they count you as a new user. Increasingly, users may visit the same website on a laptop, tablet, and phone, even to complete the same high-level task, and currently that user is counted as a separate user with every visit.

The only ethical way to link these sessions together as coming from the same user is to entice a user to create an account on your website and log in every time he or she visits. Obviously, this strategy isn't viable for many websites. Nonetheless, it is likely that analytics vendors will find ways to partially or fully address this problem because of the growth of channel-switching among users.

BETTER MEASUREMENT OF ON-PAGE BEHAVIOR

Web analytics tools will get better at capturing user behavior that doesn't result in new pageviews and presenting the data in a way that makes them easier to analyze, as websites tend to become more richly interactive.

At the time of writing, the barriers to comprehensive event tracking are less a matter of feasibility than effort in writing the necessary code. It is likely that in the future more onsite actions will be recorded without additional configuration. This is good news for anyone who works on highly interactive websites or applications that users access through a browser.

CONNECTING TO OTHER DATA SOURCES

It will also get easier to connect web analytics data to other data sources and easier to analyze them. Companies capture data about their customers in multiple systems (and, more and more often, cloud-based systems) like customer relationship management (CRM) tools, point-of-sale (POS) tools, and so on. The desire to better understand the cost-effectiveness of marketing efforts will drive the growth of integration. User experience can ride this trend to gain greater insight into who users are and what they do.

THE CONTINUING DOMINANCE OF GOOGLE

This book has used Google Analytics for examples because there is a free version that has led to it being a commonly used tool. As long as Google continues to give away a powerful tool for free, they will continue to be a dominant force in web analytics.

At the time of writing, other tools like Omniture offer features that Google does not, particularly a level of customization that may be necessary for particularly complex websites, but many organizations choose free tools that do a good enough job of meeting their needs rather than pay for tools that exactly meet their needs. As Google continues to add features to their free tool, they will further undercut their competitors and maintain the relevance of their analytics tool.

THINGS WILL KEEP CHANGING

We can be confident in predicting that things will keep changing. There will always be more to learn, tools will keep changing, and the things that are important tomorrow may catch us completely off guard.

This is not a new problem for UX professionals, though. We work in a field where we can never stop learning and adapting and applying our fundamental skills to new situations. The goal of this book has been, despite the necessity of discussing the practical use of a specific web analytics tool, to impart the fundamentals of using the kinds of data web analytics produce. These data are a great complement to other UX research methods, providing context and a way to answer more questions about user behavior.

Index

Note: Page numbers followed by "*f*", "*t*" and "*b*" refers to figures, tables and boxes, respectively.